A Pinch of This and A Dash of That...

Conversations With A Cook

by Kaye Johns

Illustrated and Designed by Diana Craft

ASPEN WEST PUBLISHING, SLC, UT. 84070-6415

First printing May 1988

ISBN # 0-9615390-5-4

Printed in the United States of America
Cover Design, SMART DESIGN, SLC, UT.

for papa...

I know cookbooks

aren't usually dedicated —

but he was my Papa,

and he taught me.

I loved him.

CONTENTS

INTRODUCTION

THOUGHT YOU'D WANT TO KNOW . . .

Someone asked about my test kitchen once. He suggested I bring some of my staff of home economists by for him to meet.

I had to laugh. "I'll call my mom and my grandmother," I said. "Maybe my sisters-in-law and brothers can come, too."

The test kitchen is where we live. The recipes are my personal collection from me, my family and friends. And, I cook them just the way the rest of you do — usually in haste, sometimes creatively, and most always lovingly for breakfast, lunch and dinner, three times a day.

I, too, am wife, mother and working woman with little time to spare. I select the recipes for my radio features from those I'm cooking and serving at home. The recipes that have found their way into this, my first cookbook, represent more than two years of radio broadcasts.

I hope you'll enjoy them and that you'll treat them as I treat recipes — creatively. Relax and have fun with them so that they'll bring you and your family the hours of pleasure they've brought me and mine.

Kaye Johnson

Save Yourself a Trip to the Store

If I'm notorious for anything, it's the creative flair I show in the kitchen when I'm trying to make it through one more meal without a trip to the grocery store.

I wish I had a nickel for every recipe I've plowed my way through only to come to a screeching halt by an ingredient I simply didn't have on hand.

Perhaps this list of substitutes will help you when you're in that predicament. My theory is — always try to make do when you can! If it doesn't turn out exactly as planned, keep it to yourself and no one will be the wiser.

Be courageous!

1 cup granulated sugar = 1 cup brown sugar, packed

Frozen whipped topping = whipped heavy cream

Evaporated skim milk = cream or sour cream in some sauces

3-1/2 tbsp. cocoa plus 1 tbsp. oil = 1 square cooking chocolate

1-1/2 tbsp. vinegar in 1 cup milk = 1 cup buttermilk (for baking)

1 tsp. dried herb = 1 tbsp. fresh herb

1 tsp. arrowroot or 2 tsp. cornstarch = the thickening power of 1 tbsp. flour

Pale dry sherry = rice wine in Chinese recipes

1 tbsp. dehydrated minced onion = 1 small fresh onion

1 tbsp. prepared mustard = 1 tsp. dry mustard

Know What's in Your Kitchen

I have a confession to make.

A couple of years ago my Aunt Titta drew my name in the Christmas drawing and gave me a lovely glass baking dish in a wicker serving basket. It was such a handy size that it immediately became one of my favorite "bake anything" dishes.

I've referred to it in print and over the air repeatedly, calling it my basic 9" x 13" pan. Still, there have been times that it puzzled me. For instance, it wouldn't quite hold all of some of my favorite casseroles. Some sheet cakes had a tendency to run over.

One day a friend asked if I was sure it was a 9" x 13" dish. "Well, sure — it's your basic rectangular baking dish," I answered.

"They do come in other dimensions," she said. "Why not measure and be sure?"

Much to my chagrin, it measures 8" x 12". What a silly goof.

Have you ever made a casserole that suggested a three-quart dish and you didn't know if you had one on the shelf? Have you ever misjudged volume and had to pour from one dish to another? Then you're my kind of person.

Let me share some words of hard-earned wisdom. If you will take thirty minutes one afternoon and measure your pots, pans and baking dishes, you'll save yourself a lot of time and trouble over the years. Take careful notes. Use a ruler and a measuring cup.

Use your measuring cup to measure the volume, filling each piece with water and counting the cups carefully. Remember there are four cups in a quart. If you will put those written notes in a favorite cookbook or your recipe file so you know where they are, it will make your life much simpler.

As you use my recipes, you'll notice pretty quickly that I have about three favorite baking dishes that I use over and over and over again. Don't you?

I'm going to show you my standard favorites, with their dimensions, so you'll know what I'm talking about when I say three-quart casserole.

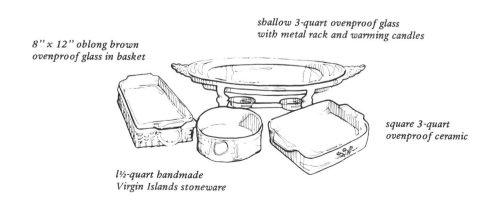

shallow 3-quart ovenproof glass with metal rack and warming candles

8" x 12" oblong brown ovenproof glass in basket

square 3-quart ovenproof ceramic

1½-quart handmade Virgin Islands stoneware

Your idea of a medium onion may be quite different from mine — a dilemma that can drive you crazy when preparing recipes.

To assist you in successfully preparing these recipes, we need to clarify a few things. For instance, green pepper is used to mean green bell peppers, not chili peppers of any kind! In the recipes that call for "green chilies" we mean the mild canned peppers and not jalapeño or other hot chili peppers. If you like very spicy food, go ahead and add some of the hot peppers to taste, but don't substitute them for the mild chilies.

For the sake of simplicity, and personal preference, most of these recipes call for butter. If you prefer, feel free to substitute margarine in any of them. However, in the two or three recipes where margarine is called for, don't substitute butter. Margarine works better in these few instances.

All this leads up to why I am including the following bits of information. I've used them as my rules of thumb in the recipes in this book. Hope they help.

Apple	1 medium	= 1 cup chopped
Banana	1 to 2 medium	= 1 cup sliced
Beans, dried	8 ounces	= 1 cup cooked
Butter or Margarine	1 pound	= 2 cups
Carrots	1 to 2 medium	= 1 cup shredded
	2 to 3 medium	= 1 cup sliced
Celery	2 medium ribs	= 1 cup sliced
Cheese, Cheddar or American	4 ounces	= 1 cup shredded
Cheese, Cottage	8 ounces	= 1 cup
Chicken, cooked	2-1/2 lb. broiler-fryer	= 2 cups diced
Chicken, canned	6-oz. can	= 1/2 cup
Chocolate Chips	6 ounces	= 1 cup
Cereal Flakes	3 cups	= 1 cup crushed
Crackers, Graham	12	= 1 cup fine crumbs
Crackers, Soda	20	= 1 cup coarse crumbs
	25	= 1 cup fine crumbs
Cream, Sour	8 ounces	= 1 cup
Heavy Cream, Whipping	1 cup (1/2 pint)	= 2 cups whipped
Flour, All-Purpose	1 pound	= 3-1/2 cups
Green Pepper	1 medium	= 1 cup chopped
Lemon Juice	1 medium lemon	= 2 to 3 tablespoons
Lemon Peel	1 medium lemon	= 1-1/2 teaspoons grated
Macaroni, Elbow	4 ounces	= 2 cups cooked
Meat, Cooked	6 to 7 ounces	= 1 cup julienne strips
Milk, Evaporated	1 small can (5.33 ounces)	= 2/3 cup
	1 large can (14-1/2 ounces)	= 1-2/3 cups
Noodles	4 ounces	= 2 cups cooked
Nuts, Shelled	4 ounces	= 1 cup chopped
Onions	1 medium	= 1/2 cup chopped
Rice, Brown	1/2 cup	= 1-3/4 to 2 cups cooked
Rice, Converted	1/2 cup	= 1-1/2 to 1-3/4 cups cooked
Rice, Regular	1/2 cup	= 1-1/2 cups cooked
Strawberries	1 pint	= 2 cups sliced
Sugar, Brown	1 pound	= 2-1/4 cups
Sugar, Granulated	1 pound	= 2-1/4 cups

Appetizers

Brandied Cheese Spread

This spread is marvelous used any number of ways — on crackers, spread on bread for bubbly cheese toast, or dropped into a steaming baked potato.

NOTE

For those of you who enjoy giving kitchen goodies as gifts, I like to pack cheese spreads like this in pretty coffee mugs or little serving dishes so that my friends will have something left when the cheese is gone. This recipe fills two fairly large coffee mugs.

8	oz. Cheddar cheese, grated
1	pkg. (3-oz.) cream cheese
1/4	cup crumbled blue cheese
2	tbsp. butter
3	tbsp. brandy or wine
1	tsp. Worcestershire sauce
	Dash of salt

Have the first four ingredients at room temperature and mix together thoroughly. Stir in the brandy, Worcestershire sauce and salt.

Pack in a container and refrigerate overnight. This will keep for two to three weeks in the refrigerator.

Makes two cups.

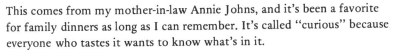

Curious Vegetable Dip

This comes from my mother-in-law Annie Johns, and it's been a favorite for family dinners as long as I can remember. It's called "curious" because everyone who tastes it wants to know what's in it.

1	pkg. (8-oz.) cream cheese, softened
1	bottle (8-oz.) Green Goddess salad dressing
1	jar (10-oz.) apple jelly
5	tbsp. prepared mustard, more to taste

Cream the cheese and salad dressing together with your electric mixer. (Don't use your blender or it will turn to soup.) Add the jelly and mustard. Taste it at this point and add more mustard, if you like. You want a good balance of sweet and tart.

Serve this dip with fresh vegetables — raw carrot sticks, pieces of celery, cauliflower, green pepper rings, slices of rutabaga and Jerusalem artichoke — whatever you like. I've found that children especially love this dip. It keeps well in the refrigerator.

Makes about three cups.

Date-Walnut Cheese Ball

Delicious double duty as cheese ball or sandwich filling.

1/3 cup chopped dates	1 pkg. (8-oz.) cream cheese, softened
1/3 cup chopped walnuts	1/2 can (3-1/2-oz.) shredded coconut

Mix dates and walnuts with cream cheese. Form into a ball.

Spread coconut on a sheet of wax paper and roll cheese ball in it, pressing slightly to make the coconut stick.

Serve with a crispy, salty cracker.

NOTE

For sandwich filling, I leave out the coconut. Especially good with Oatmeal Raisin Rolls on pg. 40.

Dill Dip

I've had two good friends give me this recipe, declaring it's the best vegetable dip they've ever had. It's very good, and doesn't taste like mayonnaise.

2/3 cup mayonnaise	1 tsp. dill weed
2/3 cup sour cream	1 tbsp. instant salad onions
1 tsp. salt	1 tbsp. dried parsley

Mix all ingredients being sure to crush the dill weed with your fingers before adding it to release more of its flavor. Refrigerate at least 24 hours to blend the flavors.

Serve with vegetable munchies.

Makes a little over one cup.

It doesn't take a lot of effort to present your food, rather than just serving it — and it's a lot of fun, not only for you, but for your guests.

If you have the time, trim and cook an artichoke, scoop out the center, and use it to hold your dip. It isn't necessary, but it's so nice!

Hot Artichoke Dip

This is unusual, delicious and a welcome change from anything with onion soup mix!

1 jar (6-oz.) marinated artichoke hearts, drained and chopped

1/2 medium red onion, chopped; or
1/4 cup chopped green onion

1 cup grated Parmesan cheese

1 cup mayonnaise

1 tbsp. lemon juice

Combine all ingredients and heat thoroughly.

Serve with chips, vegetable sticks or melba toast rounds.

Makes 1-1/2 cups.

When recipes call for well-drained ground beef or sausage, it's a good idea to put the cooked meat into a colander and press the fat out with a spoon. I set mine over a coffee can which I use for collecting grease.
    If I am very serious about making sure it is well drained, I will then dump it onto several thicknesses of paper toweling and press the grease out. Yes, it does make the meat dry; but if you are calorie conscious, it's worth it. Besides, if you combine the meat with other ingredients in a casserole or dip, this prevents the dish from becoming greasy.

NOTE
    The salt is optional because processed cheese, such as Velveeta, tends to be very salty by itself. If you are serving it with salted chips, use one of the chips when you taste it before adding extra salt.
    There is a world of difference between green chilies and jalapeño peppers; the jalapeños are much hotter and command your respect. Approach with caution.

Hot Chipped Beef Bake

The first time I served this, I took it to a family reunion. Believe me, we were well fed — but this silly, simple appetizer, served with wedges of pumpernickel bread, was the hit of the afternoon. Perhaps it should be an entrée.

1	large pkg. (8-oz.) cream cheese, softened
1	carton (8-oz.) sour cream
1	tbsp. dehydrated minced onions
1/4	tsp. garlic powder
2	jars (2-1/2-oz.) dried beef, chopped
1/2	cup chopped pecans
	Rye or pumpernickel bread, quartered (or party rounds)

Combine cream cheese and sour cream; whip until fluffy. Add onion and garlic; stir in dried beef. Spread in a fairly small baking dish; the one I use holds about three cups, and this recipe doesn't quite fill it.

Top with pecans and bake uncovered at 350° for about 20 minutes, until the pecans begin to brown and cheese is bubbling around the edges.

Serve hot with bread.

Serves approximately 20. (I say approximately 20 because the 20 of us each got a taste. If I'd brought a double — or triple — recipe, I don't think a bite would have been left!)

Nacho Dip

This dip is always a favorite, especially in cold weather.

1	lb. ground beef
1	small onion, chopped
1	lb. bulk sausage
2	lbs. easy-melting cheese (such as Velveeta)
	Dash Worcestershire sauce
1	small can (4-oz.) chopped green chilies, or 1/2 cup chopped jalapeño peppers
1	tsp. salt (optional)

Brown ground beef with onion. Drain and set aside. Brown sausage and drain. Combine well-drained ground beef and sausage with cheese, Worcestershire sauce and chilies. Heat in double boiler or microwave until cheese is melted. Stir well. Taste and add salt as desired.

Serve warm with corn chips and vegetable sticks. Makes 2-1/2 quarts.

Peanut Cheese Ball

I originally came up with this as a sandwich filling to avoid lunch box blues. It's equally good as an unusual cheese ball.

- 1/3 cup chopped peanuts
- 1/3 cup chopped stuffed green olives
- 1 pkg. (8-oz.) cream cheese, softened
- 1/2 jar (2.5-oz.) dried beef, chopped finely

Thoroughly mix peanuts and olives with cream cheese; shape into a ball.

Spread dried beef on a sheet of waxed paper; roll cheese ball in it, pressing slightly so it will stick.

Serve with an unsalted or bland cracker. Makes one 5" ball.

NOTE

It's great without the dried beef as a sandwich filling. Combine cream cheese, peanuts and olives. Spread on whole-wheat, rye or pumpernickel bread. Add lettuce or, better yet, alfalfa or bean sprouts.

Snowball Cheese Ball

This unusual cheese ball is as pretty to look at as it is delicious to eat. It's slightly sweet, and needs a plain, salty cracker to set it off. Perfect for holidays.

- 2 pkgs. (8-oz.) cream cheese, softened
- 1/3 cup crushed pineapple, drained and minced
- 1/3 cup minced green pepper
- 1/3 cup minced pecans
- 1 can (3-1/2-oz.) shredded coconut

Mix everything but the coconut together well (hands are best). Mixture will be fairly soft, but firm enough to mold into sticky balls.

Sprinkle the coconut on a piece of waxed paper. Divide the cheese mixture into two pieces and shape them into balls. Roll each in the coconut, pressing coconut into the cheese as you shape it. Wrap in plastic wrap and chill several hours or overnight before serving.

Recipe makes two cheese balls, approximately 5" in diameter. Serve with whole-wheat crackers.

Anchovy Cheese Spread

This makes a rather sophisticated hors d'oeuvre. Capers and anchovies are both strong flavors, but in this recipe you get just a delicate suggestion of each. It's really outstanding.

- 1 tbsp. dehydrated onions mixed with 1 tbsp. water
- 2 tsp. dry mustard mixed with 2 tsp. warm water
- 1/2 cup butter, softened
- 1 large pkg. (8-oz.) cream cheese, softened
- 2 anchovy fillets, minced
- 1 tsp. minced capers
  Parsley

Mix onions and water; set aside to soften. Mix dry mustard with water; set aside.

Whip butter and cream cheese together. Add onion, mustard, anchovies and capers; blend well.

This makes roughly 1-1/2 cups. You should be able to pack it into an individual soufflé dish or large custard dish. Chill it several hours or overnight, and unmold it by dipping the dish in warm water. Serve it on a plate surrounded by parsley. Good with most crackers and party breads.

VARIATION

Cook and drain a large artichoke.

Separate leaves of the artichoke and spread some of the anchovy cheese spread on the soft part of each leaf. The cheese spread should be at room temperature.

Arrange leaves in concentric circles on plates and serve as appetizers. Delicious! (And not as much trouble as you think it's going to be. Try it at least once.)

Aunt Marj's Quickie

Next time you need a quick hors d'oeuvre, try this favorite from my aunt Marj Patrick. May not sound like it, but it is delicious!

Just spread whole-wheat crackers with cream cheese and top with a sliver of sweet pickle.

Cheddar Cheese Cookies

Great munchies. Be very careful with the calories.

1-1/2	cups flour		1/2	cup chopped pecans
2	cups grated Cheddar cheese		1	tsp. Worcestershire sauce
1/2	cup butter, room temperature		1/4	tsp. cayenne pepper (less to taste)

Combine flour, cheese and butter; add remaining ingredients. Form dough into two logs, about 12" long and 2" in diameter. Refrigerate until chilled enough to slice into 1/4" slices. They don't get much larger, so you can crowd your cookie sheet and squeeze them into two batches.

Bake at 350° for about 10-12 minutes, until browned around edges. Cool on wire rack.

Makes 6-8 dozen.

Use styrofoam egg cartons to mold individual appetizers.

Chili Cheese Logs

When you want to set out something for nibbling, my mom's chili cheese log is an excellent choice. It keeps well in the freezer so doubling or tripling the recipe is a good idea.

- 2 pkgs. (3-oz.) cream cheese, softened
- 1 lb. sharp Cheddar cheese, grated
- 1 cup finely chopped pecans
- 2 cloves garlic, minced
  Chili powder

Put cheeses into a bowl with pecans and garlic. Mix together thoroughly (hands work best for this) and shape into two logs.

Pour some chili powder onto a piece of wax paper and roll the logs in it to cover. Store in refrigerator at least 24 hours. Serve in 1/4" slices with crackers.

VARIATION

You might substitute more chopped nuts for the chili powder, either alone or combined with chopped fresh parsley. Just don't use the parsley on the ones that are going into the freezer for a while.

Cinnamon Bread Sticks

My friend Phyllis Fleming served these for a light luncheon buffet, and they were a great hit. Serve them with pieces of fresh fruit.

- 1 pkg. plain bread sticks, about 16 sticks
- 1/4 cup butter, melted
- 1/2 cup sugar
- 1 tsp. cinnamon

Place bread sticks on a piece of foil and pour the melted butter over them. Combine the sugar and cinnamon and roll the buttered bread sticks in it.

Bake on a cookie sheet for ten minutes at 350°. Serve cool, using Orange Custard Sauce on Page 51 as a dip.

VARIATION

Instead of sugar and cinnamon, roll the buttered bread sticks in sesame seeds or poppy seeds. You might add a dash of garlic powder if you like, or a few drops of hot pepper sauce (such as Tabasco).

Curried Liver Pâté

This is splendid. Both the curry and the liver mellow overnight in the refrigerator. (People who think they don't like liver or curry are surprised that they like this!)

1/2 lb. chicken livers
1/2 cup butter (1/4 cup plus 1/4 cup)
1/2 cup chopped apple
1/2 cup chopped onion
3/4 tsp. curry powder (or more to taste)
Salt and freshly ground pepper
1 egg, lightly beaten

Trim and quarter chicken livers. Melt half the butter in a skillet and sauté liver, apple and onion until liver is just cooked through — about ten minutes over medium heat. Add curry powder, salt, pepper and egg, stirring until egg is set.

Pour this mixture into blender or food processor along with the remaining butter. Blend until smooth and creamy. Pour into a small bowl, about the size of a cereal bowl. Chill overnight.

Serves 8-12.

Holiday Trash

My friend Phyllis Fleming always makes the most flavorful party mix I've ever tasted. This is her recipe.

2 large boxes (12-oz.) Rice Chex
2 large boxes (15-oz.) Wheat Chex
1 large box (10-oz.) thin pretzel sticks
3 small jars (7-oz.) dry roasted mixed nuts
3 small jars (12-oz.) dry roasted peanuts
2 cups margarine, melted
6 tbsp. Worcestershire sauce
3 tsp. garlic powder
1-to-3 tbsp. red pepper sauce to taste (such as Tabasco)
Salt to taste

Divide the cereals and pretzels into three 9" x 13" pans. Add one jar mixed nuts and one jar peanuts to each pan.

Stir the seasonings into melted margarine and spoon over cereal-nut mixture, carefully salting and turning it over with a spoon.

Bake each pan at 250° for 2-3 hours, stirring every 20-30 minutes.

Store in air-tight containers. Let sit at least overnight before serving to let the flavors blend.

Jim's Potato Chips

When my husband Jim makes his potato chips, it's a Saturday afternoon project. They're so good we coax him into it as often as we can.

5   lbs. potatoes
      Oil
      Salt

You may peel the potatoes or not. Slice them uniformly, as thinly as you can, so they will cook quickly and evenly. Slice the potatoes with your food processor, the slicing edge of your cheese grater, or a good sharp knife. Put slices into a bowl of cold water to keep them from turning dark.

Heat 1/2" oil in electric skillet to 375°. Drain potato slices on paper towels before dropping them into hot oil. Fry until golden brown.

Drain on paper towels; salt while hot. Layer cooked chips between paper towels on a cookie sheet and keep them warm in oven until serving time.

NOTE
I can't give you an exact quantity because we have never made it through the cooking process without snitching. I can tell you that five of us can snack on them while they cook and then eat ample portions with our hamburgers and have a few to munch on during the evening. They never make it to the next day.

Marbleized Tea Eggs

A lovely addition to a buffet table, lunch box or picnic.

12 eggs, hard-cooked
2   tbsp. soy sauce
2   tbsp. salt (yes, I mean 2 tbsp.)
6   tea bags (or 3 family-size)

Cook eggs and gently crack shells all around them without removing any part of shell.

Put cracked eggs in bottom of large pan. Add soy sauce, salt, tea bags and enough water to cover them. Simmer them for about 30 minutes. Let them sit off heat until you can handle them.

When you peel eggs, the dark salty liquid will have soaked through the cracks, staining the egg white so that it looks like the eggs have been carved from marble. They are beautiful! And they are delicious, usually requiring no additional salt.

VARIATION
I haven't tried this; but a friend saves pickled beet liquid and uses it, diluted slightly with water, to simmer her cracked eggs. The eggs are red, instead of brown, and she says they are just as good.

Parmesan Spinach Balls

Remarkable appetizer; everyone wants the recipe. Easy to keep on hand in freezer.

- 2 pkgs. (10-oz.) frozen chopped spinach, cooked and drained
- 1 large onion, chopped
- 3/4 cup butter, melted
- 1 pkg. (8-oz.) cornbread stuffing mix
- 5 eggs, well beaten
- 1/2 cup grated Parmesan cheese
- 1 tbsp. garlic powder (tablespoon is correct)
- 1 tbsp. freshly ground pepper
- 1 tsp. thyme
- 1 tsp. salt

Cook and drain spinach; set aside.

Sauté onion in butter until transparent. Add onions and spinach to stuffing mix in a large bowl along with eggs, Parmesan cheese and seasonings.

Mix thoroughly with your hands, and chill until you can handle it easily. Roll into balls about the size of walnuts. Place them on a cookie sheet and freeze them; store covered in freezer until you are ready to serve them.

Put frozen spinach balls on a cookie sheet and bake at 400° for about 15-20 minutes. If you bake immediately after preparing, 350° for 15 minutes should be sufficient.

Makes about 8 dozen.

NOTE

If thyme isn't one of your favorite herbs, use parsley or sweet basil instead.

Quick Pâté

Keeps well in the refrigerator. Great to have on hand during holidays.

- 1 roll (8-oz.) liverwurst
- 4 green onions, chopped (green part only)
- 1 small can (4-1/4-oz.) chopped black olives
- 2 tbsp. cream cheese
- 1-to-2 tbsp. brandy

Combine all ingredients in bowl of food processor using plastic blade; do not over-process. If blending by hand, use a pastry blender.

Chill, and serve with whole-wheat or rye crackers or spread on fresh

NOTE

When you buy a can of chopped olives, there is not enough juice to drain. If you substitute sliced olives or whole olives and chop them yourself, be sure to drain them first.

vegetable sticks.

Excellent on fresh dark bread with hot mustard. (See Page 50.)
Makes about 1-1/2 cups.

Roquefort Quiche

This is unusual, but very good. I like to serve small wedges with crisp slices of fresh apples, either as an appetizer or part of a picnic lunch.

- 3 eggs
- 1/4 cup heavy cream
- 1 cup ricotta cheese
- 3 oz. Roquefort cheese
- 1/2 tsp. your favorite herb — dill weed, sweet basil or parsley
   Dash cayenne pepper, or a few drops red pepper sauce (such as Tabasco)
- 1 8-9" pastry pie shell, pre-baked

Beat eggs; add cream, ricotta and Roquefort. Stir in seasonings; pour into pre-baked pie shell. Bake at 400° about 25 minutes. Center should be firm enough not to jiggle, and it should be lightly browned.

Serves 12 as an appetizer.

Sugared Popcorn

If you love popcorn as much as we do at our house, you are going to want to try this recipe. It is very different — and very good.

- 1/3 cup popcorn
- 1/4 cup water
- 3 tbsp. bacon drippings
- 1/3 cup sugar

Put unpopped corn into water and set it aside while you heat bacon drippings and sugar together in a large and heavy saucepan. When sugar has dissolved, add popcorn and water. Watch out for splatters. Cover and shake. And shake. And shake. I don't know why it takes longer to pop, but eventually it will, and it's worth the wait.

Watch it carefully and remove from the heat before it is quite through popping — sugar burns easily.

This popcorn is just a touch sweet. It doesn't resemble caramel corn at all. It is the lightest, most tender popped corn I've ever eaten.

Store in air-tight container (if there's any left).

NOTE

When pre-baking any pie crust for quiche, be sure to brush unbaked crust with a little of the beaten egg. Keeps it crisp.

Pre-bake at 450° for 7-10 minutes; long enough to bake, but not brown.

NICE TO KNOW . . .

When using a quiche pan with a removable bottom, stand the pan on a large can after the quiche is baked and the ring will slip off. The quiche can then be easily sliced, or removed to a pretty platter.

Alsatian Onion Pie

NOTE

Paint unbaked pie shell with a little of the beaten egg. Bake it at 450° for 7-10 minutes; long enough to cook but not brown. The egg keeps it crisp after it's filled.

To be honest, you have to like onions. If you do, this is a winner! The combination of onions and cream makes a rich, delicious appetizer.

6	slices bacon, sliced in 1/4" pieces, cooked and drained
1	tbsp. reserved bacon fat
6	cups thinly sliced onions (about 2-1/2 lbs.)
1/4	tsp. salt
1/4	tsp. freshly ground pepper
1	tbsp. flour
1	cup heavy cream
4	eggs, beaten
1/8	tsp. freshly grated nutmeg
1	pastry pie crust, pre-baked but not browned

Cook and drain bacon. (I prefer to slice it first because it's easier to cook.)

Discard all but one tablespoon bacon fat and add onions to skillet. I used my electric skillet and it was almost overflowing with onions. I was sure just one tablespoon bacon fat wouldn't be enough, but it was. Cook onions until soft and translucent, about 12-15 minutes; stir occasionally. Season with salt and pepper.

Remove from heat and toss with flour. Add cream and mix to blend. Add eggs and nutmeg and mix well.

Pour into pre-baked pastry pie shell and bake at 400° for 35-40 minutes, until firm in center. Cover edge of crust with foil to prevent it from getting too brown. Serves 8-12 as an appetizer.

Artichokes with Cheese Soufflé

NOTE

The first time I made these, I laboriously scooped out the chokes *before* I cooked the artichokes— because that's what I read to do in several cookbooks. It took my brother Brian Patrick to figure out it's much easier to cook the artichokes first. He simply didn't know any better. Believe me, his way is best!

This recipe is typical of me. I saw a picture in a magazine years ago showing artichokes stuffed with cheese soufflé. I looked and looked for that recipe, and never did find it. So I improvised one night, relieved that they were a great hit. When you really want to do something special, try this as a first course, or perhaps as a luncheon entrée.

4	large artichokes	1	cup milk
	Piece of fresh lemon		Salt to taste
1/4	cup butter	2	cups grated Cheddar cheese
1/4	cup flour	4	eggs, separated

Slice one inch from the top of each artichoke with a sharp knife. Trim stem off at base of artichoke. Clip thorn from top of each leaf with kitchen shears. Rub cut edges with lemon. Simmer for 30-45 minutes in 1-1/2" salted water, until leaves near the base can easily be pulled off.

Remove from heat and drain. When cool enough to handle, carefully pull the artichoke open and scoop out the choke with a spoon; discard this middle part.

Make soufflé filling by cooking butter and flour in a saucepan over medium heat for 2-3 minutes. Remove from heat and stir in milk with a whisk. Add salt and return to heat until it boils and thickens. Stir in cheese until melted and, again, remove from heat.

Separate eggs and beat egg yolks until frothy and lemon colored. Add a spoonful of the cheese mixture to yolks, then gradually stir yolks into cheese mixture.

Beat egg whites into stiff peaks and fold into cheese mixture. Spoon this soufflé batter into center of artichokes. Using a small spoon, tuck what is left in among the leaves of the artichokes.

Bake uncovered at 350° for 30-40 minutes, until soufflé has completely set in the center and is lightly browned. Serve immediately, encouraging everyone to dip each artichoke leaf into the soufflé as they eat it.

What a lovely dining experience! Serves 4.

Gnocchi

The first time I made these delicious little dumplings, I was sure they would be more trouble than they were. They hold beautifully in the oven and make a delightful first course.

1	lb. frozen chopped spinach	1/2	cup grated Parmesan cheese
1	lb. ricotta cheese	1	cup flour (1/2 cup
1	egg, lightly beaten		plus 1/2 cup)
1/2	tsp. freshly grated nutmeg	1/4	cup unsalted butter, melted
1	tsp. salt		

Thaw, drain and mince the spinach. Combine with ricotta cheese, egg, nutmeg, salt, Parmesan cheese, and 1/2 cup flour.

Put remaining 1/2 cup flour on a sheet of waxed paper. As you roll pieces of the spinach mixture into little marble-size dumplings, drop them into the flour and roll them around. Add more flour as needed.

To cook, bring a large pot of salted water to a boil. Drop in the dumplings one by one until they cover the bottom of the pot. They will rise to the top when they are done.

Take them out of the water with a slotted spoon and drain them on paper towels. Put them in a large casserole, drizzle them with melted butter, and keep them warm until serving time. They keep well. Can be refrigerated overnight.

Yields 60-80 dumplings, enough for 6-8 people.

By Special Request...

"P" FOR POP

I loved my grandfather Pop.

He always took me Christmas shopping, just the two of us. Late in the afternoon, my grandmother Nano would take me to Pop's barber shop on Main Street, right in the middle of downtown, and drop me off. I still remember the sweet smell of bay rum as I sat on the bench amidst the curling old magazines and watched in fascination as he clipped away.

When it was time to go, Pop would sweep the great clouds of hair from the floor and pull the shades down over the windows and the door. Hand in hand we'd take to the street.

Do you remember the way store windows used to be? Full of Santa's elves, animated and exciting? Every store had something special, and we'd always stop to look.

Pop carried my purse for me; so, as we shopped and I checked off my list, it never ran out of pennies.

I remember one year in particular. We had gone into a dime store, the kind with the wooden floor and that special popcorn smell. There was a man selling neckties — oh, such special neckties! They had initials on them, to make them personal. So, I told Pop to turn his head and took my purse up to the counter to buy him a tie.

His name was Harley Grandstaff, and I bought him the most beautiful red, initialed tie. It said, "P" — for Pop — and he wore it for a long, long time.

ISLAND PLANE RIDE

We had been waiting at the airport in Puerto Rico for about seven hours.

The airline we were scheduled on to St. Thomas had gone out of business — the day before we arrived.

We waited for another plane, not knowing it had lost its door during take-off somewhere else in the Islands when one of the passengers hit the emergency alarm. They never did find that door, but they did fit the plane with an extra one and sent the plane back for us.

Finally, our '30s vintage, eight-passenger plane was ready. We settled into our rump-sprung seats as the pilot hurried up the aisle muttering something about seat-belts.

He revved up the engines. They roared and backfired and spewed sparks everywhere as we lifted off into the nighttime sky. There was nothing so formal as taxiing out for clearance. We just heard the pilot gun the engines and go.

The cabin of the tiny plane was completely dark. The cockpit dials cast an eerie glow, and outside the stars were so bright we could have read by them. The engines were so loud we couldn't talk, and the sparks continued to fly.

Though we couldn't see him, we all knew our pilot must have flung a scarf around his neck to flutter in the night air.

It was a memorable ride.

Original Kaye Johns Radio Scripts

14

Beverages

Coffee Brewing Tips

It's easy to brew a full-flavored cup of coffee whether you like your coffee strong or weak. The best way to do it is to make your general rule of thumb two tablespoons ground coffee for each cup of coffee. If you don't like your coffee that strong, add hot water after it has brewed — you'll have a much better flavor. If you like it strong enough to chew (as we do at our house), just add a little more ground coffee per cup until you find the amount you prefer.

There are a couple of alternative methods to the electric or stove-top percolator that I would like to mention. One is the paper filter method. We've used this for years. I personally prefer it because it's so easy to make just one or two cups. That way you always have fresh coffee without leaving any to go stale in the coffeepot. It is, however, more trouble if you need to serve a lot of people. In that case, I almost always make one pot of coffee to hold in our thermos and one pot fresh; it keeps perfectly in the thermos. You can buy paper filter holders at most gourmet shops or in the housewares department of large department stores. They come with or without pots. My favorite is an individual cup holder so that I can make myself one cup of fresh coffee whenever I like. All I need is boiling water to pour through the ground coffee.

There is also a cold water method of brewing coffee. You can buy the equipment for making your concentrate at special coffee houses, gourmet shops and, perhaps, at larger department stores.

The principle is simple. You pour a whole can of ground coffee into the appliance. Then pour in the cold water which drips slowly through the coffee overnight. In the morning you have a very concentrated black liquid which looks like soy sauce. You keep this small bottle of concentrate in the refrigerator and, when you want a cup of fresh coffee, you add 1-2 tablespoons liquid coffee concentrate to a cup of boiling water.

I've been served coffee made this way and it was very good. It is different in flavor — though I can't describe the difference — but you can tell it isn't quite like any coffee you've ever had before.

One of the selling points of brewing coffee this way is that it is supposed to remove most of the acid, making the coffee a little easier on the digestive tract. Like the paper filters, it has the advantage of giving you a fresh cup of coffee whenever you like — and tasting better than instant.

Frozen Fruit Milkshakes
(Calorie Conscious)

Rich, creamy milkshakes with roughly 100 calories each.

FOR EACH SERVING

- 1/2   cup *canned* evaporated skim milk
- 1/2   tsp. vanilla extract
- 1   cup *frozen* fruit, diced
-       Artificial sweetener to taste

Canned evaporated milk has half the water removed. This leaves the milk slightly thick, so that it whips almost as well as cream. It does taste canned, so it's important to use vanilla to cut this canned taste.

Put canned milk (do not add water), vanilla, sweetener and frozen fruit into your blender and purée until the consistency of a milkshake. Sometimes it's too thick for your blender. If this happens, add ice water, one spoonful at a time until it's whirling again.

Holiday Coffee Punch

Very rich, but not too sweet. A delight at holiday time.

1	pint vanilla ice cream		Rum or Kahlua to taste
7	tsp. instant coffee granules		(optional)
	(4 tsp. plus 3 tsp.)	8	oz. heavy cream
1/4	cup hot water	2	tbsp. honey
2	bottles (10-oz.) club soda,		Cinnamon, for garnish
	very cold		

Spoon ice cream into punch bowl; chop with a spoon so that it's in fairly small pieces. Dissolve four teaspoons instant coffee granules in hot water and drizzle it over the ice cream. Add club soda and rum or Kahlua.

Whip cream with honey and remaining three teaspoons instant coffee. Whip it to soft peak stage, then fold half into ice cream mixture. Drop the other half in large soft dollops over the top. Dust with a sprinkling of cinnamon and a few granules of instant coffee.

Serve right away, unless you have room in your freezer to chill it. If you put it in the freezer, watch it carefully, stirring in ice crystals that may form around sides of bowl. It's really better if you chill it in freezer for an hour or so before serving; stays cold longer. You may want to hold last half of whipped cream (for topping) until serving time.

Serves 15-20.

VARIATIONS

Literally any frozen fruit or fruit combination will work, within your diet requirements. Just a little banana adds a lot of richness to both flavor and texture. Be sure to dice fresh fruit and freeze pieces on a cookie sheet. Once frozen, they can be stored in a covered container and the separate pieces scooped out as needed. Suggestions:

1. Use one cup frozen strawberries with 1/2 cup frozen bananas.
2. Try 1/2 cup frozen blueberries (alone or with 1/2 cup frozen bananas).
3. Mix 1/2 frozen fresh medium orange with one slice frozen canned unsweetened pineapple.
4. One frozen peach or nectarine.

NOTE

I once tried frozen cantaloupe. That's the only fruit I don't recommend. I love cantaloupe, but it makes a lousy milkshake.

There are a couple of things you can do to ensure crystal-clear iced tea.

1. Brew your tea according to notes on hot tea: one rounded teaspoon for each serving, plus one for the pot.

2. Pour the warm steeped tea into a pitcher of cold water and it will be perfectly clear.

3. If you have leftover tea in the refrigerator, you can almost always clear it by adding a little boiling water.

I've never been a sun tea fan, although I know it is a good way to make tea. I've always thought it took more tea per serving, making it more expensive; and it requires planning ahead, which I don't always do.

Something I think is a good idea, and wish I would do more often, is to freeze ice cubes made from tea. They don't dilute your iced tea as they dissolve. I know some people who go a step further, freezing twists of lemon or orange peel or sprigs of mint in the cubes. Not only adds flavor, but color.

Hot Buttered Nog

This recipe makes a thick, rich batter you can keep for weeks in the freezer. Makes a satisfying hot drink for any cold evening, much appreciated by guests.

1	box (1-lb.) powdered sugar	1	quart vanilla ice cream, slightly softened
1	box (1-lb.) light brown sugar		Rum or brandy
2	cups butter, softened		Boiling water
1	tsp. freshly grated nutmeg		
1	tsp. cinnamon		

Cream sugars and butter together with nutmeg and cinnamon. Stir in ice cream and mix well.

Store this batter in an air-tight container in your freezer. It won't freeze solid; you can spoon out some whenever you like.

To serve, mix one heaping tablespoon of the batter in a warm mug with an ounce or two of rum or brandy and fill with boiling water.

If you prefer, add a little more batter and a touch of vanilla extract in place of rum.

Makes 2 quarts, approximately 70-80 servings.

Iced Tea Punch

This is an unusual punch recipe that is a traditional favorite at my friend Rita Browning's church. It's perfect for receptions.

6	cups water (2 cups plus 4 cups)
2	large family-size tea bags
3	cups sugar
2	cups lemon juice
1	large can (12-oz.) frozen orange juice concentrate, thawed
16	oz. pineapple juice
2	bottles (32-oz.) lemon-lime soft drink, such as Sprite

Brew a strong tea using two cups water with two tea bags. (Rita recommends using a sun tea jar if you have one. I use boiling water steeped for five minutes.)

Add sugar and stir until completely dissolved. Add juices, four more cups water, and chill overnight. Just before serving, add Sprite.

Makes 40-45 punch cups full.

Old-Fashioned Eggnog

I went two years without making eggnog because I'd lost my favorite recipe. Here it is — I found it!

6	eggs, separated (set aside whites)	1	tsp. vanilla extract
		1	cup light rum
1/2	cup sugar	1	pint heavy cream
2	cups milk		Freshly grated nutmeg to taste

Whip egg *yolks* with sugar until light, fluffy and lemon colored. Add milk, vanilla extract and rum. If you choose not to use the rum, be sure to add another cup of milk. You may prefer bourbon or brandy. Chill mixture overnight to let flavor develop.

A couple of hours before serving time, beat egg *whites* until stiff, but not dry. Whip cream until soft peaks form; fold both into milk mixture. Grate fresh nutmeg over the top.

Set bowl in freezer and chill for 1-2 hours before serving. Check it every 20-30 minutes. Stir in ice crystals that have formed around the edge of the bowl. Chilling in the freezer isn't necessary; but eggnog stays cold longer.

Serves 6-10

Orange Spice Tea

Versions of this recipe have been around for years and they are always popular in cold weather, or as a coffee substitute year round. I'm including my version because I think it's a little less sweet than some I've seen, and you may prefer it. This is something children can make from scratch, put in inexpensive jars and give as holiday gifts. (So can Mom!)

1	jar (1-oz.) instant tea, such as Lipton	1	envelope lemon or lemon-lime powdered drink mix (.39-oz.), unsweetened
1	jar (9-oz.) instant orange breakfast drink, such as Tang	1/2	cup sugar
		1	tbsp. cinnamon

Combine all the ingredients and stir to blend well. This easily fits into a clean coffee can.

This is one of those recipes you adapt for your personal taste. Some recipes add powdered cloves; I don't because I don't care for them. You can use more or less of the powdered lemon drink and, if you are counting calories, you might buy low-calorie artificially sweetened brands and experiment with taste until you're satisfied.

To serve, add 1-2 tablespoons of mix to each cup boiling water.

Always throw away eggs which have even the slightest crack. Bacteria can enter the egg and, although you can't smell or taste it, it can be dangerous.

CALORIE-CONSCIOUS VARIATION

For those of you who love this type of drink but are counting calories, I suggest you experiment as I have done. Count 1/6 (1-oz. liquid) of a 6-oz. can of frozen orange juice concentrate as one fruit exchange on your eating program.

Add this thawed orange juice concentrate to your cup along with a teaspoon of instant tea, a dash of cinnamon, and a squeeze of lemon, and artificial sweetener to taste. It's an excellent substitute. I sometimes hold out my ounce of concentrate when I'm making the family's juice in the morning— just leave it in the can and use it later in the day.

Perfect Pot of Tea

Do me a favor. If you ever drink or serve hot tea, whether by the individual cup or by the pot, be sure you always use water that has been brought to a full, rolling boil. Not simmering, not just hot, but boiling!

If you're not already careful about this, make two cups side by side — one with boiling water, one hot or barely simmering. Taste the difference!

Rules of thumb about tea are simple.

1. Always use fresh cold water. Fresh rather than what's left in the tea kettle, because it tastes better. Cold, rather than hot, because hot water sometimes picks up sediment from the hot water heater.

2. Always have the water at a full rolling boil. It is usually said, "Take the pot to the water, not the water to the pot." Meaning, don't let the water cool even the short amount of time it takes to walk across your kitchen.

3. It's best to warm your cup or your tea pot by rinsing with very hot water before you add the tea. This helps keep the boiling water very hot while the tea is steeping.

4. Use one rounded teaspoonful (or tea bag) for each cup. If you're making several cups in a teapot, add one rounded teaspoonful for each cup, and one extra for the pot.

5. Cover your cup with a lid. If you're making a pot of tea, use both lid and a tea cozy or kitchen towel to hold the heat in. A tea cozy is a simple cover (usually quilted) much like the covers you can buy for your blender or other appliances.

6. Brew tea by the clock, not by its color. Many teas are light in color even when fully brewed. Most teas require a full five minutes steeping time.

7. If you do end up with tea that's too strong for your taste, add a little hot water to your cup. You'll have the benefit of the full flavor without having it full strength. If you shorten the steeping time, you won't have the full flavor.

8. I've found that sometimes I forget my tea, and it gets a little bitter if it steeps over five minutes. I add a splash of milk. It cuts the bitter taste beautifully, but is not enough to change the color of the tea.

9. Use milk instead of cream with tea because the fat in the cream will float on top of the tea. Use milk or lemon, not both. Lemon curdles the milk, and that's really unappetizing.

If you enjoy hot tea, I encourage you to experiment. There are many different types of tea available today, each unique. Makes it a lot more fun.

Canadian Blueberry Tea

Try this on a cold winter's evening and you will know why it is popular in Canada. Amazingly, it tastes like blueberries.

PER PORTION

1	oz. Grand Marnier
1	oz. Amaretto
3/4	cup freshly-brewed, strong, very hot tea

Combine ingredients in a large cup and sip slowly.

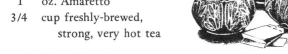

B&B and Tea

This is another variation of a delightful after-dinner drink using tea.

PER PORTION

1-1/2	oz. B & B
3/4	cup freshly-brewed, strong, very hot tea

Dollop of whipped cream

Combine the B & B with the tea in a large cup and top with the dollop of whipped cream.

By Special Request...

TAKING OFF FOR CAMP

Our daughter Shannon was accepted for a two-week camp that's totally paid for by the Lions Club. It's a camp for special kids, kids with problems.

It's some distance from our home, an eight hour drive or so, in the Hill Country of South Texas.

For years the Lions Club has not only sponsored the camp, but they have worked with a local businessmen's flying club to see that our kids are flown to camp in private planes. What a thrilling experience, and what a wonderful plus for the parents.

Last Sunday we drove our daughter to the small general aviation airport early in the morning. We gathered outside the small terminal to wait with the other parents and their children.

It was a pretty subdued group. Some of the kids had been to camp before, some hadn't. They were all looking forward to going, but I think they all shared our Shannon's feelings.

"Mom," she said, "It's kind of strange, but part of me feels like I want to go and part of me feels like I want to stay." I understood.

Finally, our pilot was ready to take off. The three girls who were to go on his plane scrambled aboard, one very slowly as the others held her crutches. The pilot got on board himself, looking every bit the kindly grandfather as he waved through the window at us and revved the engines.

And when that little plane taxied off and lifted into the sky, three mothers stood with lumps in their throats.

GIFT FROM CAMP

It was awards night at the Texas Lions Clubs' camp for crippled children, and I'd like to tell you what we saw.

One hot shot, maybe eight years old, ran across the rough ground to get his award. He runs with a four-legged walker for support. The secret of his speed is that two of the legs have wheels — does he scoot.

One thirteen-year-old boy played the piano so beautifully we sat spellbound, not even noticing he was blind.

The older children were graduating from camp, and were called to the stage individually to receive plaques. There were about twenty of them, and it took quite a while for them to walk that far.

Crutches were such a struggle for one lovely girl that the counselors carried her to the stage. One of them sat with her so she wouldn't feel awkward while the others stood. It wasn't good enough for her. She sent the counselor after her crutches and struggled to her feet, balancing precariously but proudly, as the others got their awards.

Our daughter isn't on crutches. Hers is a hidden handicap, mild cerebral palsy, that's enough to make her different from other children. Friends are hard to come by.

Her gift from the camp? Friendship. Acceptance. And the look of absolute, unqualified joy as she hugged her loving counselors good-bye.

Some money, you see, does buy happiness — when it's given away.

Original Kaye Johns Radio Scripts

LOVE STORY

It's a rather remarkable love story. They're both legally blind, although he can see enough shapes and colors to steer through a room. He takes care of her.

They met at the doctor's office, the eye doctor, chatting in the waiting room about the weather, the doctor and how lonely each was living alone. She'd lost her husband, he'd lost his wife.

A few weeks later they met again at a vocational training program for the blind. They had a splendid day together, chatting and building a friendship.

When they were driven home she asked him, rather coyly, why didn't he call her some time? And when he did, she asked him over. "I'll fix you some supper," she said, and he came in a cab. Once a week, then twice, three times or more. And the cab fares mounted.

One day he said, "Ethel, I believe I'm falling in love with you." And when she loved him too, he said, "Why don't we just put a stop to these cab fares and get married?"

So they did.

She's my grandmother, and they were married when she was eighty-three. They've just celebrated their seventh anniversary.

My incredible grandmother, who lost her husband of sixty-five years, and her sight, never forgot what living was about. Lovely and loving in her age, she whispered to me not long ago, "I'm happier than I've ever been in my life."

SPECIAL CHILD

Today my heart is with my daughter.

She's fifteen, a lovely, gangling, immature fifteen. A child with eyes that twinkle and dance, a smile that is always ready and easy. A child hungry to touch and be touched, hug and be hugged . . . a child with "mild cerebral palsy".

Whatever that means, technically.

What it has meant to us, has meant to her, is years of going slower than the rest — taking longer to skip and to run and to jump rope and ride a bike, because muscles wouldn't work right. It's meant years of being misunderstood because talking was such a chore with a tongue that was hard to control and wouldn't do right. It's been years of painstaking printing when others were breezing through cursive penmanship, and swinging at pinatas and missing because visual perception wasn't there.

It's been teachers and school administrators and doctors and diagnosticians who couldn't figure out what was wrong, who tried and couldn't help.

There are a lot of you out there who have a special child who doesn't fit the mold, who, as one expert told us, falls in the cracks because there really isn't a place for her that seems right. I want to say, don't give up, never stop trying. The next thing may help.

It's been a fifteen-year-long struggle for self-confidence, from "I can't," to "I think I can," to "I can, I will, I did." It hasn't been our struggle, it's been hers. And I want to say to our Shannon, and for our Shannon, what a bright kid to have come so far when it was so hard.

Original Kaye Johns Radio Scripts

Breads

Lemon Biscuits

These are delightful biscuits with baked chicken or fish. The lemon doesn't make them tart, but gives them almost a lemon drop flavor without being sweet.

    2   cups biscuit mix
    1/2 cup minced fresh parsley (or 2 tbsp. dried parsley)
         Grated rind of one fresh lemon
         Juice of one fresh lemon
         Water, added to lemon juice to equal 2/3 cup

Combine biscuit mix, parsley and lemon rind. Stir in lemon juice and water. Knead lightly about ten turns, adding biscuit mix as needed to keep dough from sticking. Roll dough out to a thickness of about 1/2 inch.

Cut with biscuit cutter and bake on oiled cookie sheet at 425° for ten minutes, or until lightly browned. Serve hot with butter.

Makes 12.

Mom's Perfect Biscuits

I've always used my mom's biscuit recipe. My brother Brian says Grandma Ethel is the only one who can top it — but he's remembering summer camping trips in the mountains of Colorado when Grandma baked her biscuits in a wood-burning stove. That's not fair competition!

    2   cups flour   2   tsp. sugar
    4   tsp. baking powder   1/2 cup shortening
    1/2 tsp. cream of tartar   2/3 cup milk
    1   tsp. salt

Combine dry ingredients and cut in shortening until size of peas. Add milk all at once and stir only to moisten ingredients.

The secret, if there is one, is in the handling of the dough. I turn mine onto two pieces of plastic wrap, adding only enough flour to keep it from sticking to the plastic. Knead it about ten quick turns and roll it between the sheets of plastic to about 1/2" thickness. Cut with biscuit cutter and bake at 450° for 10-12 minutes, until lightly browned.

Using plastic wrap not only makes for a quick clean up, but keeps you from adding too much flour, which makes the biscuits heavy. These, I promise, almost float off the plate!

Makes 12 biscuits.

Scones

Scones are rich, barely sweet biscuits, much like fruit shortcake. Best served hot out of the oven with lots of butter.

2 cups flour	1/2 cup butter
2 tbsp. sugar	1 egg, beaten
3 tsp. baking powder	2/3 cup milk or half-and-half
1/2 tsp. salt	

Mix first four ingredients, then cut in the butter until crumbly. Stir in egg and milk; dough will be sticky. Drop by spoonfuls onto a greased cookie sheet.

Bake at 450° for about ten minutes.

Makes 12 biscuits.

NOTE

You may use 1/2 cup milk rather than 2/3 cup; dough will be stiff enough to roll out. Bake at 450° for about ten minutes.

Cinnamon-Bran Coffee Cake

Without question, one of our favorites. I like it as well the next day as I do hot out of the oven.

BATTER

1 cup flour	1 tsp. baking soda
1 cup bran (not cereal, but natural bran flakes, from the health food store)	1 cup buttermilk (or 1 cup milk plus 1 tbsp. vinegar)
1/2 cup brown sugar, packed	1/2 cup oil
3 tsp. baking powder	1/2 cup chopped pecans

TOPPING

1/4 cup butter, melted
1/4 cup sugar
1   tbsp. cinnamon
1   tbsp. flour

Mix flour and bran together; add brown sugar, baking powder and baking soda. Blend well, mashing most of the lumps out of the brown sugar.

Combine buttermilk with oil; stir into dry ingredients and mix just until moistened. Add pecans and put into a three-quart casserole or large 10" pie plate.

Spread melted butter over top of the batter and sprinkle with combined sugar, cinnamon and flour.

Bake at 350° for about 30 minutes, until firm in center.

NOTE

Prepare batter, complete with topping and refrigerate overnight, if you like. Bake next morning, allowing an extra 20-30 minutes.

NICE TO KNOW . . .

Keep your shelled nuts in plastic bags in the freezer to prevent their becoming rancid.

NOTE

Jill's Monkey Bread sounds stickier —and sweeter— than it really is. The pieces of dough pull apart easily and are just sticky enough to be marvelous. Add some chopped pecans if you like. I haven't tried it but I think you could use larger pieces of biscuit dough.

My sister-in-law Jill Kelly served us this outstanding coffee cake one weekend when we spent the night with them. I loved the idea of using canned biscuit dough because it's so easy to keep on hand.

    4   cans refrigerator biscuits (10 biscuits each)
    3/4 cup sugar
    1   tsp. cinnamon

SAUCE

    3/4   cup butter, melted
    1-1/2 tsp. cinnamon
    1   cup sugar

Separate biscuits and cut each one into fourths. Mix sugar and cinnamon together and roll biscuit pieces in it. Drop them in a one-piece Bundt pan. Do not use two-piece angel food pan, as butter may leak out and could catch on fire.

Melt butter, add cinnamon and sugar for sauce and heat, stirring until sugar is dissolved. Let cool a minute and pour over dough in the pan.

Bake at 350° for about 45 minutes, or until brown on top and firm to the touch. When you remove the pan from the oven, let it stand for five minutes or so before inverting it onto a plate.

Margaret's Honey Nut Rolls

VARIATION: QUICK PECAN CRISPIES

Another idea is to take the biscuit rolls after you have sugared and cut them in half and put them on a buttered cookie sheet, cut edge up. Press them flat with your hand and sprinkle with chopped pecans.

Bake at 350° for about ten minutes, until lightly browned. These are delicious little pecan crispies.

Margaret Ackerman taught Home Ec for over 30 years and she has many wonderful recipes. This one is typical — it starts with something as simple as canned biscuits, but no one would guess! They melt in your mouth.

    1/2 cup brown sugar
    1/2 tsp. cinnamon
    1   can (10 count) refrigerator biscuits
    5   tbsp. butter, melted (3 tbsp. plus 2 tbsp.)
    2   tbsp. honey
    2   tbsp. chopped pecans

On a piece of waxed paper, mix brown sugar and cinnamon. Dip biscuits in three tablespoons melted butter and roll in cinnamon mixture.

Flatten biscuits a bit with the heel of your hand. Roll each biscuit like a little jellyroll and cut in half.

In a pie plate or 9" cake pan, put remaining butter. Stir in honey, pecans, and any remaining cinnamon mixture.

Arrange biscuit pieces on top and bake at 350°for 20 minutes, or until puffed and slightly browned on top. Center rolls should be firm to the touch.

Invert pan on a plate and let sit a minute so the gooey part ends up on top.

North Texas U.B. Coffee Cake

U.B. stands for Union Building where we used to hang out at North Texas State University. The coffee cake was more than a tradition, it was sustenance for thousands of students through the years.

My roommate talked one of the cooks out of the recipe, which originally called for many pounds of ingredients. We cut it down to size and it comes as close to the real thing as memory allows. After studying all night, it was a just reward.

BATTER
- 2 cups flour
- 2 tsp. baking powder
- 1/2 tsp. salt
- 1 cup sugar
- 6 tbsp. oil
- 3/4 cup milk
- 1 egg
- 1 tsp. vanilla extract

TOPPING
- 1/4 cup butter, melted
- 1/4 cup flour
- 3/4 cup sugar
- 1 tbsp. cinnamon

Combine batter ingredients in bowl and beat with the mixer for at least three minutes. It should be light like cake batter.

Pour batter into a greased 8" x 8" pan and spoon on the melted butter.

Mix flour, sugar and cinnamon and sprinkle over batter. As it bakes, the butter and cinnamon make little rivulets through the batter. It's wonderful, even without the memories.

Bake at 350°for 30-40 minutes until firm enough in center to spring back when lightly touched.

NOTE
    I usually make the batter the night before; it keeps well overnight in the refrigerator. If you do, increase the baking time, since the batter will be so cold. It should bake in 45-60 minutes. When it's firm in the middle, it's done.

Pull-Apart Coffee Cake

NOTE

Do *not* use angel food pan as butter could leak out and cause a fire in your oven.

VARIATION

Leave out cinnamon and add 1/2 cup chopped pecans.

Unbelievably easy, remarkably delicious! Serve this when you have overnight guests.

1	pkg. frozen cloverleaf yeast rolls (about 25 rolls)	1/2	cup brown sugar, packed
		4	tsp. cinnamon, less to taste
1/2	cup butter, melted		
1	pkg. vanilla pudding (not instant) four-serving size		

Butter a Bundt cake pan heavily (use about 1/4 cup soft butter).

Separate each roll into three pieces and put these frozen pieces into cake pan. Pour melted butter over them.

Combine pudding mix, brown sugar and cinnamon; sprinkle this *dry* mixture over frozen dough. (Do not add milk to pudding mix.)

Leave cake pan out overnight on kitchen cabinet, uncovered. The next morning, bake it for 20 minutes at 375°. Remove from oven and let pan rest for 3-4 minutes, then invert it over serving plate.

These rolls pull apart, but they are very sticky, so be sure to serve with forks. Amazingly, they aren't overly sweet — just incredibly rich and delicious!

Sour Cream Coffee Cake

NOTE

You can make the batter the night before. Go ahead and top with melted butter and sugar mixture. Cover the dish and refrigerate. Bake at 350° but allow more time because the batter is cold — usually almost an hour. Begin checking after 45 minutes.

Do you ever forget to take the butter out of the refrigerator in time for it to soften?

I've found that if I cut it into chunks and use my pastry blender, it's easy to mix the butter and sugar. I cream it with the pastry blender until my arm gets tired, then switch to the electric mixer. By then it's soft enough.

People absolutely rave about this coffee cake.

2	cups flour	1	cup sugar
2	tsp. baking powder	2	eggs
1	tsp. baking soda	1	cup sour cream
	Pinch of salt	1	tsp. vanilla extract
3/4	cup butter, softened		

TOPPING

1/4	cup butter, melted	1/2	tsp. cinnamon
1/4	cup brown sugar, packed	1/2	cup chopped pecans

Combine flour, baking powder, baking soda and salt in one bowl. In larger bowl, cream together butter and sugar; add eggs one at a time. Beat until light and fluffy.

Add dry ingredients to creamed ingredients alternately with sour cream. Stir in vanilla.

Pour batter into well-buttered 8" x 12" baking dish. Spoon melted butter over top of batter. Combine brown sugar, cinnamon and pecans; sprinkle over butter.

Bake at 350° for about 30 minutes, until it's firm in center and pulling away from sides of baking dish. Serve warm. If not serving immediately, cool to room temperature and cover.

Cornmeal Griddle Cakes

These are my favorite pancakes, served with warm maple syrup.

1	cup flour	2	eggs, separated
1	cup yellow cornmeal	1-1/2	cups buttermilk (or regular
2	tsp. baking powder		milk plus 1-1/2 tbsp. vinegar)
3	tbsp. sugar	2	tbsp. butter, melted
1	tsp. salt		

Mix dry ingredients in a bowl and set aside. Combine egg yolks with buttermilk and add dry ingredients to this egg yolk mixture. Stir until moistened. Add butter.

Whip egg whites until they hold stiff peaks, and fold into batter.

Bake griddle cakes on a hot griddle or electric skillet set at 425°. Pile them on a platter to keep warm in a 200° oven until you serve them. Serves 4.

NOTE

I always bake all the pancakes at once so I can eat with the family.

If I have any left over, I stack them in a bread wrapper and keep them in the freezer. I can pull out as many as I need to reheat on busy mornings.

Crêpes

These are great to have in the freezer. Once you discover how easy they are, you'll want to always keep them on hand.

1/2 cup unsifted flour
1/2 tsp. salt
  3 eggs, beaten
  1 cup milk

Slowly beat the flour and salt into the eggs, then add the milk. (Or mix everything in your blender.) When batter is smooth, cover and let "rest" in the refrigerator for at least 30 minutes. (I don't know why.)

Lightly grease your pan (can be any skillet) for the first few crêpes. After that it won't be necessary.

Pour in small amount of batter and cook until lightly browned on the underside. They don't need to be turned over.

Stack them, as you cook them, between layers of plastic wrap or waxed paper.

Refrigerate (several days) or freeze (several weeks) until you need them. The whole stack can be rolled.

Makes 8-12 crêpes, depending on the diameter.

NOTE

Crêpe pans are wonderful, but not neccessary. I made these crêpes for years in my *square* electric skillet; I simply shaped them as I poured them. Don't get too hung up over having "proper" utensils.

NOTE

Recipes using crepes are Burgundy Beef, Page 104; Kevin's Blintzes, Page 138; and Vi's Custard Crepes, Page 190.

Waffles

This is a wonderful basic waffle batter. I don't even add syrup, just lots of melted butter.

    2   cups flour
    1   tsp. salt
    1   tsp. baking soda
    1/2 tsp. sugar
    2   eggs, lightly beaten
    2   cups buttermilk
    2   tbsp. melted butter

Mix dry ingredients together in a mixing bowl and stir together with the eggs, buttermilk and melted butter.

Fill your pre-heated waffle iron with enough batter to make a full waffle, but not enough to run out the sides. Do not overcook.

Makes 4-6 large waffles, depending on the size of your waffle iron.

VARIATION

Add 1/2 cup chopped pecans to the batter for delicious pecan waffles.

Whole-Grain Pancakes

A delicious new flavor and texture. You expect them to be heavy, but they are surprisingly light.

    1/2 cup whole-wheat flour
    1/2 cup white flour
    1/2 cup rolled oats
    1/2 cup flaked bran (not cereal)
    1   tsp. baking soda
    3   tsp. baking powder
    1/2 tsp. salt
    3   tbsp. sugar
    2   eggs, separated
    1-1/2 cups buttermilk (or regular milk with 1-1/2 tbsp. vinegar)
    1/4 cup butter, melted

Measure dry ingredients by spooning lightly into measuring cup and leveling. Combine with baking soda, baking powder, salt and sugar.

Whip egg whites separately. Combine lightly beaten egg yolks with buttermilk; add to dry ingredients. Stir in melted butter; fold in egg whites.

Bake pancakes on lightly oiled griddle or electric skillet set on 425°.

These pancakes will keep well on a platter in a 200° oven. They are

You can lighten any pancake batter by whipping the egg whites separately and folding them in.

Be careful not to overmix the batter if you do. You should have little fluffs of egg white visible in the batter.

Mix batter for pancakes as little as possible; it should be slightly lumpy. Otherwise? Pancakes could be heavy and tough. Light and tender is better.

slightly sweet, so you may not want to add syrup. We tried them with just a little strawberry jam and that seemed perfect.

Makes 16 four-inch pancakes; serves 4.

Banana Bran Bread

I developed this recipe years ago when my husband took his breakfast with him every morning. It's not only portable, but nutritious and delicious.

1	cup flour
1	cup bran (not cereal)
1/2	cup powdered milk (the concentrated kind from the health food store)
2/3	cup brown sugar, packed
3	tsp. baking powder
3-to-4	small, very ripe bananas
1/2	cup oil
2	eggs
1/2	cup chopped pecans

In one bowl mix together first five ingredients. In another bowl mash bananas and mix in oil and eggs. Gradually add dry mixture to banana mixture and stir to mix completely; add pecans.

Pour batter into a greased one-pound loaf pan and bake at 350° for 50-60 minutes, until firm in center and pulling away from side of pan. Cool slightly in pan and invert onto cake rack. When cool, wrap in plastic.

Slice into 16 slices.

NOTE

Flaked bran can be bought by the bag in health food stores and some large grocery stores. Store in freezer.

Peeled bananas won't turn dark if you toss them with a little pineapple juice.

ALL ABOUT BANANAS

Did you know you can freeze bananas? If you peel and dice them and scatter the pieces on a cookie sheet to freeze, you can pick them up and store them in plastic baggies until needed.

Or even easier, freeze them in their skin. It turns black and awful looking, but the bananas are fine and well protected. The peeling comes off easily while they are still frozen, and they are easy to chop in their frozen state.

Use them for calorie-conscious milkshakes or with sweetened ricotta cheese over toast.

Bananas can be refrigerated. If you are like me and prefer them a little green, this is a good idea because the cold temperature stops the ripening process.

One word of warning. The skins turn black, which makes them unappetizing. Peeled, no one can tell the difference.

Blueberry Muffins

Everybody loves these!

    2   cups flour
    1/4 cup sugar
    3   tsp. baking powder
        Pinch of salt
    1/3 cup oil
    1/2 cup milk
    1   egg, well beaten
    1/2 cup individually frozen blueberries, still frozen

Combine dry ingredients, then liquid ingredients. Add liquid mixture to dry and stir briefly, just to moisten. Add frozen blueberries at last moment.

Fill greased muffin tins 1/2 — 2/3 full and bake at 400° for about 25 minutes, until golden brown.

Serve immediately with butter.

Makes 12 muffins.

VARIATION

Add one tablespoon minced onion and two tablespoons of poppy seeds or sesame seeds.

Cheese Bread

This recipe comes from my sister-in-law Jo Johns. She served it with her homemade vegetable soup, and it was wonderful.

    2   cups biscuit mix
    2   tsp. dry mustard
    1-1/2 cups grated Cheddar cheese
    2   eggs
    3/4 cup milk (or water)
    2   tbsp. butter

Combine biscuit mix, dry mustard and one cup cheese.

Add eggs to milk and combine with dry ingredients; mix thoroughly.

Turn dough into a well-greased loaf pan. Dot with two tablespoons butter and sprinkle with remaining cheese.

Bake at 350° for 45 minutes; cool in pan for 15 minutes. Remove from pan and let cool completely before slicing, as it has a tendency to crumble.

Cheese Puffs

These are like cream puff shells, with cheese. Lovely change from dinner rolls.

1 cup water	4 large eggs
1/2 cup butter	1 tsp. dry mustard
1 cup flour (1/2 cup white, 1/2 cup whole-wheat is best)	Several shakes cayenne pepper
1/4 tsp. salt	2/3 cup grated Swiss cheese
1/4 tsp. sugar	

In medium saucepan boil water with butter until butter melts. Stir flour in all at once, beat with wooden spoon until it forms a thick, glossy dough that leaves the sides of the pan. Add salt and sugar. With pan off the heat, beat in the eggs, one at a time. (Your arm may get tired.)

Add the mustard, pepper and grated cheese; blend well.

Drop by teaspoonfuls onto a greased cookie sheet. Bake at 375° for 30 minutes, until they are puffed and golden brown.

Makes about 28 puffs. Serve hot with butter.

NOTE

Cool cheese puffs on wire rack and fill with chicken salad for a delightful luncheon dish.

Connie's Zucchini Muffins

Connie Crockett brought me this recipe, knowing how crazy I am about zucchini. These muffins are very moist and very sweet. Everyone loves them, and no one guesses they have zucchini in them except *my* family. They think I put zucchini in *everything*.

3 eggs	2 cups sugar
1 cup oil	2 cups flour
1 tbsp. vanilla extract	1-1/2 tsp. baking soda
2 medium zucchini squash, unpeeled, grated	1/4 tsp. baking powder
1 cup chopped pecans or walnuts	1 tsp. salt
	1 tbsp. cinnamon

In large mixing bowl combine eggs, oil, vanilla extract and grated zucchini.

In medium bowl combine pecans, sugar, flour, soda, baking powder, salt and cinnamon, stirring until well blended. Gradually stir this dry mixture into the zucchini mixture until well moistened.

Fill muffin tins with paper liners (or grease them well). Fill each muffin cup about 3/4 full. Bake at 400° for 15-18 minutes, until muffins have risen and are browned on top and pulling away from sides of muffin tin. Makes approximately 2-1/2 dozen.

Ginger Muffins

NOTE

It's great for small families to keep this batter on hand for freshly baked muffins; however, I prefer to bake the muffins all at once. Leftover muffins can be frozen, or put in plastic bags for two to three days. I personally think muffins are as good toasted in a toaster oven the second day as they are baked fresh.

Either way, these muffins are so moist they keep well.

This batter keeps two to three weeks in the refrigerator which makes it especially nice for small families. Simply bake them as you want them, and have them deliciously fresh.

1/2 cup sugar	2 cups flour
1/2 cup butter	1 tsp. baking soda
1/2 cup molasses	1/2 tsp. *each* salt, ginger and cinnamon
1/2 cup buttermilk	1/2 cup raisins or dates (optional)
2 eggs	

Cream sugar and butter until light and fluffy. Add molasses, buttermilk and eggs; mix well.

Combine dry ingredients; add them to creamed mixture and blend thoroughly. If you like, stir in raisins or dates. Bake in muffin tins (1/2-2/3 full) at 375° for about 20 minutes or until firm to touch. Increase baking time if batter is chilled.

Makes 12-18.

Hot Water Cornbread

My husband grew up with this wonderful fried cornbread. His mother, of course, didn't have a recipe. I had to watch and learn. Now it's our son's favorite, too.

1 cup cornmeal	1 tsp. salt
1 tbsp. flour	Boiling water
Pinch of baking powder	Bacon fat

Mix all the dry ingredients together in a bowl. While you are waiting for the water to boil, heat the bacon fat in a skillet to a depth of about 1/2". Pour just enough of the boiling water into the cornmeal to stir into a thick paste. Make sure all the cornmeal is moistened.

Keep the cold water tap running so you can rinse your hands under it while you quickly make cornmeal patties out of the thick dough. You won't burn your hands if you work quickly and keep rinsing your hands in the cold water. Form into 12-16 patties about 4" in diameter.

Fry the patties a few at a time in the bacon fat until they are browned on both sides. The thinner the patties, the crisper they are.

Keep warm in the oven until you are ready to serve — with lots of butter.

Serves 4, barely. Doubles beautifully.

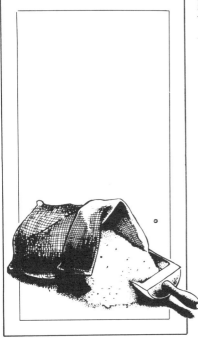

Irish Soda Bread

Similar to, but heavier than, biscuits. You'll find it perfect for a weekend brunch.

3 cups flour	1 cup raisins
3 tbsp. sugar	1-1/2 cups buttermilk
1 tbsp. baking powder	2 tbsp. sugar, dissolved
1/2 tsp. baking soda	in 2 tbsp. hot water
1/2 tsp. salt	

Mix dry ingredients together, including raisins. Stir in buttermilk. Mix until this becomes a sticky dough and then turn it out on a floured board and knead about ten times.

Shape into a round or oblong loaf and place it on a well-greased cookie sheet. Cut an X across top of loaf with a sharp knife, and bake it at 375°.

After about 35 minutes, it will begin to brown. At that point remove from oven and brush top with sugar water and return to oven. Bake ten minutes longer, or until golden.

NOTE
Traditional Irish soda bread has caraway seeds in it. I don't care for them, so I left them out. If you like, add one teaspoon caraway seeds.

Jiffy Irish Soda Bread

This comes from my friend Sue Dill. She knows how much I love it, and this recipe is so quick, it's a real treat!

2 cups biscuit mix	1 egg, lightly beaten (reserve 1 tbsp.)
1/2 cup whole-wheat flour	2/3 cup buttermilk (or add 1 tbsp.
2 tbsp. sugar (plus some	vinegar to 2/3 cup regular milk)
for top of bread)	1/2 cup raisins
2 tbsp. butter	

Combine biscuit mix with whole-wheat flour in a large mixing bowl. Stir in sugar. Cut in butter with your pastry blender.

In a small bowl combine egg and buttermilk. Add to dry ingredients, along with raisins. Stir until well blended.

Knead the soft dough about 20 times on a well-floured counter top. I like to use plastic wrap to guarantee easy cleanup.

Form the dough into a round ball and put it on a well-greased cookie sheet. Brush it with reserved egg and sprinkle it with sugar.

Bake at 350° for about 50 minutes, until it sounds hollow when you thump it. Watch it carefully. If the bottom seems too brown, turn down the heat.

Serve hot with butter — and don't expect leftovers!   Serves 4-6.

NOTE
Irish soda bread has more texture than biscuits, and it's heavier. I mention this in case you've never had it, so you'll know what to expect.

Jo's Zucchini Bread

I've tasted many different zucchini breads, but my friend Jo Ramey's is the best. Perhaps it's because she grows her own zucchini.

1	cup cooking oil	1/4	tsp. baking powder
2-to-3	cups fresh coarsely chopped zucchini squash		Pinch of salt
3	cups flour	3	eggs
1	tbsp. baking soda	2	cups sugar
1	tbsp. cinnamon	1	tbsp. vanilla extract

Pour oil into blender and add enough zucchini (don't peel it) to fill container to three-cup mark; purée.

In mixing bowl stir together flour, baking soda, cinnamon, baking powder, and salt.

In another larger bowl beat eggs with sugar until they are light and fluffy, and add vanilla extract. Mix in half the dry ingredients, then half the zucchini, and so on until you have a moist batter.

This is a fairly large recipe and can be baked in a variety of ways. You may use two loaf pans, three 1-lb. coffee cans, six or more 1-lb. vegetable cans. Be sure to fill containers about 2/3 full and don't forget to grease them carefully.

Bake at 350°; time will depend on the size pan used. Bread is done when lightly browned and firm in center. Sides should be pulling away from pan.

Loaf Pan	Approximately	—	50-55 minutes
Coffee Can (1-lb.)	Approximately	—	50-55 minutes
Vegetable Can (1-lb.)	Approximately	—	45-50 minutes

Lemon Tea Bread

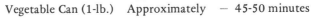

I'll go to the trouble of grating *two* lemon rinds for this tea bread, so you know it must be good. I love the slightly tart glaze.

1/2	cup butter, softened	1	tsp. baking powder
1	cup sugar	1/2	cup milk
2	eggs	1	pkg. (2-1/2 oz.) finely chopped walnuts
	Freshly grated peel of 2 lemons		
1-1/2	cups flour		

GLAZE

1/4	cup sugar		Juice of 2 lemons, about 1/3 cup

Cream butter and sugar until light and fluffy. Add eggs one at a time, and the grated lemon peel.

Combine flour and baking powder; add to creamed ingredients, alternately with milk. Add walnuts and pour batter into well-greased loaf pan.

Bake at 375° for about 60-65 minutes, until bread is golden on top and firm in middle.

While the bread is baking, combine sugar and lemon juice. Stir until sugar is dissolved. As soon as you remove bread from oven, poke holes in it with a meat skewer or something that will reach through bread to the bottom of pan. Drizzle lemon mixture over hot loaf and let it soak in the pan for about ten minutes.

This is a delicate bread, so remove from pan carefully and let cool before slicing. Glaze keeps it beautifully moist.

Makes one 1-lb. loaf.

When you select lemons at the store, compare several to see how heavy they are. By holding two, one in each hand, you can select the one most likely to contain the most juice.

Lemons, oranges and other citrus fruit are juicier when they seem relatively heavy. The lighter they are, as a rule of thumb, the drier.

You'll get more juice out of lemons if you'll roll them on the counter top before slicing. Press down hard with the heel of your hand.

Oatmeal-Bran Muffins
(Calorie Conscious)

When you are seriously counting calories, muffins like these are a welcome treat.

2/3 cup flour	1 tbsp. baking powder
2/3 cup rolled oats	2/3 cup skim milk
2/3 cup bran (not cereal)	2 tbsp. oil
3 tbsp. fructose	1 egg
Pinch of salt	

Mix the dry ingredients; combine milk, oil and egg and stir into flour mixture. Fill muffin tins 2/3 full.

Bake at 350° for 20 minutes.

Makes 12 muffins, 64 calories each.

NOTE

In this recipe rolled oats and bran have been substituted for part of the flour. Any time you substitute rolled oats for flour, you save calories. Substitute bran, and you save more. Both rolled oats and bran add flavor and texture.

Most large grocery stores carry fructose now. It has about the same calories as sugar, but is sweeter.

Puffed Cheese Ring

NOTE
You aren't likely to have any left over, but if you're lucky enough that you do, split and toast it the next day. Wonderful!

This cheese bread is like a cheese-flavored cream puff pastry. Light as a feather, and excellent with soup or salad.

1 cup water	1/2 tsp. salt
1/2 cup butter	4 eggs
1 cup flour	6 oz. Gruyère cheese, diced (1-1/2 cups)

Put water and butter in a saucepan and bring to a full, rolling boil over medium-high heat. Remove from heat and stir in flour and salt *all at once.* Stir like crazy (wooden spoon, if you have one) until well blended. Keep stirring until dough is glossy and elastic and doesn't stick to pan.

Let cool for about five minutes then beat in eggs, one at a time; stir in cheese.

Dampen your baking sheet with cold water and drop large spoonfuls of dough onto the sheet, forming a ring of dough.

Bake at 400° about 30 minutes, or until the cheese ring is puffed and browned. Serve immediately.

Serves 4-6.

Anadama Bread

NOTE
This is a fairly heavy bread with just the suggestion of sweetness. Makes marvelous toast.

When you're measuring sticky liquids like molasses or syrup, it's a good idea to measure the oil or other liquids first. If you use the same measuring cup, the molasses will slide right out.

This recipe comes with a traditional story. A fisherman had a wife, Anna, who was too busy to bake his bread, so he baked it himself. But he grumbled about it, and every time he put a loaf in the oven, he muttered under his breath, "Anna-dama, Anna-dama". The name stuck, and the bread, which was easy enough for the fisherman, is delicious.

1/2 cup cornmeal (plus	1 pkg. dry yeast
2 tsp. for pan)	1/4 cup warm water
3/4 cup boiling water	1 egg, beaten
3. tbsp. oil	2-3/4 cups flour (1-1/4 cups
1/4 cup molasses	plus 1-1/2 cups)
1 tsp. salt	

In large mixing bowl, combine 1/2 cup cornmeal, boiling water, oil, molasses and salt; cool to lukewarm.

Sprinkle yeast over warm water and stir to dissolve. Add this dissolved yeast, egg and 1-1/4 cups flour to cornmeal mixture. Beat with electric mixer for two minutes. With spoon, stir in remaining flour; batter will be very stiff.

Grease one-pound loaf pan and sprinkle with two teaspoons corn meal. Spread batter evenly in pan; cover and let rise in warm place until it reaches top of pan, about 1-1/2 hours.

Bake at 350° for 30-35 minutes, until loaf sounds hollow when thumped. Cool on wire rack.

Dilly Bread

You're going to love this wonderful yeast bread because it's a batter bread which doesn't require kneading. It's an outstanding addition to a buffet dinner.

1	pkg. dry yeast	2	tsp. dill seed
1/4	cup warm water	1	tsp. salt
1	cup cottage cheese	1/4	tsp. baking soda
2	tbsp. sugar	1	egg, beaten
1	tbsp. dehydrated minced onion	2-1/4	cups flour, plus 1/4 cup if needed
1	tbsp. butter, softened		

Soften yeast in warm water and set aside. Heat cottage cheese until lukewarm and put in large mixing bowl. Add sugar, onion, butter, dill seed, salt, baking soda, egg and yeast. Stir until completely blended.

Add flour about 1/2 cup at a time, reserving the last 1/4 cup flour. Stir until the flour is absorbed and a stiff dough forms. You should have enough flour in the dough that it makes a sticky ball of dough which follows the spoon around the bowl. If it isn't that stiff, add the last 1/4 cup flour. Cover the bowl and set to rise in a warm place until doubled in bulk, about 60 minutes.

Stir the dough down, form it into a ball, and place it in a well-greased oven-proof bowl or soufflé dish. Turn the dough once to lightly grease the top. Cover and let rise for another 40 minutes.

Bake at 350° for 40 minutes, or until the top is well browned and loaf sounds hollow when you thump it.

Remove from soufflé dish immediately and let cool on a wire rack. Brush warm loaf with melted butter and sprinkle with salt.

Serve sliced into 16-20 wedges.

An ideal place for bread to rise is inside an oven with a pilot light with the door closed.

If your oven doesn't have a pilot light, turn the oven on and as soon as you hear it ignite (gas oven) or as soon as you feel it begin to heat (electric oven), turn it off.

NICE TO KNOW . . .

All cheeses are at their flavor peak at room temperature. Remove from the refrigerator about one hour before serving.

Cheese is "cooked" when it is melted. Heat at low temperature to avoid stringiness.

Oatmeal Raisin Rolls

NOTE
See pg. 3 for Date-Walnut Cheese Ball. One Christmas I had the cheese ball and rolls for separate occasions. I combined both leftovers into marvelous sandwiches.

I don't bake many yeast breads because with my busy schedule I seldom find time to plan for rising time, in the same day.

The first time I made these Oatmeal Raisin Rolls, I simply put them on the baking sheet and refrigerated them overnight before the final rising.

The next morning, I set them out in the kitchen just long enough to bring them to room temperature, about thirty minutes to an hour, and baked them according to the recipe.

They were fine.

NOTES

These have delightful flavor and firm, chewy texture. The second day I either toast them with butter or split and serve them with cream cheese and dates.

2-1/2 cups whole-wheat flour (1 cup plus 1-1/2 cups)
1 cup rolled oats
1 cup bran (not cereal, but natural bran flakes from the health food store)
3/4 cup raisins
2 pkgs. dry yeast
1/2 tsp. salt
2 cups water
1/2 cup honey
1/4 cup butter
2 cups white flour (approximately)

Combine *one* cup whole-wheat flour, rolled oats and bran. Add raisins, yeast and salt; mix well.

In a small saucepan combine water, honey and butter; heat to lukewarm. Add to flour mixture and mix well.

Stir in remaining 1-1/2 cups whole-wheat flour and roughly two cups of white flour — enough to make a fairly stiff dough. Knead 6-8 minutes; cover, let rise until doubled and punch down. This is a heavy dough, so it will probably take an hour or so.

Let the dough rest ten minutes; divide into 12 pieces and shape into round or oval rolls. Place on greased cookie sheet and let rise until doubled, about another half hour.

Bake at 350° for 25 minutes, or until rolls have begun to brown on top and around the bottom edge.

Makes 12.

Swiss Cheese Bread

Homemade bread is so delicious it's worth the effort — especially if you have a simple recipe like this one. Don't be afraid of using the beer, you will hardly know it is there when you bake it. It's wonderful bread!

- 1 can (12-oz.) beer
- 1/2 cup water
- 2 tbsp. sugar
- 2 tbsp. butter
- 1 pkg. (8-oz.) pasteurized process Swiss cheese (not the kind with the holes), grated
- 5 cups flour (2 cups plus 3 cups)
- 2 pkgs. dry yeast

In a large saucepan warm the beer, water, sugar, butter and grated Swiss cheese. Stir until cheese just begins to melt and remove from heat; cool to lukewarm.

Add two cups flour and the two packages of yeast to cheese mixture and beat it with your electric mixer for about three minutes. Stir in the rest of the flour by hand to make a stiff dough.

Turn onto a floured surface and knead until smooth and elastic, about five minutes. Let rise in a covered, greased bowl until doubled in size — about one hour. Punch down, divide in two and put in greased loaf pans to rise again until doubled in size.

Bake at 350° for 40-45 minutes. Loaf is done when tapping the top with your finger makes a hollow sound.

Makes 2 loaves.

NOTE

The reason for using "processed" Swiss cheese instead of natural is that it melts better. I haven't tried it, but I imagine processed Old English cheese would be great in this recipe as well.

When I was a girl, we were taught to sift everything. These days, most recipes suggest you simply "spoon and level". I've gone to the extreme of always spooning and leveling, and none of the recipes in this book will suffer if you measure that way.

One important note. I do fluff the flour in the canister, lightly tossing it with a spoon, before I lightly spoon it into my measuring cup. Never shake the cup to level it or press it down with a spoon or you will end up with too much flour.

Always level with a straight-edged knife or ruler.

By Special Request...

END OF CHILDHOOD

I think I notice it more in his hands than anything else. My twelve-year-old son suddenly has a man's hands, still awkward with boyish clumsiness and looking too big, really, for his arms.

I wasn't prepared for it. I doubt any mother is, no matter how much we think we are. After all, he is twelve. I knew the teenage years were coming. He'd grown a couple of inches over the summer . . . but it wasn't until his soccer team photos came in that I really saw it so clearly.

In team photos taken six months ago, he was still at the end of his childhood, the tall one in the back row, grinning widely. Still a boy, my baby.

But now, a soccer season later, the end of childhood is over. And the gangly youth, now towering from the back row, is clearly in the beginning of his new age, the teen years.

The gregarious, open kid now begins to slouch down and look out the window, or up at the ceiling, when Mom tries to talk with him. His answers are suddenly, "Yeah, I guess so. I dunno." And information has to be dragged out word by word.

He's pulling away. I know he should. I want him to, but I have this terrible sense of loss. I know we'll have him back, but it will take a few years of learning, of working through the peer pressure, of discovering the man he's turning into.

I hope it doesn't take too long.

BAW PAW'S TAPE

Recently we spent an evening with my husband's brother, Dick. He said, "I have something I want you to hear," and he pulled out his cassette recorder and pushed the button. The recording was rough and full of static, the voice slightly distorted. Jim strained to listen, but he couldn't quite tell who it was.

Finally Dick said, "It's Baw Paw." Baw Paw was their grandfather, pastor of a church, pillar of the community in his day. "No, it doesn't sound like him."

"Yes, it does — listen." And I saw a disbelieving grin spread across Jim's face. It was Baw Paw.

We sat absolutely spellbound. Baw Paw was seventy-eight the year he recorded it. He would have been one hundred and thirteen this year, so it was thirty-five years old. He'd made it as he reminisced with a Sunday School class.

We heard Baw Paw talk about his youth, how he was orphaned in Ireland and came alone on a boat to live with an uncle in Louisiana when he was just ten years old. We heard him tell about the day he was to preach his first sermon at a new church, and he forgot his notes. He told how scared he was, and how he wrestled over whether he should try it without the notes — or run. He found the courage, and I know just how he felt.

I met Baw Paw for the first time through that recording. And I met him as a warm, human person. For a little while, he was alive.

Original Kaye Johns Radio Scripts

Soups, Sauces, & Sandwiches

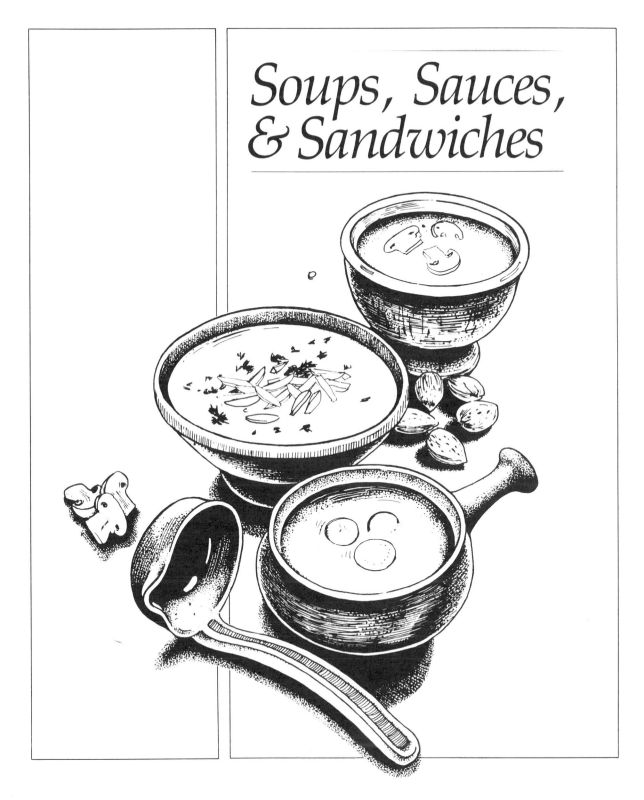

Beer Cheese Soup

I can't imagine going through a cold weather season without serving this rich, filling soup. Everyone loves it.

1/4	cup butter	8	oz. cheese, grated (Cheddar,
1	large onion, sliced thinly		Swiss)
1/4	cup flour		Salt, freshly ground pepper and a
6-to-12	oz. beer		few drops red pepper sauce
2-1/2	cups milk		(such as Tabasco) to taste

Melt butter in a fairly large saucepan and sauté onion until it's translucent, but not browned, about ten minutes. Add flour. The flour makes the onions kind of pasty, but if you watch it carefully, and stir constantly, the flour will cook without burning.

Add beer and milk, stirring with a spoon or whisk, then the grated cheese. Heat until the soup thickens slightly and cheese has melted. Taste and add seasonings.

This should be made ahead of time because it mellows as it ages. Overnight is perfect.   Serves 4.

Any soup tastes better if left overnight in the refrigerator. This gives flavors a chance to blend. Stews, goulash and chili also benefit from this extra holding time.

One advantage of refrigerating soups overnight is that you can lift off any fat that rises to the top and solidifies.

Cheese Chowder

This is the perfect soup for a cold winter's evening. It's a wonderful way to clean out the vegetable drawer and make it seem like you did it on purpose! Filling enough for an entrée, with only salad and bread to complete your meal. Better the second day, if you have any left.

4	large potatoes, peeled and diced	4-to-6	cups milk
4	large carrots, peeled and diced	2	cups grated cheese
1	large onion, diced		Salt to taste

The basic soup is really no more than a potato soup with cheese.

Place potatoes, carrots and onion in large soup pot and just cover with water. Simmer until tender, about fifteen minutes. Drain and mash coarsely with your potato masher.

Add milk. I start with a quart and add to it, depending on the other ingredients I add, and how thick I want the soup to be. Stir in the milk, and add the cheese.

Be flexible with the cheese. If you have bits and pieces of hard cheese, grate it all and toss it in the pot. I recommend no less than two cups, but more is even better. You may also use loaf cheese, such as Velveeta, allowing about two ounces of cheese per serving portion. Add

VARIATIONS

1. Add other chopped vegetables such as celery, green pepper, mushrooms, zucchini, chopped spinach, broccoli or corn.

2. Add chopped meat such as ham, chicken or beef; or add either canned or leftover baked fish.

salt to taste.

Simmer soup over low heat until cheese melts, stirring frequently. Serve immediately, or set in refrigerator overnight, reheating at serving time. The flavors blend better overnight, but I don't usually plan that far ahead. Serves 4-6 as an entrée.

Chilled Curry Soup

This soup is ideal for warm weather entertaining. It can be made the day before and served in mugs or bowls. Light, but rich.

2-1/2	cups chicken broth (1 can broth, plus 1 can water)	2	egg yolks
1	large carrot, chopped	1	cup heavy cream
1	large rib celery, chopped		Curry powder to taste
1/2	medium onion, chopped	1/2	cup applesauce

Heat broth while you chop vegetables. Simmer vegetables in broth until tender, then purée in your blender.

In a small bowl, beat egg yolks and blend in heavy cream. Add hot soup mixture to the cream a little at a time until you've added about a cup of broth. Then pour the mixture into saucepan with remaining broth and heat until it thickens, about five minutes.

Remove from heat and add curry powder to taste. Stir in applesauce and chill several hours before serving — overnight is best.   Serves 4-8.

NOTE

Curry powder varies greatly in flavor. As a rule of thumb, I usually put 1/2 teaspoon curry per portion into the dishes I'm preparing. My personal taste preference is for more, but not everyone loves curry as I do. Find a brand you enjoy and stick with it, and you'll learn to estimate easily.

When recipes like this one call for egg yolks, you may want to freeze your egg whites. Some people freeze them in plastic ice cube trays and then put the "egg cubes" in a plastic carton or bag.

Cream of Vegetable Soup

Hot or cold, it's a rich, delightful soup. Very easy.

6	cups water	1	medium yellow squash, chopped
6	tsp. chicken bouillon granules	1	medium onion, chopped
2	cups peeled and chopped potato	1	tsp. sugar
2	medium tomatoes, chopped	1/2	cup heavy cream

Put water in saucepan with bouillon granules. Add vegetables and sugar; simmer until vegetables are cooked, about ten minutes. Purée vegetables in blender or food processor and return to broth. Stir in cream.

If you are serving soup hot, reheat to simmering. Otherwise, chill overnight in refrigerator. It's wonderful hot or cold.   Serves 4-8.

Egg Drop Soup

VARIATION

Add the half package of frozen chopped spinach to the soup when it comes to a boil. Add eggs at the last minute. This is really a meal in itself, with bread and butter and a nice fruit salad.

Try this when you —and the family— feel slightly adventurous. It's really delicious!

1   envelope Lipton's chicken noodle soup mix
3   cups water
2   eggs, lightly whipped with a fork
2   green onions, chopped
1/2 pkg. (10-oz.) frozen chopped spinach (optional, but good!)

Cook soup according to package directions with the water. While it is boiling, dribble eggs into soup — they will instantly cook into ribbons or strings.

Serve very hot, sprinkled with chopped green onions.

Golden Cream Soup

NICE TO KNOW . . .

A peeled potato cut up into over-salted soup will absorb the excess salt. Leave the potato in or discard it.

I've taken a lot of kidding for this soup. I love it and think you should at least give it a chance. (The night I served it, two out of four liked it, one abstained, and one turned up her nose!)

1/2 cup uncooked Cream of Wheat
6   tbsp. butter, melted
1/3 cup minced onion
1   quart chicken bouillon
1   quart milk
1/3 cup heavy cream
1   egg yolk
     Chopped chives

Add Cream of Wheat to melted butter and stir over low heat until it turns a nice golden brown. Add onion and cook until it becomes trans-lucent — about two minutes. Add the bouillon and milk; bring to a boil, stirring constantly. Simmer a few minutes and remove from heat.

In a small bowl beat cream and egg yolk together and spoon a little of the hot mixture into it, stirring. (This prevents the egg yolk from scrambling when added to soup.) Slowly add cream mixture to soup, stirring.

Serve immediately with a sprinkle of chopped chives.
Serves 4-6.

Peanut Butter Soup

Sounds crazy, but it's delicious. Very rich, so serve it with something light, like a sandwich.

3	tbsp. butter	1	tsp. chicken bouillon granules
1/2	cup chopped onion	3	cups milk
1/2	cup chopped celery	1/2	cup chunky peanut butter
2	tbsp. flour		

Melt butter in saucepan, and sauté onion and celery in butter until cooked, but crisp. Stir in flour and cook for two minutes. Add bouillon granules and milk; cook until it simmers. Add in peanut butter and stir with whisk until well blended.

When you add the peanut butter, it looks funny. At first it melts into little bits which float in the milk. Don't be alarmed; eventually they melt completely and blend with the milk.

If you don't serve the soup immediately, it will get very thick, so you might want to add a little more milk.

Serves 4-6.

Spinach Soup

This is an excellent creamed vegetable soup. Good before dinner or *as* dinner.

1	pkg. (10-oz.) frozen spinach
2	slices onion
3	tbsp. butter
1	tbsp. flour
3	cups chicken stock
	Salt to taste
1	cup half-and-half
	Pinch of freshly grated nutmeg

Cook spinach and onion slices in 1/2 cup water. Drain and purée in the blender or food processor. Set aside.

Melt butter and cook with flour for two minutes; gradually stir in chicken stock and salt to taste. Bring this mixture to a boil, add spinach and simmer for several minutes. Remove from heat; stir in half-and-half and nutmeg.

Serves 4.

NOTE

The Puffed Cheese Ring on pg. 18 is perfect with this soup.

VARIATION

Substitute a similar size package of frozen asparagus, cauliflower, squash, carrots or mixed vegetables.

Won-Ton Soup

Much as I love Chinese food, this is the first time I've ever made won-ton soup. As usual, I could kick myself for waiting so long. It's easy, fun and delicious!

1/4	lb. ground beef
1/2	cup coarsely chopped green onion (plus garnish)
1/2	cup coarsely chopped green pepper
1/2	cup coarsely chopped fresh mushrooms
2	tsp. soy sauce
	Garlic powder to taste
1	package (12-oz.) frozen won-ton wrappers (48)
6	cups beef bouillon

Put uncooked ground beef in blender or food processor with all other ingredients except won-ton wrappers and bouillon. Process until finely minced; you may also mince with a sharp knife.

Put one teaspoon beef mixture in center of each square won-ton wrapper. Moisten edges of wrapper slightly and fold one corner up over the filling to meet the other corner; you will have a triangle. Press the edges to seal them.

In medium saucepan bring the beef bouillon to a boil. Drop won-tons into bouillon; they will sink to the bottom of the pan. Stir them gently to keep them from sticking. When they float, they're done. Serve with the bouillon, garnished with chopped green onions if you like.

Serves 4-8, depending on size of bowl you use.

NOTE

Quite a few low-calorie or diet foods on the shelves must be labeled "imitation" simply because they don't conform with standard methods of preparation. In the case of at least one brand, it means that it has *too many apricots and too little sugar!*

VARIATION

For an unusual and delicious sandwich, bake boneless chicken breasts and baste with this sauce. Top with Swiss cheese, melt under broiler or in oven, and serve hamburger style on onion buns. Great!

Apricot Sauce
(Calorie Conscious)

I enjoy cooking with sauces. I think they look pretty, taste good and always make a dish seem special. I am also of the opinion that sauces don't have to be high in calories to be good.

1	cup "imitation" apricot jam (low-calorie)
4	tbsp. Worcestershire sauce
2	tsp. dry mustard

Mix ingredients, taste and correct seasonings. Heat slowly and use to top baked chicken, ham or lamb — or even fish. It's even good on meatloaf, especially if you put just a pinch of curry in the meat mixture before you bake it.

Makes one cup sauce.

Country Gravy

Jo Ann (technically my stepmother, truly my friend) was born and raised in one of the smallest of small towns, Corn, Oklahoma.

Her dad was a farmer, and she had the luxury of his farm-fresh vegetables, among them potatoes. I still remember years ago when her sister Delores came for a visit with a gunny sack of new potatoes in the trunk of her car. They were the best potatoes I ever had in my life.

Jo Ann taught me how to make the onion gravy she'd been raised with. It is so rich and good that a plateful of new potatoes smothered with the gravy is meal enough.

1/2	lb. bacon, chopped
1	medium onion, chopped
1/2	cup bacon drippings
1/2	cup flour
1	tsp. salt
4	cups milk

Chop the bacon before you cook it. Put it in a large skillet with the chopped onion and fry over medium heat until the bacon has browned and the onion is translucent and just beginning to brown.

Drain the bacon fat from the skillet, reserving 1/2 cup. Leave the bacon and onion in the skillet and stir in the flour and salt. Cook over medium heat for at least two minutes to cook the flour. Stir occasionally, taking care not to let it brown.

Remove from heat and stir in milk. When well blended, return to heat and cook until it boils and thickens.

Serve onion gravy with steamed or boiled new potatoes.

Makes enough gravy for two pounds new potatoes, which should serve 4-6.

The world is full of people who have stepped into marriages where children are involved. We call them stepparents, and they face some of the toughest responsibilities in the world.

I've experienced stepparenthood as many ways as it exists, I guess. I have a stepmother, I am a stepmother, and my children regularly visit a stepmother.

Each situation is difficult.

To accept that a parent can love someone else — what a hard thing for a child. The most important thing to give a child trying to cope with divorce and remarriage is the freedom to love the new stepparent without guilt. And then one day he can realize

that "different" isn't "bad". It's just different, and that's okay.

As a stepparent, your lesson is the same. You have to accept those children as they are, molded by another family. They can't change to fit your preconceived ideas. If you accept them first, love can follow.

I happen to know that divorce doesn't have to divide families for children — it can multiply them. They can be nurtured by two sets of loving parents, four pairs of adoring grandparents.

Nobody said it was easy — but it's not impossible.

I married a stepparent who has been wonderful with my children. Don't think I don't count my blessings every day.

NOTE

You may want to add chopped parsley or a pinch of your favorite herb. I love dill weed, sweet basil or cilantro.

When you're lucky enough to find tomatoes that are full of flavor, you can make a simple and delicious salad with this dressing. Arrange generous tomato slices on lettuce leaves and drizzle with dressing.

Honey Mustard Dressing

My mom Peg Patrick sent me this recipe. I always prefer light salad dressings, and this one is particularly flavorful. It's ideal for chef's salads, especially if you use Swiss cheese with ham or turkey.

1/4	cup mayonnaise
1	tbsp. prepared mustard
1	tbsp. vinegar
1	tbsp. honey
1/4	cup salad oil

Combine mayonnaise, mustard, vinegar and honey. Drizzle oil into mayonnaise mixture gradually while whipping it with a whisk or a fork.

This is best with the stronger-flavored salad greens like spinach and romaine, alone or mixed with iceberg lettuce.

If you like it, double or triple the ingredients. It should keep several weeks in the refrigerator. This is enough dressing for a nice-size chef's salad for four people, or to toss a dinner salad for six to eight servings (unless you use dressing with a heavier hand than I do).

Makes about 1/2 cup.

NOTE

This recipe may be too hot for some people; if so, add more mayonnaise. I love it as is!

NICE TO KNOW . . .

To prevent skin from forming on a sauce that is left to stand, butter waxed paper and lay the buttered side on the surface of the sauce.

Hot Mustard Sauce

Tangy, hot, sweet vegetable dunk or sandwich spread. This is nice to put in pretty jars to give as gifts.

1/4	cup dry mustard
1/4	cup cider vinegar
2	tbsp. sugar (or brown sugar, packed)
1	egg, lightly beaten
1/2	cup mayonnaise

Beat together the first four ingredients in a small saucepan; cook over *low* heat, stirring *constantly,* to prevent egg scrambling.

When it has thickened, remove from heat and cool to room temperature. Add mayonnaise, mixing thoroughly.

Makes approximately one cup. Can be doubled or tripled.

Lemon-Cheese Butter

This lemon butter recipe is wonderful on steamed vegetables.

- 2   lemons
- 1/4   cup butter, softened
- 1   tsp. coarse salt (Kosher or the kind for salt mills)
- 1   tsp. freshly ground pepper
- 1/4   cup grated Gruyère or Parmesan cheese
- 1/4   cup chopped parsley (or chives or fresh sweet basil)

Grate rind of two lemons. Stir rind into butter along with rest of ingredients listed, mixing thoroughly.

Spoon over hot, steamed green vegetables.

Makes about 1/2 cup.

VARIATION

1. Lemon-cheese butter is good with baked chicken. Place heaping tablespoon under skin of chicken breasts and bake at 325° for 20-30 minutes, depending on size of chicken pieces.

2. Put boned, skinned, chicken breast on piece of foil. Top with 1/4-1/2 cup sliced mushrooms and heaping table-spoon lemon-cheese butter. Fold foil into packet and bake at 325° for 20-30 minutes.

Orange Custard Sauce

This is a lovely sauce for fresh fruit, pound cake or to use as a dunk for cinnamon bread sticks. It's rich, light and delicate, with just a hint of the tangy citrus flavor. We love it with fresh strawberries — or blackberries, when we can find them.

- 4   egg yolks, lightly beaten
- 1/2   cup sugar
- 1/3   cup orange juice
- 1-1/2   tbsp. lemon juice
- 1   cup heavy cream, whipped

Combine egg yolks, sugar, orange juice and lemon juice in top of double boiler. Cook over hot — but not simmering — water until thick, about 10-12 minutes. Stir constantly with a whisk to keep it smooth. When cooked, mixture will be thick enough to coat a spoon.

Cool the sauce *completely*.

Whip cream until very stiff and fold into cooled sauce. If sauce is warm, cream won't hold its shape.

Serve as dunk for fresh fruit or Cinnamon Bread Sticks (Page 7).

Makes 2 cups.

Vanilla Crème

Sometimes I wish I'd never created this one — it's too good!

3   cups half-and-half
1   pkg. French vanilla pudding
        mix (not instant) *four-serving* size
2   egg whites
1/3 cup sugar

Combine half-and-half with pudding mix in medium saucepan and cook until it comes to a boil. Remove from heat. At this point the pudding is very thin because three cups is more liquid than the pudding mix calls for. When you add it to the egg white mixture (next step) it will thicken nicely.

Whip egg whites with sugar into fairly stiff meringue. Slowly pour hot pudding into egg whites, beating until completely blended. The heat of the pudding will cook the egg whites, so they will hold their shape as the pudding is chilled.

This pudding doesn't set firmly, but is thick enough to serve from parfait glasses or as a lovely, rich sauce over fresh fruit or cake.

Makes 2 quarts or 8 one-cup servings.

Wendy's Dijon Mustard

When our daughter Wendy was a teen, she made this mustard for everyone in our very large family one Christmas. It was much appreciated!

2   cups white wine   2   tbsp. honey
1   large onion, chopped   1   tbsp. vegetable oil
2   cloves garlic, minced   Salt and red pepper sauce
1   can (4-oz.) dry mustard   (such as Tabasco) to taste

Combine wine, onion and garlic in a medium saucepan. Slowly heat to a boil and simmer for five minutes. Pour into a bowl to cool.

When it cools to room temperature, strain liquid into a smaller saucepan and add dry mustard, beating constantly with a small wire whisk until smooth.

Heat slowly, stirring constantly, until it thickens. It will scorch easily so remove from heat as soon as it's thick.

Stir in honey, oil, salt and red pepper sauce and store in a glass container in refrigerator. Let it age several days to blend flavors.

Makes 1 pint.

White Sauce

I learned to make a white sauce in 4-H class when I was about 12. There were a half-dozen of us gathered in someone's kitchen, and she made it seem so simple. It tasted so good that I've never thought it was too much bother. I'm grateful for the lesson.

If you've fallen out of the habit of making white sauce from scratch, I'd like to encourage you to take it up again. Canned soups are a convenience, and the little packets of powdered sauce mix are very good, but nothing is better than making your own.

There are a couple of rules of thumb that make it especially easy:

1. Always cook your flour and butter for at least two minutes over medium heat. This cooks the flour and gives your sauce a delicious flavor. If you don't cook the flour, you end up with sauce that tastes like warm paste.

2. Before you add your liquid to the cooked flour and butter, remove the pan from the heat. Add the liquid all at once, stirring with a whisk. As soon as it's blended return it to medium heat, stirring until it bubbles and thickens. This is quick and easy and prevents lumps.

White sauce is made with milk, but you can use other liquids as well. For instance, you can substitute chicken broth or beef bouillon for part or all of the milk. You might want to enrich your sauce with part heavy cream, or you might want to add 2-4 tablespoons sherry or wine for part of the liquid.

You can make a fine cheese sauce by simply adding grated cheese to the thickened sauce, stirring over the lowest heat until the cheese melts. A rule of thumb is to add equal parts milk and cheese — if you use one cup milk, add one cup grated cheese. The type cheese is up to you.

THIN WHITE SAUCE

This is a good consistency for soups. If the soup sits overnight to be reheated, it may be a little too thick. Just add more milk.

  1 tbsp. butter
  1 tbsp. flour
1-1/2 cups milk
     Salt to taste

MEDIUM WHITE SAUCE

Perhaps the best consistency for sauces and scalloped vegetables.

  2 tbsp. butter
  2 tbsp. flour
  1 cup milk
     Salt to taste

THICK WHITE SAUCE

A good sauce for soufflés or croquettes.

  3 tbsp. butter
  4 tbsp. flour
  1 cup milk
     Salt to taste

Chicken Sandwiches for Sailing

We call these our sailing sandwiches because I so often take them along for our picnic lunch when we sail with my brother Brian. They're great for any picnic lunch.

    4   chicken breast halves, skinned and boned
    1/2   cup chopped onion
    1   cup chopped fresh mushrooms or one 4-oz. can chopped
            mushrooms, drained
          Pinch of herb pepper or tarragon
          Salt and freshly ground pepper to taste
    4   slices Swiss cheese
    4   onion rolls (or other buns)
          Dijon mustard
          Lettuce

Flatten chicken pieces slightly with meat mallet and sauté in non-stick skillet. (If you don't have a non-stick skillet, use whatever you do have with about one teaspoon butter per piece of chicken.) Cook chicken about five minutes on each side, until cooked through (no pink inside).

While chicken cooks, lightly steam onions and mushrooms in just a little water (about 1/4 cup). Onions should be translucent; takes about five minutes.

Season cooked chicken with herb pepper or tarragon, salt and pepper. Top with Swiss cheese, cooked and drained onions and mushrooms, and place on buns spread with mustard. Add lettuce just before eating so it won't get soggy.

Egg Sandwiches

I know this sounds like a silly thing to include in a cookbook, but I have homey, warm family feelings about egg sandwiches. They're so old-fashioned. I personally think they are fun for weekend brunches or for breakfast any day of the week, especially when you need a breakfast on the run.

SANDWICH VARIATIONS

1. *Fried egg sandwich.* When I fry the egg, I break the yolk and cook until firm on both sides. Season with salt, freshly ground pepper, and make the sandwich with lettuce and mayonnaise on white bread. (That's my husband's favorite.) I prefer mine on toast, no mayonnaise,

with a couple of slices of bacon and some tomato if I have them on hand.

2. *Scrambled egg sandwich.* Scramble two eggs with a slice of easy-melting cheese (such as Velveeta). Pile them into buttered hot dog or hamburger buns. Kids love them.

3. *Hard-cooked egg sandwich.* Mash two peeled, hard-cooked eggs with a fork. They should be hot. Add in a pat of butter, salt and freshly ground pepper, and Dijon mustard to taste. Serve open-faced on a piece of toast, preferably whole-wheat or pumpernickel bread.

Open-Faced Peanut Butter Sandwich

Sounds a little strange, but it's a real winner!

1	slice toast (sourdough bread is good)
	Chunky peanut butter
	Favorite jam or jelly
1	slice Swiss cheese

Spread toast with peanut butter, then jelly. Top with slice of Swiss cheese and broil until cheese melts.

This is delicious!

Shannon's Peanut Butter

I came home one day to find our daughter Shannon had made her own peanut butter. It was delicious and has become a family favorite.

As a matter of fact, the second time Shannon made her peanut butter, it was for her dad in Tyler. I suspect it was his favorite birthday gift that year.

1	cup dry roasted peanuts
1-1/2	tbsp. salad oil
1/2	tsp. salt

Put peanuts and oil in the blender and purée until smooth. Taste before adding salt.

This doubles easily and well.

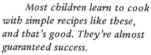

Most children learn to cook with simple recipes like these, and that's good. They're almost guaranteed success.

But no matter how often Mom lets you cook, there's so much you don't learn. We're all full of those early marriage stories, aren't we?

My friend Skip was laughing about noodles one day. "My daughter had never made noodles before, and she didn't know how much bigger they got as they cooked. So when I came home, she was in tears.

"There was this incredible blob of dough in the pot, with

noodles sticking out of it every which way, looking like the Noodles That Ate Cincinnati."

It was a typical story. I'd done it myself, but it wasn't noodles, it was pralines.

I started with something like a cup of buttermilk and whatever the other ingredients were — they fit easily into my smallest saucepan.

When it boiled over, I grabbed the next largest size, and then the next, and I worked my way all the way up to the pressure cooker, the largest pan in the house.

I made it with just a half-inch to spare, and it took forever to clean the kitchen. The pralines were good, and I never forgot the lesson.

By Special Request...

WENDY'S NEW CAR

The color on the outside almost matches the color on the inside. The paint on the dent almost matches both of them.

It doesn't matter that it isn't air conditioned. This is Texas, where summer lasts through September, but she'll get used to it. The windows, after all, do roll down.

You have to be proud of Wendy, it's a very grown-up decision on her part. She's come around from snazzy to functional the same way the rest of us do, a little painfully.

First job, first purchase — snazzy little foreign number. Cute. Clever. Expensive to buy, expensive to maintain.

Finally, with a sigh, snazzy gave way to ordinary. A second car, plain vanilla, kind of fuddy-duddy. But the parts which kept breaking went from minor to major. It was hard to be independent and keep up payments and gas and repairs. So, like so many of us before her, she decided to sell her middle of the road economy car and opt finally for cheap wheels.

It takes me back. That pitiful little car looks like our little hoopey from years ago. It had everything but reverse.

We would whiz up the driveway across the street because it had just enough incline that we could put on the brake, wait for a clearing in the traffic, and whoosh backwards into our driveway, ready for a fast breakaway in the morning.

That little car had class, too.

MOM AND MOVING

When I was a kid, my dad entered a profession that required moving so many times that I attended twenty-four elementary schools. He wasn't in the service, so there was no service housing. We simply packed a trailer and went looking for rent houses. Furnished rent houses.

This was before one in five families moved every year. Then, our transience made us oddities in our neighborhoods.

I remember the first time we set out. Mom and Dad had one of those little sports coupes with one seat and a shelf in the back, and a tiny rear window. My twin brothers went on the shelf — 18-month-old twins.

Home movies show us packing for trip after trip with a trailer hooked to the back of the car. This was before rental trailers in bright colors were available so Dad bought a trailer. Our first movies show it bound clumsily with ropes, highchair legs sticking out and everything slightly askew. Gradually, through the years, the baby paraphernalia faded away and the load grew more compact and was tucked neatly under a tarp.

In all those years of moving and living, from the northern most tip of Maine to Mexico City, the years of leaving friends behind, traveling miles and miles to be home with Grandma for the holidays, the settling-in, finding new grocery stores and new schools — in all those years, I always told my friends, "Moving? My mom loves it!"

Think about that for a minute. What a compliment, to a remarkable woman!

Original Kaye Johns Radio Scripts

Salads

NOTE

For a buffet, cover a large tray with lettuce leaves. Scatter two or three flavors over lettuce. Can double as dessert.

You may store in plastic bag in freezer.

FLAVOR SUGGESTIONS

1. Raspberry yogurt with cranberry sauce
2. Apricot yogurt with chopped apricot halves
3. Lemon yogurt with crushed pineapple

Aunt Marj's Frozen Salad

When my aunt Marj Patrick helped celebrate our Grandma Ethel Templin's 90th birthday, she asked the family to dinner. This salad was the hit of the day, and no one guessed it was made with yogurt.

BASIC RECIPE

2	cartons (8-oz.) fruit flavored yogurt
1/2	cup sugar
1/2	cup chopped pecans
1	can (approximately 1-lb.) fruit, drained
1	can (8-oz.) crushed pineapple, drained (optional)

Combine all ingredients in large mixing bowl. Spoon into paper-lined muffin tins.

Basic recipe fills 12 muffin cups very full. To serve 18 add pineapple and fill cups about 2/3 full.

Freeze several hours or overnight until solid. Paper peels off easily. Serve on lettuce leaves.

Serves 6-12.

Creamy Gelatin Salad

Describing this salad is a bit of a puzzle. It tastes light and rich, with a hint of lemon and a suggestion of pineapple. It's a perfect blending of flavors.

1	large pkg. lemon gelatin (8-serving size)
3	cups boiling water
1	can (8-oz.) crushed pineapple, drained (reserve juice)
1/2	cup mayonnaise
2	cups grated Cheddar cheese
2	cups frozen whipped topping, thawed (or 8-oz. heavy cream, whipped)

Dissolve gelatin in three cups boiling water; add reserved pineapple juice. Chill until consistency of raw egg whites.

Stir in pineapple, mayonnaise and grated cheese. Fold in whipped topping. Chill several hours, until firm.

You may pour into 9" x 13" pan to chill and cut into squares, or make it easy on yourself, as I do. I chill it in my large mixing bowl and simply spoon onto lettuce leaves. Either way, it's delicious!

Serves 12.

Frozen Cranberry Salad

This is so rich, I serve it with something light like baked chicken. It's great for a holiday buffet.

1   can (16-oz.) jellied cranberry sauce
1   pkg. (8-oz.) cream cheese, softened
1   flat can (8-oz.) crushed pineapple, drained
1/2 cup chopped pecans
1   cup heavy cream, whipped

Combine cranberry sauce and cream cheese; add pineapple and pecans. Fold in whipped cream.

Line a loaf pan with plastic wrap, pour in salad mixture and freeze. You may prefer to line a gelatin ring with plastic wrap and use it instead.

Allow a few minutes at room temperature before slicing. Serve on lettuce leaves.

Serves 6-8.

Pink Fluff

This is one of those recipes that can serve as a rich salad or a light dessert. It goes well as part of a buffet, especially with ham or turkey. It always disappears, and you hear people asking, "What's in this? It's delicious!" It's from my sister-in-law Jo Johns who is a marvelous cook.

1   can (21-oz.) cherry pie filling
1   can (14-oz.) sweetened condensed milk (such as Eagle Brand)
1   can (20-oz.) crushed pineapple, drained
1   carton (8-oz.) frozen whipped topping, thawed (or use 8-oz. heavy cream, whipped)
1-1/2 cups chopped pecans (may use less)

Mix cherry pie filling, sweetened condensed milk and drained pineapple together. Fold in whipped topping or cream. Add chopped pecans.

Chill several hours or overnight before serving. Serve small dollops on lettuce leaves for salad. Spoon into parfait glasses, top with a little reserved whipped topping or cream and a few pecans for dessert. Either way, it's wonderful.

Serves 8-10.

NOTE

I can't, in good conscience, put these two rich, delicious fruit salads on a page without some help for those of you who can't have the calories.

Here are three very simple, very low calorie fruit salads that are good enough to be a real treat. And imagine how easy these salads would be for children to make.

APPLE-CHEDDAR SALAD

Combine one chopped apple (peel and all) with 1/4 cup grated sharp Cheddar cheese. I love the combination, and usually add nothing else.

If you like, add chopped celery. One serving.

ORANGE-COCONUT SALAD

Chop a peeled orange into bite-size pieces and toss with as much flaked coconut as your calorie count will allow.

The two flavors are lovely together. One serving.

FOUR FRUIT SALAD

Combine one chopped apple, one orange in bite-size pieces, one small banana, diced, and two canned pineapple rings in bite-size pieces.

The pineapple and orange will keep the banana from turning dark if you toss the fruit thoroughly. Four servings.

No, you don't need fattening mayonnaise or whipped cream or pecans or marshmallows. I didn't say you wouldn't enjoy them, I said you don't need them. Sigh.

Have you ever gone to a restaurant salad bar and watched someone build a 5,000 calorie salad?

Seems that way sometimes, the way people pile on high-calorie shredded cheese, bacon and salad dressing. It's wonderful, if they can afford the calories. I can't.

I usually prefer my salads with just enough dressing to make the salad greens glisten. I don't like to have excess dressing pooling on the bottom of the plate.

For those of you who are serious calorie or cholesterol counters, let me suggest a good way to toss your green salads with the least amount of oil and vinegar.

Wash and dry your greens and put them in the salad bowl. Measure one teaspoon oil (or more to taste) for each serving, and toss the salad greens with only the oil — no vinegar.

The less oil you use, the more you need to gently toss and tumble the greens, but soon they will begin to glisten with the thinnest coating of oil.

By coating each lettuce leaf with oil first, you seal in the natural moisture and nutrients of the lettuce, so they aren't pulled out by the salt and other seasonings.

Add half as much vinegar as you did oil, more or less to your own taste.

Finally, add your other chopped goodies. I like to add chopped green onions and fresh mushrooms, sometimes green pepper or celery.

Toasted sesame seeds and/or toasted almond slivers are wonderful additions, with grated Parmesan cheese. Limit quantities if you're counting calories.

Annie's Spinach Salad

This recipe comes from my mother-in-law. The dressing is really exceptional.

- 1-1/2 lbs. fresh spinach leaves, washed, drained, trimmed and torn into bite-size pieces
- 1/2 lb. fresh mushrooms (you can get by with less)
- 1/2 lb. bacon, diced, fried and drained
- 2 hard-cooked eggs, sliced (optional)

DRESSING

1	uncooked egg	1	tsp. sugar
1/4	cup salad oil	1	tsp. Worcestershire sauce
	Juice of one lemon		Salt and freshly ground
1	tbsp. grated Parmesan cheese		pepper to taste
1	tbsp. Dijon mustard		

Prepare spinach and slice mushrooms into thin slices. Fry and drain bacon. Slice the hard-cooked eggs if you want to use them.

Make dressing by whipping uncooked egg with a fork and gradually adding salad oil and lemon juice. Add rest of dressing ingredients, mixing well.

Put spinach leaves into salad bowl with mushrooms and bacon. Toss with dressing and garnish with egg.

Serves 6-8.

Chef's Salad

I feel a little awkward writing a recipe for a chef's salad, because it's supposed to be made from leftovers in the bottom of the vegetable drawer of your 'fridge — at least that's the way I make it at our house. However, I do repeat this particular version with ham, Swiss cheese and a light sweet-tart dressing fairly often because it's such a favorite. Vary it, please, to suit what you have on hand.

SALAD

- 1/2 head iceberg lettuce
  Equal amount of fresh spinach leaves
- 1/2 medium green pepper, chopped
- 3 medium green onions, green part only, chopped
- 1/2 cup fresh sliced mushrooms, optional
- 1/2 cup grated Swiss cheese
- 1/2 cup chopped cooked ham

DRESSING

- 2 tbsp. wine vinegar (may use less)
- 1 tsp. sugar
- 2 tbsp. oil (may use more)
- 1/4 tsp. garlic salt
- 1/4 tsp. dill weed
- 1/4 tsp. dry mustard
  Salt and freshly ground pepper to taste
- 2 tbsp. toasted sesame seeds

Rinse, dry and tear lettuce into bite-size pieces. Rinse spinach leaves all at once in a large bowl filled with water. Remove stems and any bruised spots, dry on paper towels and tear into bite-size pieces.

Add all the other ingredients for the salad; then make your dressing.

Put the wine vinegar in a small bowl and add the sugar, stirring to dissolve. I use equal parts of vinegar and oil, but that may be too tart for your taste. If you would rather, decrease the vinegar or add more oil.

Combine the oil and seasonings with the vinegar and sugar, and whip with a fork until well blended. Pour over salad and lightly toss to coat all ingredients. Add salt and pepper to taste.

Serve on dinner plates and sprinkle sesame seeds over the top.

Fresh Zucchini Salad

This is an excellent change from ordinary green salads. Especially good for dieters.

- 4 medium zucchini, grated
- 1/2 cup *each* — chopped green onion, green pepper, celery, fresh mushrooms
- 1/4 cup oil
- 2-to-4 tbsp. vinegar
  Pinch of dill weed or garlic salt
  Salt and freshly ground pepper to taste

Grate zucchini and squeeze out moisture with paper towels. Add chopped vegetables and toss with oil and vinegar. Add dill weed or garlic salt, salt and pepper.

Serve on a lettuce leaf.

Serves 4.

VARIATIONS

1. This is easy to make for one serving. It's especially low in calories and full of flavor and texture. Use only one teaspoon of oil and vinegar to taste if you're counting calories.

2. To serve as a hot vegetable, simply leave out oil and vinegar. Heat briefly in microwave (one to two minutes) or sauté in two tablespoons butter or olive oil until tender but crisp.

3. For vegetable fritters, omit oil and vinegar and add four lightly beaten eggs and one cup bread crumbs, cracker crumbs or stuffing mix. Fry in butter like pancakes.

German Potato Salad

This is my favorite potato salad, served hot or cold.

2	lbs. new potatoes	1/2	cup salad oil
1/2	lb. bacon, diced, fried and drained	1/2	cup vinegar (less to taste)
		1/2	cup sugar
1	large onion, chopped		Salt and freshly ground
1	cup beef bouillon		pepper to taste

Boil new potatoes in jackets until barely cooked; cool and slice in 1/4" slices. No need to peel, but you may if you like.

Meanwhile, dice and fry bacon, adding chopped onion to skillet for a couple of minutes when bacon is almost done. Drain off bacon drippings. Remove skillet from heat and add rest of ingredients, mixing well. Make sure sugar is completely dissolved.

Pour hot dressing over sliced potatoes, and add salt and pepper to taste. Like most potato salads, this one is best the next day. I prefer to serve it at room temperature.

Serves 6-8.

Jim's Caesar Salad

The best way to clean romaine lettuce is to separate leaves and submerge them in a sink of cool water. Swish them carefully to remove sand and let them dry between layers of paper toweling. You can slip them, paper towels and all, into a plastic bag and hold them for several days.

This is my husband's version of our favorite Caesar Salad from a restaurant we've loved for many years.

1	large head romaine lettuce	1/2	lemon
1	clove garlic		Garlic salt, salt and freshly ground pepper to taste
1/2	small flat can anchovy fillets Worcestershire sauce		Croutons (preferably homemade, see Papa's Caesar Salad, (Page 64.)
1	uncooked egg		
1/3	cup salad oil		
1/3	cup wine vinegar		

Rinse, dry and tear lettuce into bite-size pieces.

Rub the inside of a large salad bowl with cut clove of garlic. In a smaller bowl mash several anchovy fillets with a fork; add enough Worcestershire sauce to make a paste. Crack egg into this and whip with fork to blend. Add oil, vinegar and juice of 1/2 lemon.

Place lettuce in salad bowl, pour dressing over it and toss until well coated. Add seasonings and croutons, toss to mix and serve.

Serves 4-8.

Layered Salad

This is my kind of salad. I recently made it, left it in the refrigerator overnight, and carried it over 100 miles in an ice chest — it held up beautifully for our family dinner. Thanks to Debbie Edwards for sharing.

1	head iceberg lettuce, bite-size pieces	1	cup mayonnaise
1/2	cup chopped green onions	2	tbsp. sugar (less to taste)
1/2	cup chopped celery	3	hard-cooked eggs, chopped
1/2	cup sliced water chestnuts	4	slices bacon, cooked and crumbled
1	can (15-oz.) green peas	1/2	cup grated Cheddar cheese

In a clear glass salad or mixing bowl, layer the vegetables in the order given, beginning with the lettuce.

Combine mayonnaise and sugar and spread it over the vegetables, covering them completely with a very thin layer. Add sugar a little at a time, tasting as you go, making sure not to get it too sweet for your taste.

Sprinkle with egg, bacon and cheese. Cover tightly with plastic wrap and refrigerate for 24 hours. Do not toss before serving; layers are too pretty. Serves 10.

Watch the meat counter at your local grocery store. They will probably put their store brand bacon on sale in packages of bits and pieces. Buy them when you can and slice them, a whole package at a time, into 1/4" thick pieces.

Cook these bacon bits over low to medium heat in a large skillet, stirring occasionally. Drain them in a colander when they are browned. Store the bits in a jar in the refrigerator to sprinkle over salads, eggs, omelettes, casseroles and sandwiches. Much better than soy bits.

Overnight Cauliflower Salad

This is a layered salad that is pretty in a glass bowl. It is a delicious exception to the rule that tossed salads cannot be made and dressed ahead of time, so it is perfect for a buffet or seated dinner.

1	head iceberg lettuce
1	lb. bacon, chopped, fried and drained
1/2	cup chopped green onions
1	head cauliflower, broken into flowerets
1	cup mayonnaise
1/4	cup sugar (see note)
1/4	cup grated Parmesan cheese

Tear lettuce into bite-size pieces and place them in bottom of bowl. Top with bacon, green onions and cauliflower, all in layers.

Combine mayonnaise, sugar and Parmesan cheese. Spread thinly over top, sealing the salad. Cover with plastic wrap and refrigerate overnight.

Serve salad — untossed — from clear glass bowl, if possible, so your guests can see how pretty it is. Add salt and pepper at the table. Serves 8.

NOTE
If you don't care for sweet salad dressing, add sugar one tablespoon at a time, tasting after each addition. One tablespoon may be enough.

Papa's Caesar Salad

Far as I know, this salad is my dad's original. It isn't like a traditional Caesar salad, but that is what he called it, and I wouldn't change it for the world. It's an outstanding salad that really impresses people.

CROUTONS

4	slices bread, cubed into 1/2" pieces		Garlic salt
1/4	cup oil (approximate)	1/4	cup grated Parmesan cheese

Cube the bread. Pour enough oil into a pizza pan to thinly cover bottom of the pan. Add bread cubes and stir to coat with oil. Sprinkle with garlic salt and Parmesan cheese; stir to coat.

Bake at 300° for 10-15 minutes, until dry and lightly toasted. (These are excellent croutons for any salad.)

SALAD

1	large head romaine lettuce, washed and drained	1/3	cup sour cream
1	egg, coddled	1/3	cup chopped green onions
1/3	cup salad oil	1	large avocado, diced
	Juice of a large lime		Salt and freshly ground pepper to taste

Tear romaine lettuce into bite-size pieces and put in large salad bowl.

To coddle the egg, fill a medium saucepan with water and bring it to a boil. Remove from heat and slowly lower an uncooked egg into the water. Cover pan and let sit five minutes; remove egg to cool water until needed.

Toss the romaine lettuce with salad oil, then lime juice, sour cream and egg. When lettuce is coated, add onions and avocado. Season with salt and pepper. Add croutons and serve.

Makes 4-6 large servings; 8-10 small ones.

Rice Salad

I've only recently learned what a lovely salad cooked rice makes. This one is a nice, light change of pace that can be turned into an entrée by simply adding a cup of chopped ham or chicken.

2	cups cooked rice
1/4	cup chopped green onion
1/4	cup chopped green pepper
1/4	cup grated carrot

1/4	cup chopped mushrooms
1/4	cup chopped olives (ripe or pimiento-stuffed)
4	tbsp. oil
2	tbsp. wine vinegar
	Pinch of dill weed (or favorite herb)
	Salt and freshly ground pepper to taste
1	cup chopped cooked ham or chicken, optional

Combine rice with chopped vegetables in medium bowl. Toss well with oil and vinegar. Add dill weed, salt and pepper (and ham or chicken if using).

Cover and chill several hours or overnight for best flavor. Serve cold on pretty lettuce leaves.

Serves 4 as salad, 2 as entrée.

NOTE

Rice cooked with a chicken bouillon cube has more flavor. I always cook a double batch and keep the extra for dishes like this.

Sally's Salad

My mom Peg Patrick works in an office with several women who frequently bring potluck lunches. This salad has been one of their favorites on and off for several years.

MARINADE

6	tbsp. sugar	Pinch of favorite herb (cilantro,
1/4	cup oil	dill weed, sweet basil)
6	tbsp. vinegar	

In small saucepan, combine sugar, oil and vinegar. Cook over medium heat until sugar is dissolved, stirring constantly. This takes only a couple of minutes. Add herbs and set aside to cool.

VEGETABLES

1	can (about 16-oz.) green peas
1	can (about 16-oz.) French-style green beans
1	can (about 12-oz.) white shoepeg corn
1	cup finely chopped celery
1	cup finely chopped onion or green onion
1	small jar (2-oz.) chopped pimiento

Drain cans of vegetables; put vegetables into large mixing bowl. Add chopped celery, onion and pimiento.

Pour on marinade and stir to mix thoroughly. Cover and chill for at least 24 hours, stirring occasionally.

This keeps well for several days.

Serves 10-14.

NOTE

Mom's original recipe called for 1 cup sugar, 1/2 cup oil and 1/2 cup vinegar in the marinade. Too sweet for me, but I'm including her version in case you prefer to try it. Everything else is the same.

Tomato Soup Salad

NOTE

The day I first tasted this salad my grandma's friend had added the whipped topping because she had it on hand. It isn't necessary, but it lightens the salad a bit.

This is an exceptional gelatin salad that doesn't really taste like tomato soup. In fact, the first time I had it, I couldn't imagine what was in it.

1	can tomato soup, undiluted
6	oz. cream cheese, softened
2	pkgs. lemon gelatin, (four-serving size)
2	cups boiling water
1	cup mayonnaise-type salad dressing (such as Miracle Whip)
1	cup chopped celery
4	green onions, chopped
1	medium green pepper, chopped
1/2	cup chopped pecans
1	cup frozen whipped topping, thawed (optional)

Heat tomato soup to boiling, stir in cream cheese until it melts. Dissolve lemon gelatin in boiling water and add to soup mixture. Cool to room temperature.

Add the salad dressing, chopped vegetables and pecans and mix well. Fold in whipped topping, if desired.

Pour into an oiled 9" x 13" pan and refrigerate until set.

Serves 16.

Zingy Tomato Salad

Sounds strange, I know, but it's as good as it is easy.

1	small pkg. cherry gelatin, (four-serving size)
1	cup boiling water
1	can (16-oz.) sliced tomatoes, undrained
1/2	cup sour cream

Dissolve gelatin in boiling water; add tomatoes and pour into a mold or bowl. Refrigerate until set.

Serve with a dollop of sour cream.

Serves 4-6.

NICE TO KNOW . . .

Spices arranged in alphabetical order on your shelf save time when looking for one. Also cool, dark places (inside a cupboard, for instance) are better than open racks to store spices. Heat and light hasten deterioration.

By Special Request...

NEW DIRECTIONS

If you met our son David today, you'd never know he was in and out of trouble from kindergarten on. He was a cute kid. Smart, personable, mischief dancing in his eyes.

But he couldn't handle school, for whatever reason. And school couldn't handle him. Not the teachers, not the principals, not the counselors. Ultimately, not the doctors, not even his dad or me, or his mom.

One day he was fourteen and the problems were more serious.

The Salesmanship Club threw him a rope. Those ordinary people in their suburban station wagons sent him to their camp for troubled boys. It's a camp with rough living quarters and campfires, a place for gathering wood and looking after yourself. It's a camp that shows the boys how to face nature and win — to feel self-confident, some of them for the first time in their lives.

If they ran short of food, they went hungry. If one ran away, the others brought him back. David grew and matured daily, almost visibly. That camp experience turned him around. Back to school and, in time, into the Navy.

Some of you don't even know you saved that boy's life. You may not be a member of the Salesmanship Club. Maybe you just bought a ticket to one of their fund-raising affairs. Or maybe you support the universities where those camp counselors were educated.

Isn't it nice to know you're making a difference?

LEARNING TO DRIVE

Do you remember learning to drive?

My first trials behind the wheel of the family station wagon were short jaunts down a dirt road — the center of the dirt road — in Missouri.

Before I got my license, we moved to a city in Texas where the streets had traffic and the pressures weren't the same. I remember one glorious spring day when my dad asked me to drive to the lake with him, and he handed me the keys to his '55 Thunderbird.

You remember that car, don't you? Tiny, cool. His was white, a convertible, and the top was always down. Was I hot stuff?

So my first time out on real streets, with traffic lights and several lanes going each way, I inched along 20-30 miles an hour. On the open road I goosed it up to 40, and the wind was flying through my hair. I was exhilarated, and terrified. I can feel the lump in my stomach even now.

Still, I made it. All the way to the lake and back home, with everything under control. I was so proud of myself. Then, I sailed into the driveway and into the back of Mom's station wagon.

Actually, it was a small bump, not a crash. At the time, though, I kind of wished it had been. If I were bleeding I might have gotten some sympathy.

Daddy, the master of understatement, just sat there a moment. Finally he said, "Now, why did you do that?"

I still don't have an answer.

Original Kaye Johns Radio Scripts

GRANDMA'S 90TH BIRTHDAY

When Grandma Ethel turned ninety, we had a family birthday party.

To appreciate it, you should understand that Grandma and Grandpa — my first Grandpa, who died several years ago — had four children. They all married and had fourteen grandchildren, who now have seventeen great-grandchildren (two more on the way) and one great-great grandchild. That's five generations.

We're scattered all over the country, and Grandma is the only person in the family who can give you name, address, ZIP code, phone number and birthday for everyone in the family — including in-laws. She spends her Sundays on the phone keeping us up to date on each other.

This summer we decided it's not enough for her to be the only link. We decided to do something about it. We came home for Grandma's 90th birthday.

We came from California and Florida, Ohio and Texas. It was inconvenient. It was expensive. It was a lot of bother. But we spent the whole weekend hugging each other. We made plans for a family mailing list to keep in touch, and we've started planning our next reunion.

The party was to honor Grandma, but the celebration — the celebration was for the family. It was the best birthday present Grandma ever had. I didn't have to ask. I knew.

GRANDMA WALKS AGAIN

My grandma called me the other day. You've heard me mention her before — eighty-nine years old, technically blind, and the happiest person I know. I say "technically" blind because that's what the tests show. She lost her sight about seven years ago, but she's never lived in darkness.

She was calling to tell me that she and Grandpa Dan (his sight is just a shade better than hers) have been active with the Retired Senior Volunteer Program. They go all over town talking to school children about the "olden days" when they were children in school themselves. The children love it, but not nearly so much as Grandma, the great storyteller of our family.

She's spoken to the local Lions Club, she's been interviewed on radio, and they have something to do almost every day of the week. His church group meets one day, hers the next.

Then she got around to the point of her call. "Grandpa and I are planning to walk for mankind again this year, and since I'm nearly ninety, I'm looking for ninety sponsors."

When you "Walk for Mankind" your sponsors donate a certain amount of money for each mile that you walk. "How many miles are you planning to walk?" I asked.

"Five, like last year."

She knew I'd say yes. One of my favorite photos is a snapshot of her and Grandpa Dan at the finish line last year. She was wearing her official Walk for Mankind T-shirt.

Eighty-nine years old, and technically blind. But don't ever say she can't see.

Original Kaye Johns Radio Scripts

Vegetables
& Side Dishes

Green Vegetable Casserole

NOTE

This recipe could be served from a 8" x 12" baking dish if you like. In that case I wouldn't layer the vegetables but would combine them and spread with topping. It will be a thinner topping, but just as good. Begin checking after 20-25 minutes, as it won't take as long to heat through.

This is one of the dishes on the cover of the book. I chose it because I feel it's pretty representative of the things I like to do.

• I'm a little sentimental about it because it reminds me of my dad.

• I like to serve it to our children because it's one dish with green vegetables that they eat wholeheartedly.

• I find it perfect for guests because I can make it two or three days ahead of time, and it won't suffer. It's made of simple ingredients and there's nothing complicated about the recipe itself.

Besides, it makes a grand presentation at the table. Impresses everyone — and who doesn't like a little of that?

I don't remember the time or the place, but somewhere, years ago, my dad served a dish very much like this. I loved it then, and when I asked him for the recipe years after we ate it, he couldn't remember it at all. Only recently did I run across this recipe which is as close as I think I can come.

1   pkg. (10-oz.) frozen baby lima beans
1   pkg. (10-oz.) frozen green peas
1   can (16-oz.) French-style green beans, drained
3   medium green peppers, thinly sliced
    Salt and freshly ground pepper to taste
1   cup heavy cream, whipped
1   cup mayonnaise
1   cup grated Parmesan cheese (reserve 1/3 cup)

Cook and drain frozen vegetables according to package directions. Open and drain green beans; slice peppers. Simmer the peppers in a little water for about 5-7 minutes, until tender but with texture. This seems like a *lot* of green pepper, but when the completed dish is baked, it's not too much.

Use a two-quart, clear glass baking dish, if you have it, for the most elegant presentation. The layers of vegetables and the puffed topping are beautiful.

Layer the vegetables in any order you like, seasoning to taste as you go.

Whip cream very stiff and fold in mayonnaise and 2/3 cup Parmesan. Spoon half the mixture over the top of the vegetables. Using a table knife, gently work some of the topping down through the vegetables.

Add remaining topping and sprinkle with remaining Parmesan. At this point you may cover and refrigerate overnight, or even two or three days.

Bake uncovered at 350° for about 30 minutes (slightly longer if chilled), until lightly browned on top and heated through. The top will be slightly puffed, like a soufflé.

Serves 10-12.

Matchstick Vegetables

Not always, but sometimes, I'm in the mood to chop vegetables. When I am, I chop a bunch of carrots, zucchini and crookneck squash into julienne (matchsticks) and keep them in covered plastic containers in the refrigerator. I can toss them into salads or casseroles, or I can sauté them in remarkably little butter in my non-stick skillet. They're delicious that way.

FOR EACH SERVING

- 1 tsp. butter
- 1/2 cup julienne (or chopped) vegetables

Melt butter over medium heat in non-stick skillet. (It's not enough butter for another type of skillet. If you aren't counting calories, you may prefer to add more anyway — but the one teaspoon really is enough.)

Add vegetable sticks and stir to coat evenly with the butter. Cook over medium heat, stirring frequently until vegetables are tender-crisp. Serve hot, with or without adding salt and pepper.

VARIATIONS—

1. One-fourth cup chopped onions sautéed in butter for 2-3 minutes, then add 1/2 cup squash.

2. One-half cup chopped onions sautéed in butter for 2-3 minutes. Add 1/2 cup julienne carrots for 2-3 minutes; then add one cup squash (or mushrooms or celery or all three) for 2-3 minutes more. Add one cup cooked rice if you like.

Rich Scalloped Vegetables

Delicious with all three vegetables, or with just one or two. Select your favorites.

- 8 oz. each — fresh broccoli, cauliflower, carrots, bite-size pieces
- 4 tbsp. butter
- 4 tbsp. flour
- 2 cups milk
- 4 oz. Gruyère cheese, cubed (or Swiss)
  Salt to taste
- 2 oz. almond slivers, toasted (or more to taste)

Slice vegetables into bite-size pieces and steam them until cooked but still fairly crisp.

Melt butter, add flour, cook over medium heat two minutes. Remove from heat and stir in milk; cook over medium heat until thick. Add cheese and stir until melted. Salt to taste.

Combine vegetables and cheese sauce; top with toasted almond slivers. Bake uncovered at 350° for 15-20 minutes, until cheese bubbles. If made ahead, add almonds just before baking, and increase baking time to about 25-30 minutes.

Serves 4-6.

NICE TO KNOW . . .

When making a cheese sauce, always stir the grated cheese into the sauce after the sauce is cooked. Let the cheese melt into the sauce over low heat and serve.

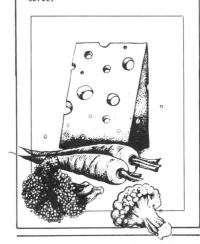

Some artichokes are all green; some have purplish tips on their leaves. The ones to avoid are those which have begun to turn brown, or which have leaves that are beginning to split.

Look for artichokes with leaves which are fairly tightly closed. The more they open, the older — and tougher — they are.

All the books tell you to use artichokes right away; they don't keep well. Sometimes I just don't get around to them right away, and I've had good luck keeping mine up to a week or ten days. I don't recommend it, but so far, I've been lucky with mine.

NOTE

You eat artichokes by pulling off individual leaves and dipping the bottom part of each leaf in lemon butter. Scrape the leaf against your teeth and eat what comes off. Discard the rest. The closer you get to the center, the more of each leaf is edible, until you get to the choke itself.

Remove the choke by cutting under it with your knife and lifting it off. What's left is the heart, the best part.

Vegetable Luncheon Casseroles

Perfect entrée for a light luncheon. Very pretty to serve, and easy since you can vary it many ways.

    1   cup half-and-half
    4   large eggs, lightly beaten
        Pinch of salt
        Pinch of freshly grated nutmeg
    2   cups cooked, chopped vegetables (broccoli, spinach or asparagus are all good), well drained
    4   oz. grated processed cheese (Gruyère or Old English are my favorites)

Add half-and-half to eggs, then salt, nutmeg, vegetables, and cheese. Mix thoroughly.

Generously butter eight custard cups or individual soufflé dishes; fill them 2/3 full.

Set dishes in a pan of hot water, approximately one inch deep, and bake them in a 325° oven for 30-45 minutes, until knife inserted in center comes out clean.

Serves 8.

Artichokes

For years I had no idea how simple artichokes were to prepare. You should be able to trim four in less than ten minutes. Once you do it, you'll be hooked!

    1   artichoke for each serving
        Salt to taste
    1   tbsp. butter for each artichoke
    1   tbsp. lemon juice for each artichoke

With a sharp knife, cut off the stem of the artichokes, and cut the top one inch from each artichoke.

With your kitchen shears, snip the thorn from each leaf. This takes only a couple of minutes for each artichoke. Rub all the cut edges with a piece of fresh lemon and put the stem end down in a large pot.

Add about one inch of water and salt. Cover and cook at a slow boil for 30-40 minutes, or longer, depending on size. They're done when the bottom leaves pull off easily.

Melt butter, add lemon juice and serve with the artichokes.

Baked Asparagus

This is a very rich dish, so serve it with something simple like baked chicken, ham or fish. Don't be limited to these ingredients, but experiment with what you have on hand; it's hard to go wrong.

2   cans (1-lb. each) asparagus bits and pieces, drained
1/4 cup asparagus juice from the can, reserved
2/3 cup chopped pecans
2/3 cup Monterey Jack cheese, grated
1-1/2 cups saltine cracker crumbs
1/2 cup butter, melted

Assemble your casserole in layers. First use half the asparagus, topped by half the nuts, half the cheese and half the crackers. Drizzle with half the butter.

Repeat layers, ending with crackers and butter on top.

Bake uncovered at 350° for 20-25 minutes, until cheese has melted and casserole is bubbling around the edges. If it seems too dry as it bakes, add the reserved liquid from the can.

Serves 6.

VARIATIONS

1. Change the vegetable — cauliflower or yellow squash?
2. Change the cheese — cream cheese or Cheddar?
3. Change the nuts — toasted almonds or peanuts?
4. Change the crackers — round or flavored?

Pickled Beets
(Calorie Conscious)

These are delicious for non-dieters, too. I especially like to serve them with casseroles or grits soufflé, both for color and flavor.

1   can (16-oz.) beets, any style
2   tbsp. cider vinegar
1   tsp. brown sugar substitute
1   tbsp. cornstarch

Drain beets, pouring beet juice into a small saucepan. Add vinegar and sugar substitute, then whisk in cornstarch.

Simmer beet juice until it thickens. Add beets, cover and heat through, about five minutes.

Serves 4.

NICE TO KNOW . . .

If something cooks over onto the floor of your oven and catches fire, sprinkle it lavishly with salt or baking soda. This smothers the fire and stops the smoke.

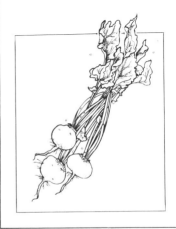

Broccoli Puff

VARIATION

Substitute a 10-oz. package of other favorite frozen vegetable (asparagus, squash, cauliflower) or substitute two cups of left-over cooked vegetables.

This is not only an unusually good broccoli dish, but it is easy to assemble in ten minutes.

    1   pkg. (10-oz.) frozen broccoli spears
    1   can cream of mushroom soup
    1/2 cup grated Cheddar cheese
    1/4 cup milk
    1/4 cup mayonnaise
    1   egg, lightly beaten
    1/2 cup crushed salad croutons

Cook broccoli according to package directions until barely done; omit salt. Drain on paper towels and cut each spear into three pieces. Arrange in 8" x 8" baking dish or 9" pie plate.

Combine soup, cheese, milk, mayonnaise and egg. Pour over broccoli and top with crumbs.

Bake at 350°, uncovered, for 35-40 minutes, until crumbs are lightly browned. Serves 6.

Carol's Broccoli

Toasted almond slivers and toasted sesame seeds are two staples in my refrigerator. Just a few tossed over vegetables or into salads and casseroles makes a great deal of difference. It's a convenience to have them already toasted.

I remember this dish from a family gathering at my sister-in-law's several years ago, it was that good. Carol's an excellent cook and, like me, she prefers recipes that are quick and easy.

    2   pkgs. (10-oz.) frozen chopped broccoli, cooked and drained
    1   stack of round crackers, crushed (about 20 crackers such as Ritz)
    1/2 cup butter
    1   lb. easy-melting cheese (such as Velveeta), in 1/4" slices

Cook and drain broccoli. (Don't salt it because the crackers and cheese are salty enough.)

Combine cracker crumbs and melted butter in skillet. Stir over medium heat until cracker crumbs begin to brown, about ten minutes.

Butter a two-quart casserole dish and assemble the ingredients in layers. Make two or three layers, depending on size and shape of your dish. Begin with broccoli, then cheese and crackers, ending up with crackers on top.

Bake uncovered at 350° for 20-30 minutes, until bubbly around the edges and browned on top. Serves 6-8.

Aunt Libba's Marinated Carrots

These carrots are simply sensational. They keep for days, they are perfect for buffet dinners, and everyone loves them — children included. Almond flavoring sounds strange, but it works!

1/2	cup sugar	1	small onion, sliced thinly
1/2	cup oil	3/4	cup of bottled Italian
1/4	cup vinegar		salad dressing
1	tsp. sweet basil, crushed	1	lb. carrots, sliced thinly
1	tbsp. almond extract		or julienne
	(tbsp. is correct)		

Combine everything but carrots in a small saucepan and heat until sugar dissolves.

In larger saucepan simmer carrots in 1/2 inch of water until tender-crisp about 10-15 minutes; drain.

In medium bowl combine carrots with marinade, stirring well. Let sit in the refrigerator at least overnight, stirring occasionally.

Drain and serve cold. I suppose you could serve them warm, but they're so good cold, I've never tried them warm. Serves 6-8.

NOTE
Sweet red onion is best in this recipe if you can find it. It cooks just enough that it isn't raw, but it's still crisp, which helps solve the digestion problem for some people.

You might try slicing vegetables like carrots on the diagonal, as the Chinese slice food for wok cooking. Slices are not only more attractive, but there is more surface exposed for cooking and marinating.

I usually cut julienne strips of vegetables about 1-1/2" to 2" long and about 1/8" wide by 1/8" high, about the size of wooden matchsticks.

Yes, it takes a little time. Sometimes I'm in the mood, and sometimes I'm not — but it's always worth it.

Carrots Madeira

I served them at our family holiday dinner, and everyone went back for seconds, even the children.

3	lbs. carrots, scraped and chopped
	Pinch of sugar
	Pinch of salt
1/4	cup butter
2	tbsp. heavy cream
2	tbsp. Madeira, cream sherry or port

Cook carrots in water to cover; add pinch sugar and salt. Simmer 10-15 minutes or until done. Drain and purée in small patches in blender or food processor with butter, cream, and Madeira.

Pour carrots into a well-buttered 1-1/2 quart casserole and bake at 300° until hot, about 20 minutes.

Serves 12-16.

NOTE
If you would like to make them ahead, they keep well in the refrigerator. Allow 30-35 minutes to heat.

Nano's Carrots
(Old English Carrots)

Maude Grandstaff was my Nano, and this was her specialty. It's the perfect make-ahead dish — excellent for freezing. Use it to accompany your turkey at holiday time or with chicken or ham at any time during the year.

1	lb. carrots, sliced on the diagonal	1	tsp. salt
4	green onion tops, chopped	2	cups milk
6	tbsp. butter, melted	1	pkg. (8-oz.) Old English cheese (do not substitute), grated
6	tbsp. flour	1/2	cup crushed potato chips

Steam or boil carrots and onion tops in salted water until tender-crisp; drain.

Make sauce by melting butter, adding flour and stirring for two minutes over low heat. Add salt and milk; stir with a whisk until bubbling and thick. Stir in grated cheese and continue heating until cheese is melted.

Combine drained carrots with sauce, turn into a two-quart casserole and top with potato chips.

Bake at 350° until browned and bubbly around the edges, about 30 minutes.

Serves 4 - 6.

Creamed Cucumbers

NICE TO KNOW . . .

Use red pepper sauce, such as Tabasco, as seasoning in sauces, mayonnaise and Hollandaise. That way you won't have black specks.

Peeled, seeded and lightly cooked, these cucumbers are delicate in flavor. The rich cream sauce is the perfect touch. Serve them hot or cold.

2	large cucumbers (about 1-lb. each)
	Salt to taste
1/2	cup heavy cream
	Freshly grated nutmeg to taste
	Hot pepper sauce to taste (such as Tabasco)
2	tsp. minced fresh sweet basil (or other favorite herb to taste)

Peel cucumbers and slice in half lengthwise. Scoop out seeds with small spoon; slice. Cover with water, add salt to taste, and boil rapidly for one minute. Drain and add cream, nutmeg, and hot pepper sauce (I'm generous with mine). I don't add additional salt or pepper, but you may.

Cook at rapid boil for about three minutes, until cream reduces and thickens into sauce. Add sweet basil and stir. Serve hot or cold. I like this dish hot with the Curried Chicken Casserole on Page 123.

Serves 4.

Spicy Green Beans
(Calorie Conscious)

This is a nice change of pace for green beans — lots of flavor.

1	can (16-oz.) Italian-style green beans
1	small tomato, chopped
1/2	small onion, chopped
1/2	green pepper, chopped
	Dash of garlic salt
	Pinch of oregano

Combine all ingredients in a small saucepan; simmer about 5-10 minutes, until onions are cooked.

Serves 2-4.

Steamed Green Beans
(and Other Fresh Vegetables)

There is nothing like the fresh flavor and crisp texture of lightly steamed vegetables. The difference in green beans is remarkable.

1-to-2	lbs. fresh green beans, washed and snapped
1-to-2	lbs. fresh new potatoes, scrubbed and halved
2	large purple onions, peeled and quartered
2-to-3	large summer squash, washed and sliced
	Butter to taste
	Salt and freshly ground pepper to taste

In vegetable steamer (or big saucepan with just a little bit of water, an inch or so) cook beans, new potatoes and onions for about ten minutes, covered. Add squash and cook about five minutes or longer. Vegetables should be cooked, but still fairly crisp.

Serve with butter, salt and freshly ground pepper. Cottage cheese and a fruit salad or slice of melon complete a light, simple, highly nutritious meal.

Serves 4-6.

Ordinary canned green beans can be greatly improved with a dab of butter, dash of garlic powder and shake of grated Parmesan cheese.

Somehow it doesn't seem enough to say that Nano was my mom's mother.

I spent all summer, almost every summer of my childhood years, with Nano and Pop.

I remember how patient she was with me. She would stand me in a chair by her little kitchen table and let me play with a bowl full of flour.

When she made pie crust, I rolled and rerolled the scraps. When she made fried chicken,

she let me stir the gravy with her special silver spoon.

I'd give anything to have that spoon now. It was worn completely flat along one edge from stirring so much gravy in that black, cast-iron skillet.

And she had a paring knife that I loved, with a short, worn blade, and a rolling pin with dents and nicks and no handles.

We spent many long and wonderful hours in her tiny kitchen. I remember how she loved me, and I loved her back.

Sweet and Sour Green Beans

These are a nice change of pace, especially good with grilled chicken or beef.

1-1/2	lbs. fresh green beans, snapped into 1-1/2" pieces
2	cups water
1-1/2	tsp. salt (1 tsp. plus 1/2 tsp.)
4	slices bacon, chopped before frying
2	cups chopped onions
1	tbsp. dry mustard
1/4	cup brown sugar, packed
1/4	cup vinegar

Simmer green beans in water and one teaspoon salt until cooked but still crisp, about ten minutes. Drain, reserving one cup cooking liquid.

Cook bacon pieces over medium heat until browned. Drain, leaving one tablespoon bacon fat in skillet. Sauté onions in bacon fat until translucent, about ten minutes. Add dry mustard, remaining salt, brown sugar, vinegar and reserved cooking liquid; simmer until sugar dissolves.

Combine onion mixture, bacon and beans. Simmer for 15 minutes, drain and serve hot.

Serves 8-10.

I had always taken okra for granted, until I saw it featured as an "exotic" vegetable in a national magazine.

If you aren't familiar with okra, the Okra Patties are an excellent way to get acquainted.

You might also want to slice the okra pods 1/2" thick, toss to coat with yellow cornmeal, and fry in bacon fat until crisp. Drain, salt, and serve as a vegetable side dish.

Okra Patties

These cornmeal patties are similar to hot water cornbread, but lighter in texture. They are still fairly chewy, and the okra is a delicious touch. Perfect with purple hull, crowder, black-eyed or cream peas.

2	cups sliced fresh okra
1-1/2	cups water
1	tsp. salt
1	cup cornmeal
2	tbsp. butter
	Freshly ground pepper to taste

Simmer okra in salted water, covered, for five minutes. Stir in cornmeal. This will be a stiff but moist mixture.

Drop pieces of batter the size of small eggs into buttered electric skillet set on 400°. Use butter sparingly, adding more as you cook more patties.

Flatten batter into patties with back of spoon. Fry until golden on

NOTE

When you simmer the okra, the water becomes the consistency of uncooked egg whites. Don't worry, it'll be absorbed by the cornmeal.

When you buy fresh okra, look for bright, clear green pods. If the okra pods feel limp or look bruised (brown spots), avoid them.

As you are trimming fresh okra, if you run across a pod that seems fibrous, throw it away. It'll be worse than eating straw.

both sides, remove to platter and keep warm in oven. Serve with butter and pepper.

Makes 12 patties.

Brian's Grilled Onions

This is my brother Brian Patrick's way of taking care of the onions for charcoal-grilled hamburgers. They're wonderful!

2	large onions, sliced 1/2" thick
4	tbsp. butter
2	tbsp. water

Stack onion slices with pats of butter in between, on squares of foil. Sprinkle a little water over them and seal up foil. Cook foil packets along with the hamburgers (or steaks) on outdoor grill. Keep them on grill as long as meat cooks. The onions should be cooked, but still have texture. Serve on hamburger or along with steak.

Serves 4.

Onions Baked in Cream

This is very rich — the cracker crumbs soak up the half-and-half and the butter. It is a great side dish with almost any meat.

4	cups sliced onions
2	tbsp. butter, melted
1	cup crushed saltine crackers
1	cup half-and-half
	Salt and freshly ground pepper to taste

Mix ingredients together and put into a one-quart casserole or 10" pie plate. Bake covered at 350° for about 40 minutes. Onions should be cooked but still have a fairly crisp texture.

Serves 4-6.

A WORD ABOUT BROTHERS

Scattered throughout this book, and mentioned often on the air, are my three brothers — Brian, Bruce and Kevin Patrick.

We all have fun in the kitchen, none of us taking ourselves too seriously. I think we're lucky because Mom and Dad rubbed off on us a lot.

Mom is fried chicken and mashed potatoes that float off the plate. Her pie crust is something I've tried to live up to.

Dad was Caesar salad and Welsh rarebit, fried shrimp and crêpes suzette.

I can't tell you how many hours I spent looking over their shoulders or how much I picked up their sense of joy at just being in the kitchen.

But I know I got a big dose of it, and so did my brothers because we all get such a kick out of cooking now.

Brian has a lot of fun with food, serving whatever he makes with remarkable flair, even on his sailboat. Make that "especially" on his boat.

Bruce is definitely debonair. Formal, gourmet, trying to do too much and always succeeding — elegantly and deliciously.

Kevin's recipes are wonderful. He's the only one of us who's ever cooked professionally, working his way through school as a short-order cook who ended up as sous chef for a country club.

He's carrying a marvelous collection of recipes in his head, but he's hard to pin down. When I finally do, it's worth the effort.

Baked Potato Shells

VARIATION

1. These shells are good filled with scrambled eggs, creamed chipped beef or chicken à la king.

2. Also good sprinkled with grated Cheddar or Parmesan cheese.

Baked potatoes are a favorite of mine. I especially like these because most of the calories are gone, while the flavor remains!

FOR EACH SERVING

1   baked potato, halved lengthwise
1   tsp. butter
     Salt and freshly ground pepper
2/3 cup cottage cheese
1   green onion, chopped

Bake potatoes, halve lengthwise and scoop out the meat of the potatoes, leaving about 1/4" thick shell. Put shells on cookie sheet, dot with butter, salt and pepper, and bake at 425° for 5-10 minutes, until lightly browned and crisp. (Save scooped potato for hash browns or potato salad.)

Spoon 1/3 cup cottage cheese into each shell and top with green onions. A delicious substitute for baked potatoes!

Serve two shells per person.

Cheesy Potato Bake

VARIATION

Fold in one cup chopped, cooked ham. Leftover fish would be good too — something like broiled cod or turbot. You might try salmon or tuna, unless you're as tired of tuna as I am.

A light and easy entrée. My family loves anything with mashed potatoes.

2   lbs. potatoes, peeled, chopped and boiled for mashing
1/2 cup butter (6 tbsp. plus 2 tbsp.)
6   tbsp. heavy cream (or sour cream)
     Salt, pepper and freshly grated nutmeg to taste
2   eggs, lightly beaten
4   oz. whole-milk Mozzarella cheese, cubed (about 1 cup)
1/4 cup grated Parmesan cheese
1   cup fresh bread crumbs

Drain cooked potatoes and mash with six tablespoons butter and cream. Heavy cream is best, but you may substitute sour cream if you don't have it on hand. Season with salt, pepper and nutmeg.

Fold in eggs, Mozzarella and Parmesan cheeses; stir to blend well. Spoon into well-buttered 10" pie plate. Sauté bread crumbs in remaining butter until lightly brown, about 5-7 minutes over medium heat. Sprinkle over potatoes.

Bake at 350° for 20 minutes, until sizzling around the edges and browned on top. Serve in wedges.

Serves 4-6.

Gruyère Potatoes

These may be the best scalloped potatoes I've ever eaten. Light, delicate, rich — much more subtle than the usual cheesy, scalloped potatoes with onion. Perfect with a simple entrée such as baked chicken. Outstanding.

The recipe I clipped from the newspaper is at least 15 years old, and I don't know why you cook the potatoes in milk — it didn't explain. But, they were so good, I have to recommend it.

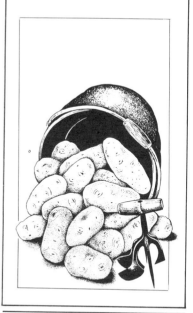

4	large potatoes (3-4 lbs.)	1	cup heavy cream
2	cups milk	1	cup grated Gruyère cheese
	Salt to taste	1/4	cup grated Parmesan cheese

Peel and thinly slice potatoes. Soak in cold water to avoid discoloration. Drain and place in medium saucepan with milk, and salt to taste. Simmer until they are about half done, 10-12 minutes. Drain them again and place in a one to 1-1/2-quart baking dish.

Add cream and sprinkle with Gruyère, then Parmesan. Bake uncovered at 350° until potatoes are completely cooked and top has begun to brown, about 20-25 minutes.

Serves 6.

Potatoes in Foil

This is an easy, delicious change from plain baked potatoes. I always make extras because leftovers make marvelous hash browns. Easy to adapt for the calorie conscious.

FOR EACH SERVING

1/2	medium potato, diced		Salt and freshly ground pepper
1/2	medium onion, diced		to taste
1	tbsp. water	1	tbsp. butter

Dice and combine potatoes and onions. Tear aluminum foil into squares approximately 8" x 8". Put potatoes and onions on the square, sprinkle with water, salt and pepper; dot with butter. Fold foil into packet, carefully rolling and tucking edges so water will not leak out. Prick top with tines of fork to let steam escape.

Bake packets at 350° for 25-30 minutes, long enough to cook potatoes and onions.

Leave potatoes and onions in packets for serving; fold foil back. Sour cream is nice, but not necessary.

VARIATIONS (Calorie Conscious)

1. It's obvious, but cut back on the butter to meet diet requirements. The potatoes and onions have so much flavor, that's easy.

2. Substitute yellow crookneck or zucchini squash for the potatoes, or add them to a small amount of potatoes to expand the serving.

Potatoes Romanoff

Everyone loves these rich, different potatoes. It's a recipe I treasure from my aunt Theresa McCauley.

6	cups sliced potatoes, about 2 lbs.
1	cup chopped green onions
2/3	cup sour cream
2/3	cup cottage cheese
1/3	cup mayonnaise
	Salt and freshly ground pepper to taste

Peel and slice potatoes. Bring potatoes and onions to boil in salted water; reduce heat and simmer until barely tender, about ten minutes.

While potatoes cook, combine sour cream, cottage cheese and mayonnaise in large mixing bowl. Drain cooked potatoes thoroughly in colander; pour into mixing bowl. Stir carefully until potatoes are thoroughly coated. Taste; add salt and pepper as needed. Place in buttered two-quart or 8" x 12" casserole.

Bake uncovered at 350° for 20 minutes, until completely heated through. If you chill it overnight, increase baking time to 30-40 minutes, until hot in center.

Serves 6.

NOTE

If you use canned skim milk straight from the can, you'll add extra protein with very few extra calories.

VARIATION

Add one cup grated sharp Cheddar or Parmesan cheese.

Potato Soufflé

This is not only a fairly low-calorie main dish, but it's pretty to serve as well. If calories are not a problem, add some cheese.

4	medium potatoes (about 1-1/2-lbs.)
1/2	cup milk
1-1/3	cups cottage cheese
	Salt and freshly ground pepper to taste
4	eggs, lightly beaten
2	tbsp. dried onion flakes (or chopped green onion)
1	jar (2-oz.) pimientos, chopped

Peel, boil and mash potatoes. Add milk, cottage cheese, salt, pepper, and eggs. Stir in onion and pimiento. Pour into a well-greased 8" or 9" pie plate and bake at 350° for about 30 minutes — until it is golden brown and fairly firm in the middle.

Serves 4.

Vi's Hash Brown Casserole

This recipe from my friend Vi Moslein is simple enough for beginning cooks, quick enough to throw together at the last minute, and delicious enough to make everyone think it took all day!

1	pkg. (2-lbs.) frozen hash brown potatoes	1	tbsp. minced onions
8	oz. sour cream	1	tsp. salt
8	oz. Cheddar cheese, grated		Freshly ground pepper to taste
1	can cream of chicken soup, undiluted	1/2	cup butter
		1-1/2	cups crushed cornflakes

Place frozen hash browns in bottom of buttered three-quart casserole. Break them into small pieces and mix thoroughly with sour cream, cheese, soup, onions, salt and pepper.

Melt butter in skillet and add crushed cornflakes; stir until lightly browned. Spread over casserole.

Bake uncovered at 350° for 30 minutes, until bubbling around edge. Serves 6.

VARIATIONS

1. Use whatever cheese you have on hand, perhaps a combination of cheeses. You may use less than eight ounces.
2. Substitute cracker crumbs or bread crumbs for cornflakes, or use another flaked cereal.
3. Add other vegetables — 1/2 cup of chopped green pepper, celery or pimientos.

Three-Cheese Spinach

My first thought, when my friend Nancy Morrison shared this recipe, was that it would be a cheese dish with spinach flavoring. I didn't doubt how good it would be, but I didn't think there would be enough spinach to be able to taste it. She was right — just enough spinach, just enough cheese. I serve it as an entrée.

1	pkg. (10-oz.) frozen spinach, thawed and drained	1	cup ricotta or cottage cheese
1/2	cup butter, melted	1	cup grated Swiss cheese
3	eggs, lightly beaten	1	cup grated Cheddar cheese
1	tsp. salt	6	tbsp. cracker crumbs
		3	tbsp. flour

Thaw spinach in a colander and press the moisture out with the back of a spoon. It takes a lot of pressing.

Combine with butter, eggs, salt, cheeses, cracker crumbs and flour until well blended. Put in well-buttered 8" x 8" shallow casserole.

Bake uncovered at 350° for 20-25 minutes, until lightly browned on top and firm to the touch and bubbling around the edges.

Serves 4-6 as entrée, 6-8 as side dish.

NICE TO KNOW . . .

Use extra seasoning in dishes you plan to freeze because freezing reduces the strength of flavors.

Sprouts

You don't need fancy equipment to grow your own delicious sprouts for salads and sandwiches.

    1   clean, empty glass jar — 1 quart size (mayonnaise jar is great)
    1   tbsp. seeds — such as alfalfa, radish, mung bean, sunflower
                        kernels, wheatberry
    1   6" square of pantyhose material
    1   rubber band
         Water

Put seeds in bottom of jar. Cover top of jar with pantyhose material; anchor it in place with rubber band.

Rinse seeds with lukewarm tap water and drain thoroughly. Rinse seeds three or four times a day until you harvest them.

Put jar in a cabinet with the door closed so they are in the dark. In about four days they should be roughly 1/2" long and ready to leave in the sun for a few hours, so the leaves will turn green.

When they are green, take them out of the jar and cover them in plastic wrap, like lettuce — and keep them in the refrigerator. You can begin another crop while you enjoy them on sandwiches and in salads.

Beware of radish sprouts — they can carry a kick. Very radishy and very hot if you eat them alone. Best on sandwiches, especially with cream cheese.

Acorn Squash with Apples

An excellent combination of flavors. Especially good with chicken or ham.

    2   acorn squash, about 1-lb. each   Pinch of salt
    2   small apples, chopped   Pinch of cinnamon
    1/4 cup chopped onion   1 cup grated Cheddar cheese
    1/4 cup water

Cut acorn squash in half. Scoop out seeds and place halves in shallow baking dish. Cover with foil and bake at 350° for 25-35 minutes, or until squash is easily pierced with fork.

While squash bakes, core and chop apples. Combine with onion and water; simmer in small saucepan until apple is tender, about 5-7 minutes. Drain. When squash is done, scoop out meat and combine with cooked apples, salt, cinnamon and cheese. Don't overmix — just toss lightly.

Fill squash shells with mixture and return to 350° oven, uncovered.

Bake long enough to melt cheese, about 15 minutes.
Serves 4.

Easy Crookneck Squash

This is quick, easy, and extremely appealing to people who aren't normally fond of squash.

1   lb. yellow crookneck squash, sliced
1   medium onion, sliced
1   egg, lightly beaten
1   cup cubed easy-melting cheese (such as Velveeta)
1   cup crushed cracker crumbs
2   tbsp. butter, melted

Steam squash with onion until tender, but not mushy. Combine with egg and *half* the cheese. Place into a buttered 8" x 8" casserole and top with the cracker crumbs, remaining cheese and butter.

Bake at 350° for about 20 minutes until lightly browned on top and bubbling around edges.
Serves 4-6.

Summer squash (such as yellow crookneck or zucchini) is best when picked small and tender. Generally, the larger the squash, the more seeds.

Pattypan Squash with Chilies

This dish is as pretty as it is unusual. It's light, a little rich, and absolutely delicious. Lovely for a buffet.

6   pattypan squash, about 3" to 3-1/2" in diameter
6   oz. cream cheese, softened
3   tbsp. chopped green chilies
2   tbsp. green chili juice from the can
1/2 cup grated Monterey Jack cheese
     Salt to taste

Cut top from squash and scoop out centers, leaving about 1/2" shells. Either steam them for 5-10 minutes, until fork-tender, or put them in microwave on high for five minutes.

Combine cream cheese and chilies with green chili juice and mash with fork until well blended. Add in grated cheese and mix thoroughly.

Salt squash shells and fill them with cream cheese mixture. Return to the microwave for about three minutes, or bake in a 350° oven for about ten minutes, until cheese melts and bubbles.
Serves 6.

NICE TO KNOW . . .

Never peel mushrooms. If they are slightly grimy, wipe with a damp, not wet, paper towel.

Sour Cream Summer Squash

When my brother Bruce Patrick shared this recipe with me, he said, "This is the best squash I've *ever* tasted." Many of your friends will agree.

2	lbs. summer squash (yellow crookneck), about 6 cups sliced
1	cup green pepper, thin 1" long slices
2/3	cup chopped green onions
2	cups grated carrots
3	tbsp. chopped parsley
3	tbsp. butter (no more)
1	tsp. salt
	Freshly ground pepper to taste
1	tsp. crushed sweet basil
1	cup sour cream
1	cup grated Parmesan cheese

Slice squash into bite-size pieces. Prepare and measure all other ingredients.

Melt butter in large skillet. Sauté green onion and green pepper over medium heat for *three minutes*. Add carrots and parsley and sauté *three more minutes*. Add squash and sauté *three more minutes*, stirring constantly.

When you add the squash, the skillet will be *very* full. You may think you need to add more butter, but it isn't necessary, and too much butter will separate when it bakes.

When squash has cooked three minutes, season with salt, pepper and sweet basil; fold in sour cream and Parmesan cheese.

Bake uncovered in three-quart casserole at 350° for 30-40 minutes, until it's hot in the center.

Serves 8-12.

Spaghetti Squash

If you haven't discovered what fun spaghetti squash is, you're in for a treat.

It's called *spaghetti* squash because when cooked, the inside literally unravels and looks like spaghetti; use the tines of a fork to scrape it into serving dish.

It smells a little like pumpkin when you first cut into it, and it tastes like a slightly sweet, more delicate yellow crookneck squash. Very low in calories.

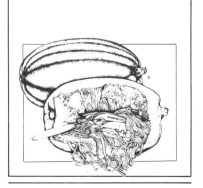

Whatever method of cooking you use, it's done when you can pierce it with a fork. Judge cooking time according to size. An 8"-10" squash should be ample for four people.

To cook, slice lengthwise into two pieces; scrape out seeds with spoon. Simmer in two inches water, cut side down; or bake cut side down on buttered baking dish at 350°. Time varies, but begin testing after 15-20 minutes.

To serve, unravel squash with fork. Toss with butter, salt and pepper to taste. Some people like to add a tablespoon or so of brown sugar; others prefer spaghetti sauce with grated Parmesan cheese.

Spectacular Squash

This is a wonderful company dish — tastes even better the second day.

1	pkg. (8-oz.) stuffing mix (herb or cornbread)
1/2	cup butter, melted
2	lbs. yellow crookneck squash (6 cups, sliced)
1/2	large onion, sliced
1	can cream of chicken soup (undiluted)
1	cup sour cream
1	cup grated carrot
	Salt and freshly ground pepper to taste

Combine stuffing mix with melted butter; press *half* of it into a 8" x 12" or three-quart casserole.

Lightly steam squash and onion until barely cooked. Drain thoroughly.

Combine soup, sour cream and carrot. Fold in cooked squash and onions. Add salt and pepper to taste. Spoon mixture over stuffing mix in casserole dish and top with remaining stuffing mix.

Bake uncovered at 350° until stuffing mix begins to brown and casserole bubbles around edge, about 30 minutes.

Serves 6-10.

NOTE
I prepare mine without additional salt or pepper; the stuffing mix seems salty enough.

It's so much better to steam vegetables rather than boil them. Steamed, they retain more texture, flavor and nutrients.

You can purchase inexpensive vegetable steamers which are designed to fit several sizes of saucepans. Simply put vegetables in the steamer over about one inch of simmering water. Cover the pan and check after two or three minutes. Time will vary according to vegetable (carrots and green beans take 10-15 minutes), but all should be served when they are easily pierced with a fork, but still fairly crisp.

If you don't have a steamer, you can get the same effect by using very little water in the saucepan — no more than 1/2 cup. Simmer the vegetables covered. One word of caution. Your vegetables have to be watched closely as the water can evaporate quickly, leaving them scorched. That's one reason I prefer the convenience of the steamer.

Stuffed Zucchini

Always leave soft-skinned summer squash slightly crisp when cooking, whether boiling, steaming or sautéing in a little butter. The hot squash continues to soften after it's removed from the heat and overcooked it turns to mush — very unappetizing.

Sweet potato recipes always remind me of holiday or special-occasion cooking.

Seems to me ham is the ideal choice for holidays, if you can eat it. I love turkey, but it requires dressing, giblet gravy and mashed potatoes or it just isn't complete.

With ham all you need is sweet potatoes baked in their shell — or a simple sweet potato casserole like this.

The greatest compliment I can pay these recipes is that non-squash lovers ask for more, including my very own children. Our family couldn't decide which version they liked best, so I'm including both.

BASIC RECIPE

4	large (10"-12" long) zucchini squash
2	cups cooked rice
	Salt and freshly ground pepper to taste

Wash and trim ends from zucchini, simmer until tender. Cut in half lengthwise and scoop out middle, leaving shells about 1/4" thick. Chop and save scooped-out part.

Place zucchini shells in large, flat baking dish and lightly salt and pepper. Mound one of rice fillings given below in squash cavities.

Bake at 350° for about ten minutes, until cheese melts.

Serves 4-8.

CHEESE AND BACON RICE STUFFING

4	slices bacon, chopped in 1/4" pieces before frying
1	cup chopped onion
1	cup grated sharp Cheddar cheese

Fry bacon and onions together until bacon is browned and onions are cooked. Drain and combine with grated cheese, reserved squash and cooked rice. Salt and pepper to taste.

GRUYÈRE CHEESE WITH ALMOND STUFFING

1	cup diced Gruyère cheese
1/2	cup chopped green onions (green part only)
1/2	cup toasted almond slivers

Combine Gruyère cheese, onions, almond slivers with reserved squash and cooked rice. Salt and pepper to taste.

Sweet Potatoes with Marshmallows

The only way I got this excellent recipe was to look over my mother-in-law's shoulder. She doesn't measure. It's the only dish of its kind I really like.

5	medium sweet potatoes
4	tbsp. butter

4   tbsp. brown sugar, packed
     Pinch of salt
1   tsp. cinnamon
1/2   tsp. ground ginger
12   large marshmallows, plus more
     marshmallows to cover top of casserole

Peel the sweet potatoes, cut into quarters and boil in salted water until tender enough to mash. Drain and mash them with electric mixer. While beating the potatoes, add butter, brown sugar and spices. Add 12 marshmallows, one at a time; they will melt right into the hot potatoes.

Turn the potatoes into a well-buttered 8" x 12" baking dish. Cover them with a layer of single marshmallows. Bake uncovered at 350° for 20-30 minutes, until marshmallows are large, soft and golden brown. Ideal with chicken, ham or turkey.

Serves 8.

Baked Tomatoes

I've always enjoyed baked tomatoes. This recipe is simple, and I think the pepper sauce makes a real difference. Use it generously.

4   medium tomatoes
     Red pepper sauce to taste, such as Tabasco
     Salt and freshly ground pepper to taste
1-1/3   cups fresh bread crumbs
1/2   tsp. crushed herbs — such as dill weed, oregano, sweet basil
     or parsley
1/4   tsp. garlic salt
1/4   cup grated Parmesan cheese, plus more for garnish

Remove stem and top from tomatoes and scoop out seeds and pulp, leaving tomato shells.

Sprinkle the inside of each tomato shell with red pepper sauce, as generously as you dare. I usually shake in 6-8 drops per tomato for adults, and less for the kids. For very young children, none.

Season inside of tomato shells with salt and pepper. Combine bread crumbs, herbs, garlic salt and Parmesan cheese. Fill tomato shells with bread crumb mixture and sprinkle with more Parmesan cheese for garnish.

Bake uncovered at 350° for 15-20 minutes, until tomatoes are heated through and cheese has browned on top.

Serves 4.

Sautéed Cherry Tomatoes

Without question, one of my favorite vegetable dishes. Colorful and delicious — you won't even recognize the cherry tomatoes, they are *that good.*

1	carton (1 qt.) cherry tomatoes	2	tbsp. butter
		1	clove garlic, minced

Rinse cherry tomatoes and remove stems. Drain them on paper towels while you melt butter in a skillet with the garlic.

Add cherry tomatoes to garlic butter and stir or shake them over medium heat for just three or four minutes. As soon as you see the skin pop on one of the tomatoes, take them off the heat and serve.

Barley Casserole

Barley is a nice change of pace from rice or pasta. My family would call it "interesting".

3-1/2	cups water	1	can (14.5-oz.) plum tomatoes, drained, chopped
2	bouillon cubes (beef, chicken, vegetable)		Other vegetables as you like
1	cup uncooked barley		Salt and freshly ground pepper to taste
	Pinch of herb (sweet basil, dill weed)	1/4	cup butter, optional
1/2	large onion, chopped	1	cup grated cheese (Cheddar, Monterey Jack), optional
2	ribs celery, chopped		
1	medium green pepper, chopped		

Dissolve bouillon cubes in water.

Put everything but butter and cheese in three-quart casserole dish and bake covered at 350° for 45 minutes to an hour (until barley is tender and liquid absorbed).

Taste to see if it needs salt; correct seasoning.

Add butter or easy-melting cheese. Cover casserole until cheese melts; stir briefly with fork to mix, and serve hot.

It's delicious with or without the cheese. Serves 4.

When you get garlic or onion odor on your hands, simply rinse them under cool water as you rub them with the side (not edge) of a stainless steel knife.

I have no idea why it works, but the odor disappears. Every time.

Best Baked Beans

I've always thought baked beans were kind of ordinary, until this recipe. These are the best baked beans in the world! My thanks to

Lee Craft who inspired the recipe.

4	cans (16-oz.) pork and beans, partly drained	1	cup chopped onion
1/2	lb. bacon, sliced into 1/4" pieces before cooking	1	cup chopped green pepper
		1/4	cup brown sugar, packed
		4	tsp. dry mustard

Put beans in 8" x 12" casserole. Chop and fry bacon. Drain, leaving one tablespoon bacon fat in skillet. Put bacon in beans, and sauté onion and green pepper in bacon fat over medium heat until onions are translucent, about ten minutes.

Stir onions and peppers into beans. Add brown sugar and dry mustard and stir to blend well.

Bake uncovered at 350° for 45 minutes. Beans should be very hot and bubbling. Serves 6-8.

Grandma's Pinto Beans

Someone asked me for my pinto bean recipe recently, and it took me by surprise. I've never had a recipe for them; I've made them instinctively all my life. I began to think about where I learned to make beans and came up with, of course, my Grandma Ethel. Her beans are so good that I have to share a story with you.

When I was in college, we had an Academic Banquet. Those who made A's ate steak. Those who made B's ate hamburger. Everyone else sat at a table with a bowl of beans. Since I was the only married member of the group, I was elected to make the pot of beans.

Truth was, everyone wanted the beans, even the A students. That's how good my Grandma's beans are. And they're simple, too!

1	pkg. (2-lbs.) dried pinto beans	Salt to taste
1	large onion, chopped	Chili powder to taste
1	large green pepper, chopped	Garlic salt to taste
1	pkg. (3 or 4) ham hocks	

Put the pinto beans in a large stew pot and cover them with water. Let them sit overnight. Pour off the water and rinse the beans before cooking.

Add the onion, pepper, ham hocks, salt, chili powder and garlic salt to the beans in the pot. Cover everything with water.

Simmer covered for 3-4 hours, stirring occasionally and adding water as needed. Be generous with your seasoning, and taste periodically.

Before serving, remove ham hocks and pull the meat off the bone. Discard bones and fat; stir meat into beans.

Serve with cornbread and fresh green onions. Ideally, put the cornbread in the bowl and be generous with the pot liquor! Serves 6-8.

Sybilara Beans

The last night of our bareboat charter on the Sybilara in the Virgin Islands, I created these beans out of the tag ends of our provisions.

    1/2   medium onion, chopped
    1/2   medium green pepper, chopped
    1/4   cup butter
    2   cans (16-oz.) pork and beans, partly drained
    1   tsp. curry powder (more to taste)

Sauté onion and pepper in butter until onions are translucent, about ten minutes. Add beans and curry and simmer for 10-15 minutes more.

These beans were the best beans we'd ever eaten. Do you think the sunset had anything to do with it?

Serves 3-4.

Baked Fruit with Curry

This is a fine side dish for ham, turkey or any meat. It has the added plus of having few calories.

    1   can (16-oz.) Freestone peaches, drained
    2   medium bananas, not too ripe, sliced
    1   tsp. curry powder (or to taste) — use one with fairly hot flavor

Combine and bake at 350° for ten minutes.

Serves 4.

Fried Apple Rings

These make an outstanding side dish for a leisurely weekend brunch. Truthfully, I wouldn't try to serve them to more than four people because I think they are best hot out of the skillet.

    3   large apples, cored and sliced into 1/2" thick circles (with skins)
         Bacon fat
         Cinnamon sugar

I'm sorry if this sounds vague, but I'll just have to tell you what I do. I usually can get four slices out of each apple, two large ones from the center and two smaller ones from the ends. I can barely squeeze them into

my electric skillet. Your skillet may hold more or less, or you may have a griddle which would hold a good deal more. Each person should get at least two slices, and most will eat three or four slices if they are offered.

Heat bacon fat to medium, and put apples in it. You should have about 1/4" fat in skillet. Cook until apples have begun to brown on bottom, about 3-4 minutes. Turn only once, sprinkling with cinnamon sugar after you turn them. Cook second side only until browned, just 2-3 minutes usually.

Serve hot.

Serves 4.

Sautéed Apples

I like to serve apples for breakfast. They're quick and easy, and usually available all year. They're great with eggs.

| 2 | large apples | Cinnamon |
| 1 | tbsp. butter | |

Chop the apples, skin and all, and sauté them briefly in the butter in a non-stick skillet. Keep the heat on medium and stir occasionally. This takes about five minutes.

Sprinkle with cinnamon.

Serves 4.

Grits Soufflé

I've made this recipe countless times over the years and everyone loves it. It's a big favorite with our children.

4	cups salted water	Garlic salt to taste
1	cup grits	Butter
4	eggs, lightly beaten	
1	cup (4-oz.) easy-melting cheese, cubed (such as Velveeta)	

Gradually add grits to boiling water, stirring constantly. Simmer uncovered until thick, stirring occasionally — about five minutes. Remove from heat and gradually add eggs, cheese and garlic salt, stirring until cheese melts. You can return to very low heat if you'll stir constantly.

Pour into well-buttered three-quart casserole or 10" pie plate. Bake uncovered at 350° for about 30 minutes or until set in middle.

Serve as entrée with colorful vegetable and salad, or as a side dish with baked ham or roast pork. Serve with butter.

Serves 4 as entrée, 6-8 as side dish.

My husband Jim knows the very best way to eat apples — crisp and cold with a bowl of hot, salty popcorn. And, preferably with your feet propped up in front of Sunday football on TV. Don't forget the fire in the fireplace.

Remember when entertaining, especially around Christmas holiday time, that many people are faced with one rich meal after another.

Simplify your life by serving a bowl of polished apples for dessert, with or without a brick of cheese. Bet your family and friends will relish the change of pace!

NOTE

Go easy on the salt. Cheeses such as Velveeta are pretty salty by themselves.

VARIATION

Use a 6-oz. roll of garlic or jalapeño cheese.

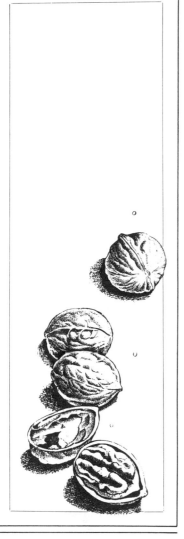

Brown Rice-Spinach Casserole

Don't some recipes fascinate you? They sound good, but because of a peculiar set of ingredients, you really aren't sure. This is one of those interesting recipes. Good, but — *interesting.*

2	tbsp. butter, melted
2	tbsp. flour
2	cups milk
1/2	cup vinegar
1/2	cup grated Swiss cheese
	Salt and freshly grated nutmeg to taste
6	cups cooked brown rice
1	pkg. (10-oz.) frozen spinach, cooked and drained
1/2	cup buttered bread crumbs

Melt butter in a small saucepan. Add flour and cook over low heat for two to three minutes, stirring occasionally. Add milk and then the vinegar.

I was concerned that the vinegar would curdle the milk. It did, but it didn't hurt anything. As you heat the sauce and stir it, it begins to smooth out. It needs to cook only long enough to come to a boil. Don't worry if it seems a little thin. Stir in the Swiss cheese and when it melts, add salt and a little nutmeg.

Combine the rice, spinach and sauce in 9" x 13" casserole and top with the bread crumbs. Bake at 325° for about 30 minutes, or until heated through.

Serves 4-6.

Raisin Rice

Lovely with ham, chicken or turkey. Great way to use up bits and pieces from the refrigerator.

1	rib celery, chopped
1	small carrot, chopped
1	small onion, chopped
1/4	cup raisins (or chopped dried apples)
1	cup uncooked rice
	Water and salt, from directions on rice box
4	oz. cream cheese, cubed
1/4	cup chopped walnuts

Place chopped vegetables and raisins in your favorite three-quart casserole. Add uncooked rice, water and salt; stir together and bake covered in microwave for 25 minutes on high. In a conventional oven, bake covered at 350° for about 45-60 minutes, or until rice is tender and water absorbed.

Stir in cubed cream cheese, cover and let it sit long enough for the cream cheese to melt. Add walnuts and toss to mix.

Serves 4-6.

Rice Pilaf

Few side dishes are as easy as rice pilaf. The basic recipe is easy to vary and goes well with many different meats.

1	cup uncooked rice
2-1/2	cups boiling water
2	bouillon cubes
1/4	cup chopped onion
1/4	cup chopped green pepper
1/4	cup chopped celery
1/4	cup chopped mushrooms

Stir rice, bouillon cubes and boiling water together in three-quart casserole dish. Bake at 350° for an hour or microwave for 25 minutes.

Halfway through baking time, stir in chopped vegetables. (You can put them in first if you like. They're crisper when served if added halfway through.)

Serves 4-6.

NOTE

I almost always bake my rice because it's so easy. If you're not sure if it's done, taste it. Cook until the water is absorbed.

Instead of serving this as a side dish, add one to two cups ham, turkey, or chicken and serve as an entrée.

NOTE

1. Brown rice is more nutritious and flavorful than white, but a little chewy for some family tastes. Try mixing your rice half white, half brown and see what you think.

2. Add one cup orange juice or apple juice for part of the water. Especially good with ham or chicken.

3. Leftover rice pilaf is a great base for poached eggs. Try it, too, for stir-fried rice.

4. Add one cup chopped meat or grated cheese to your baked rice pilaf when you want to serve it as an entree.

NOTES

Spinach-Tomato Casserole

When you serve it, the cheese oozes deliciously onto the plate.

1-1/2	cups rice, cooked according to package directions
1	can (14.5-oz.) tomatoes, drained and chopped
1	pkg. (10-oz.) frozen chopped spinach, cooked and drained
1/3	cup chopped green onion
	Salt and pepper to taste
8	oz. whole-milk Mozzarella (or other easy-melting cheese), sliced into 1/2" thick slices

Cook the rice. Drain tomatoes and spinach very well. You may want to set the tomato juice aside for another use — you'll have about a cup of it left over.

Lightly toss rice, tomatoes, spinach, onion, salt and pepper together. Put half this mixture into a well-buttered three-quart casserole and top with thick slices of Mozzarella cheese. Top with remaining rice mixture.

Bake uncovered at 350° for about 30 minutes — long enough to melt the cheese.

Serves 4-6.

Three-Color Rice

This is such a unique idea, I have to pass it along from my friend Sushma Agarwal.

Sushma came to the United States from her home in Kanpur, U.P., India; and, naturally, she brought many recipes with her. She tells me that this vegetable rice dish has been a favorite in her family for a long time, and that it is very traditional — with one exception. The food coloring and special presentation are ideas Sushma and her sister Manju Bansal came up with on their own.

When I tried this dish, I couldn't help but think how lovely it would be for a buffet — or what fun it would be for the family, especially children.

1	cup uncooked rice, cooked according to package directions	2	bay leaves	
		2	whole cloves	
		1	cup frozen mixed vegetables	
2	tbsp. oil		Salt to taste	
1/2	tsp. cumin seeds		Red and yellow food coloring	
1/2	tsp. ground allspice			

Cook rice and set aside.

Heat oil in skillet over medium heat with cumin seeds, allspice, bay leaves and cloves. Stir in frozen mixed vegetables and sauté until vegetables are tender, stirring occasionally.

While vegetables cook, divide cooked rice into three equal parts. Mix one part rice with yellow food coloring, one with red, and leave the third white. Use food coloring drop by drop until you have a nice bright color.

When vegetables are tender, remove bay leaves and cloves. Add salt to taste and divide into three parts, mixing each part with 1/3 of the rice.

To serve, make a mound of the white rice in the center of a round platter. Surround it with a ring of red rice, and then make a final ring of yellow rice. Garnish with parsley.

If you don't want to use a round platter, use a square or rectangular dish and make three colored rows of rice. They could run horizontally or diagonally.

Doesn't it sound like fun? And delicious, too.

Serves 4-6.

Tomato and Corn Casserole

Not as strange as it sounds. Give it a chance and you'll be surprised — it's really good!

1	cup brown rice, cooked according to package directions
1	can (16-oz.) corn, drained
1	can (17-oz.) stewed tomatoes, drained — use tomato juice as part of rice cooking liquid
2	cups grated Cheddar cheese

Cook the rice and combine with corn, stewed tomatoes and cheese.

Place mixture in well-buttered three-quart casserole. Bake uncovered at 350° for 30 minutes, long enough to melt cheese.

Serves 4-6.

This Tomato and Corn Casserole reminds me of a perfect dish to recommend for those of you who are organized enough to plan through your menus and do a lot of your family dinner cooking ahead of time.

I love it when I am able to take the time. I'm always dashing in at the last minute, and it's a joy to have dinner waiting in the refrigerator.

Sunday afternoons are the best time for me to cook ahead. It saves time for me to chop my onions, celery and other add-in ingredients all at the same time.

Sometimes I cook several pounds of ground beef, or poach a couple of chickens to pick from the bones for casserole dishes. If I don't complete the casseroles, I can at least divide the cooked meat into small portions for easy thawing later.

You can spread your cooked and drained ground beef on a cookie sheet in the freezer, and then store the frozen pieces in a carton or bag.

You can also freeze thin layers of cooked ground beef in compact squares, say in the bottom of a foil-lined 8" x 8" cake pan. Once frozen, the square of meat can be wrapped and stacked in the freezer.

That works with casseroles, too. If you have a favorite casserole dish you like to use, line it with foil, fill it with a casserole, and freeze it. The frozen chunk can be removed, wrapped, and several of them can be stored in the freezer — all to be baked individually when the time comes, in your favorite dish. Saves on dishes and storage space in the freezer.

Curry Stuffing

NOTE

If curry isn't your favorite thing, substitute dry mustard. Gives it a little zip.

I learned an important lesson the first time I made this recipe. I had begun my evening intending to make rice, not stuffing. I had the green pepper, onion, raisins and orange juice ready. Reached for the rice, and found I was out.

Undaunted, I used stuffing mix instead.

We didn't get to eat it because the butter I used — my last stick — had gone bad.

The second time I prepared and served it, it was delicious! Check your butter — and good luck!

1/2	cup butter, melted
1	medium green pepper, chopped
1	medium onion, chopped
1/2	cup raisins (optional, depending on how you feel about raisins)
	Orange juice (to replace water for stuffing mix)
1	tsp. curry, or to taste
1	pkg. (8-oz.) cornbread stuffing mix

Melt butter and sauté green pepper and onion until onion is translucent. If you are using them, add the raisins. Pour in orange juice and curry and mix well. Add stuffing mix and stir until moistened.

Serve with Orange Soy Chicken, Page 127, or serve with any baked chicken, turkey or ham. It's different, but delicious.

Serves 4-6.

ATTITUDE IN THE KITCHEN

I have to say something about this recipe because it represents something important to me about attitude in the kitchen.

I think we should have fun, and give ourselves permission to try things just for the heck of it.

I'm always at my most creative when I'm trying to put off going to the grocery store one more day. I have nothing against grocery stores, it's just that by the time the cupboard is really bare, it's developed into a sizeable chore. Sometimes I'm just too tired to face it.

That was exactly the situation when I attempted this curry stuffing for the first time. Even if it didn't work out, the idea of it was fun. Why not use stuffing mix with orange juice and curry?

It does work — when you have good, fresh butter. Not everyone is going to like it, and that's okay. The point is to please yourself some of the time, to relax and try things just to see what they're like.

You can always bring out the peanut butter and jelly.

PEACE HILL

We went to the Virgin Islands to charter a sailboat for a week — husband Jim, brother Brian, and me. Two of our friends, Gary and Margaret Peacock, were married while we were there. It was a remarkable wedding.

Imagine, for a moment, a very high hill. You can only reach the top by jeep and then by foot, up a steep rock-strewn path that's almost completely hidden from the road. And, when you finally reach the crest, you are on Peace Hill, St. John Island.

You overlook several bays and other islands in the distance. Not too far away, your boat is anchored. You stand at the base of an ancient windmill and an enormous stone statue of Christ, more than 200 years old.

It was a lovely day, full of sunshine and blue sky, and that unbelievably blue water. As we gathered, we watched a squall form over the islands and begin to drift our way. But it didn't matter.

The retired Army chaplain opened his Bible. Vows and rings were exchanged, and then the kiss. And there on the top of Peace Hill with the squall blowing visibly closer, my brother threw back his head and sang the Lord's Prayer like it had never been sung before.

The rain hit as we were running down the hill, slipping and sliding, laughing and awed by the sheer romance of it all.

We knew we would never forget.

EGG-THROWING CHAMPS

Son Warren was just a tyke when he joined the Indian Guides, and Dad was willing to give it a go. Some fathers take to Indian Guides like they were born in the woods. His, doesn't. Just to survive was an accomplishment.

The second night of the campout there was an egg-throwing contest. The Indian Guides were divided into six Indian nations at the camp, and the contest was very important. The winner won the honor of leading the torch parade to the Mess Hall, and that meant his Indian nation got to eat first.

So they began tossing their raw egg back and forth, stepping farther and farther apart, and would you believe who won? The city slicker and his kid! My family — heroes of the camp.

We've told and retold that Indian Guide experience. What father-son camaraderie. What wonderful togetherness. We were so proud.

The subject came up recently when I was in the kitchen with the now-teenage ex-Indian Guide. "You mean we won?" he said. "Dad and me won the egg-throwing contest?"

"What do you mean, did you win — don't you remember?"

He shrugged his shoulders a little self-consciously. "Well, I sort of remember camping and all . . . "

It's okay. He remembers they were together. That's enough. And his Dad can keep on telling the story about the night they were egg-throwing champions at a camp in the woods . . . .

Original Kaye Johns Radio Scripts

MISSING THE PLANE

I wasn't used to the airport.

I asked the ticket agent if his counter was the place to get our boarding passes. He said it was, so I waited there for my friend.

The minutes ticked by. I didn't know my watch was running slow (it had run fast for ten years). Until I heard my name over the loudspeaker, instructing me to come to the gate, I didn't realize that the ticket counter wasn't the only place to get boarding passes.

I dashed to the security checkpoint and started through the screening device — just as another late passenger pushed his way through. We set off the bell.

"Go back through, please," said the guard. I tried to hurry, but so did the other passenger, and we danced through the gate together again. And we rang the bell again, too.

By the time I got through and hurried down the hall, the plane was on its way.

Undaunted, I returned to the ticket counter to change my ticket to a later flight that was to leave in twenty minutes. By the time the paperwork was completed, I had only five minutes to make it to the gate. The agent pointed me toward a hall marked Gates 1-9.

Thank goodness, I thought. I leave from Gate 2. I ran down the hall, already out of breath. I came to Gate 9, then Gate 8, then Gate 7 . . . .

IT'S OKAY TO FAIL

Isn't it wonderful that our minds are geared to remember our successes and forget our failures. How else would we learn to walk? Or ride a bike? Think of all the falls we made before we got the hang of it!

Sometimes it hurt when we fell, but we lived through it. We learned from it. Why is it that as our children grow, we're so tempted to come to their rescue and not let them fail?

Forget your lunch money or library book? Leave your homework at home? It's so much easier for Mom to dash off to school. But it's not fair to the kids.

What is fair, what is right, is to let them learn they can fail and live through it. Paying the consequences may hurt, but not for long. And all of this builds courage and self-confidence.

Fear of failure is what holds most of us back as adults. We don't try because we might not succeed. The real point is, so what? So what if you don't succeed. At least you gave it your best show, whatever it was. You won't go to your grave thinking, "if only I had tried . . . . "

And that, in itself, is a success no one can ever take from you.

Original Kaye Johns Radio Scripts

Entrées

Baked Steak

There are times when you don't want to crank up the charcoal grill and, believe me, baking your steak is a delicious alternative.

1   sirloin steak 2" thick, with bone
     Meat tenderizer, optional
     Salt and freshly ground pepper to taste
     Garlic salt to taste
1/4 cup Worcestershire sauce
1/4 cup butter, in pats

I prefer to tenderize sirloin steak a bit, but it isn't necessary — suit your personal taste, and follow the directions on the tenderizer bottle.

When you are ready to bake your steak, season it with salt, pepper and garlic salt and place it in a shallow casserole dish (size depends on size and shape of your steak).

Pour Worcestershire sauce over steak and dot with butter.

Bake uncovered at 425° for 30-35 minutes for a medium-done steak; alter time according to how you like your steak. Slice steak before serving, and pour sauce over slices.

Serves 4-6.

VARIATIONS
Instead of Worcestershire sauce try Cognac.

NICE TO KNOW . . .

Deglaze a hot cooking pan with wine to lift the brown particles and make a quick sauce. The wine will evaporate and become thick. Stir in a little heavy cream or sour cream just before serving, if you like.

Beef and Broccoli

Stir-frying is a delicious and nutritious method of cooking that really stretches the budget. A splash of dry sherry or red wine in the bouillon is nice, if you have it.

1   cup sliced sirloin (2" x 1" x 1/4") or flank steak
      Meat tenderizer
2   tbsp. soy sauce
2   tbsp. oil (1 tbsp. plus 1 tbsp.)
2   cups chopped fresh broccoli
1-1/2 cups chopped onion
1   cup beef bouillon
1   tbsp. cornstarch
1   tbsp. water

Sprinkle sliced meat with tenderizer and soy sauce; set aside while you chop vegetables.

Heat one tablespoon of oil very hot in your wok or skillet. Add meat and stir-fry until pink is gone. Remove meat, add other tablespoon of

NOTE
Sirloin and flank steak are interchangeable in this recipe. Flank steak has many fewer calories.

oil, and stir fry vegetables for about four minutes — make sure they are still crispy.

Return beef to vegetables, pour in bouillon and bring to a simmer. Dissolve cornstarch in water, pour into skillet and simmer just a minute until thickened.

Serve over hot rice.

Serves 4.

Beef Curry

This is splendid! It's from my brother Brian Patrick. He loves to serve it aboard his sailboat, Moon Shadow. Preferably in the moon's shadow.

2-1/2	lbs. sirloin, sliced thinly
1/2	cup flour
	Salt and freshly ground pepper to taste
1/4	cup butter
1	medium onion, thinly sliced
1	medium green pepper, thinly sliced
2	beef bouillon cubes
1/2	cup water
1	can (14.5-oz.) whole tomatoes, not drained
1/2	tsp. cayenne pepper (more or less to taste)
1	tsp. ground cumin
1	tsp. curry (more or less to taste)

Slice sirloin thinly, on the diagonal, Chinese-style. Dredge in flour seasoned with salt and pepper. Brown meat in butter. Remove beef as it browns and sauté onion and green pepper in same skillet, adding more butter, if needed.

In a small saucepan, dissolve bouillon cubes in water.

Return beef to skillet with vegetables; add tomatoes with juice, bouillon, and seasonings; simmer over low heat until thickened. Correct seasonings.

Serve over hot rice.

Serves 6-8.

It isn't necessary to have a wok to stir-fry food. A non-stick skillet is the next best choice. You'll be amazed how little butter or oil it requires.

Remember, the secret is high heat and constant stirring. It doesn't take long to cook to tender-crisp perfection.

NOTE

This recipe doesn't knock you over with curry; you may prefer to add more. I use at least three teaspoons.

Cayenne pepper should always be treated with respect. It's an essential part of this recipe, but taste as you go.

NICE TO KNOW . . .

Any way you look at it, sirloin steak is expensive.

Sometimes, though, you can cut costs with sirloin and other steaks by watching the meat section of your supermarket carefully.

When meat is exposed to light, its surface turns dark. After a couple of days, it seems so dark that many people won't buy it, so the market people reduce the price for quick sale.

There is nothing wrong with the beef, it's just that a lot of people don't know that. Take advantage of these good prices when you find them and stock up.

To slice meat or poultry thinly, freeze it slightly first and it will be easier to cut.

The story behind this recipe is that when Brian gave it to me, I tried it a couple of times and loved it. I called to thank him, and told him I would use it on the air.

He laughed and said I should give one of his cookbooks credit. Then he thought and said, "But I changed several things." I told him that was okay, because I had too.

When I went back to compare our two recipes, of all the ingredients he had given me, I matched only one exactly. Don't get me wrong — they were slight changes. I doubt you could tell the difference, if any. It's just that both Brian and I are expedient — if creative — cooks!

Bruce's Italian Sauce

My brother Bruce Patrick is an exceptional cook. This sauce is his specialty, and it's perfect for any pasta. The secret is in the long simmering.

1	clove garlic, minced
1	large onion, chopped
1	large green pepper, chopped
1	lb. fresh mushrooms, chopped
1/4	cup olive oil (more as needed)
1 to 1-1/2	lbs. ground beef (or bulk Italian sausage)
	Pinch of oregano, sweet basil or Italian herb blend
	Salt to taste
3	cups dry red wine
1	can (15-oz.) pear-shaped tomatoes
1	can (14.5-oz.) tomato sauce with tomato bits
2	cans (14.5-oz.) herb seasoned tomato sauce
1	small can (6-oz.) tomato paste
2	tbsp. brown sugar, packed

Sauté garlic, onion, green pepper and mushrooms in olive oil until vegetables have cooked down to small bits.

Add meat, seasoning and salt; when meat has browned, add red wine. Boil over medium heat until wine has completely cooked away.

Add tomatoes, tomato sauce and tomato paste along with brown sugar; simmer covered for 5-8 hours, stirring as needed. Sauce should be thick, but not dry. When you put it on spaghetti, no liquid should run on the plate. Doesn't it sound wonderful?

Serves 8 with spaghetti; more with lasagne.

Burgundy Beef

One of my brother Brian Patrick's favorite dishes.

1/4	cup butter
1/2	cup chopped onion
2	cans (4-oz.) sliced mushrooms, drained (reserve liquid from cans)
1	lb. beef (flank steak, rib eye or tenderloin) sliced 1/4" thick
1	cup mushroom liquid from cans
2	tbsp. cornstarch
1/2	cup Burgundy

1   cup beef bouillon
Salt and freshly ground pepper to taste
1   cup sour cream
1   pkg. (12-oz.) noodles, cooked *al dente,* drained

In large skillet melt butter over medium heat. Sauté onion until translucent, about 5-7 minutes; add mushrooms and beef, cooking until beef is no longer red, but still pink in the middle.

Stir cornstarch into mushroom liquid. Add Burgundy to meat and simmer for 2-3 minutes. Stir in mushroom liquid and bouillon; simmer for one minute after it thickens. Add salt and pepper to taste.

Reduce heat and stir in sour cream; do not let boil. When sour cream is hot, stir in noodles.

Serves 4-6.

VARIATIONS
   Brian serves his Burgundy Beef with crêpes. I use noodles, and you may use frozen ones (which I prefer) or regular dry ones in either 8-or 12-oz. packages, depending on how many you want to serve. You could also use rice. The point is — make it easy on yourself. You can't go wrong with a recipe like this, it's too good.

Chicken-Fried Steak

Wonderful eating!

4 small chuck steaks,	Salt and pepper to taste
4-6 oz. each	2 eggs
(or pieces of round steak)	Shortening, melted to
Flour	1/2" in electric skillet

Trim steaks of gristle and fat. Tenderize them with meat tenderizer pounded in with your meat mallet.

Season flour with salt and pepper. Lightly whip eggs in a pie plate. Dip the steaks first in flour, then into the eggs and back into the flour. Coat well.

Let the steaks rest on waxed paper for about ten minutes. Heat the shortening in your electric skillet to 375°. Fry steaks like chicken, about 5-7 minutes a side (depending on how thick your steaks are). It's okay to leave them pink in the middle — in fact, I recommend it.

CREAM GRAVY

4   tbsp. drippings left in pan after cooking steaks
4   tbsp. flour
2   cups milk (or more)
Salt and pepper to taste

It's difficult to give an exact recipe for gravy, but I'll try. Pour off excess fat, leaving about four tablespoons in skillet. Stir in flour and cook two minutes. Add milk all at once and stir with whisk. If it gets too thick, add milk until it's the consistency you want. Salt and pepper to taste, and serve with steaks.

A good rule of thumb is to always make twice as much gravy as you think you'll need. I never have any left.

NOTE
   Generally chuck steaks come from the same area as a chuck roast. They aren't naturally tender, but when you tenderize them before cooking, they are delicious. We like them better than the traditional round steak in this recipe, but you may use the round steak if you prefer.

NOTE FOR NORTHERN FRIENDS —
   Southwest tradition calls for crisp, batter-coated chicken to be served with rich cream gravy and mounds of mashed potatoes.
   Chicken-fried steaks are cooked the same way — batter-coated and fried in oil. They should have a crunchy crust and be served with the same mashed potatoes and gravy.

Corn tortillas are too stiff to roll without breaking unless you steam them or soften them by briefly frying them in 1/2" oil.

If you have a microwave, simply prick the plastic bag the tortillas come in to allow steam to escape and heat them on high for one minute. If the last few cool too quickly, heat them a second time for about thirty seconds.

You may also steam them in a vegetable steamer for about five minutes. To keep them from getting too soggy, I line the bottom of my steamer with a piece of aluminum foil, and cover the top tortilla in the stack with another piece of foil.

Truthfully, it is easier to soften them in oil. Use medium heat and fry them individually. It takes only a moment. You want the tortillas to soften, but not brown. You may want to turn them once, briefly.

VARIATIONS

1. Try this with flour tortillas, chopped chicken, sautéed onion and Monterey Jack cheese.

2. The night I first tried this recipe, I didn't bother to roll my enchiladas. I simply tore the tortillas into pieces, added the ground beef, taco sauce, and stirred it together with the green sauce. I topped it with the cheese and baked it. Worked fine!

Creamed Confetti Beef

This is sneaky, but a delicious way to get children to eat vegetables. (They never guess what's in the sauce.)

- 1 pkg. (10-oz.) frozen mixed vegetables
- 2 cups medium white sauce (see Page 53.)
- 1 jar (2-1/2-oz.) dried beef, chopped
  Cornbread (or toast, biscuits, rice or noodles)

Cook mixed vegetables according to package directions and drain thoroughly. Mince vegetables and add to the white sauce along with chopped beef. Heat thoroughly.

Wonderful served over hot cornbread. Children like it over noodles, spaghetti, rice or baked potatoes.

Serves 4.

Green Enchiladas

A mother invented this delicious, unusual sauce. I know it was a mother, because I know how we think — anything to sell spinach!

- 12 6" corn tortillas
- 1 lb. ground beef, cooked and drained
- 1/2 cup taco sauce
- 3 cups grated Cheddar cheese (reserve one cup)

SAUCE

- 2 pkgs. (10-oz.) frozen chopped spinach, cooked and drained
- 2 cans cream of chicken soup
- 4 green onions, chopped
- 2 cans (4-oz.) chopped green chilies
- 1/2 tsp. salt
- 1 pint sour cream

Steam the tortillas, or soften by frying briefly in 1/2" oil over medium heat. Combine ground beef and taco sauce. Divide taco filling and 2 cups grated cheese equally among tortillas. Roll tortillas; place seam side down in a 9" x 13" baking dish.

Combine sauce ingredients in blender or food processor and purée. Pour over enchiladas and sprinkle with remaining cheese.

Bake uncovered at 350° for 30 minutes, until cheese is melted and casserole is bubbling around edges.

Serves 6.

Italian Beef Pie

This is a great dish for entertaining. It's a quick, rich dish which is sure to make an impression. It's my friend Cheryl Winters' recipe.

1	lb. ground beef
1/2	medium onion, chopped
2	packages frozen spinach (chopped broccoli or mixed vegetables)
1	can (8-oz.) mushrooms, drained
1	can cream of celery soup
1	cup sour cream
	Salt, freshly ground pepper, and garlic salt to taste
	Pinch of oregano or sweet basil
8	oz. Mozzarella cheese, grated or sliced

Brown meat and onion; drain well. Cook and drain spinach. Combine beef, spinach, mushrooms, soup and sour cream; season to taste.

Pour into oiled 9" x 13" casserole; top with Mozzarella. Bake uncovered at 350° for about 30 minutes, until cheese has melted and is lightly browned.

Serves 6-8, generously.

VARIATION

1. Try it sometime with a poached fryer, boned and chopped, instead of beef. Broccoli is good with chicken.

2. Feel free to use cream of chicken soup or cream of mushroom soup instead of cream of celery.

GRACIOUS ENTERTAINING

When you have guests for dinner, make it easy on yourself. Plan ahead and choose dishes, like this one, which can be made ahead of time and which don't require last minute attention.

When we have friends over, I like to enjoy their company. If I were serving dinner with this entrée, here's how I would do it.

I would have the entrée in the oven, filling the house with wonderful aromas as the guests arrive; a fresh green vegetable cleaned and sliced in the steamer, set over water and waiting to be cooked; tossed salad greens in a plastic bag with green onions chopped, sesame seeds toasted and cheese grated in little bowls waiting for the last minute tossing of the salad.

Rolls would be ready to be heated, already in the pan. Dessert would be chilling in the 'fridge, and since I don't have a percolator, I'd have the coffee waiting in the thermos.

Five minutes before dinner I would pour the water, toss the salad, take the entrée out of the oven so I could put in the rolls, turn on the water under the vegetables, light the candles — and call our guests to the table.

By the time I cleared the salad plates, the rolls would be ready, the vegetables steamed, and everything would be ready to set on the table.

See how easy? Keep your menu simple and well organized and entertaining will be as much fun for you as your guests. And it should be!

Mexican Flank Steak

My friend Charleen Donelson brought me this recipe to try. I'll be honest. I took one look and said, "Canned tamales? With flank steak? Surely not!" But, I trust Charleen's judgment — and her family loves it — so I gave it a try. She was right, the combination works.

2	beef flank steaks, about 1-lb. each	1/4	cup boiling water
	Salt and freshly ground pepper to taste	1	can (8-oz.) tomato sauce
			Dash of hot pepper sauce (such as Tabasco)
	Garlic salt to taste	1/4	tsp. ground cumin
1	can (15-oz.) tamales in sauce	1/2	tsp. chili powder (more to taste)
1	beef bouillon cube		

Trim steaks of fat and pound on both sides with meat mallet; add tenderizer if you like.

Season steaks with salt, pepper, garlic salt. In a small bowl, break tamales (with paper removed) into pieces and toss with sauce from can.

Spread the tamales over the surface of the steaks and roll lengthwise, jellyroll fashion. Tie the steaks together with string and place in 9" x 13" baking dish.

Dissolve bouillon cube in boiling water and stir into tomato sauce. Add several drops hot pepper sauce, ground cumin and chili powder. Spoon sauce over meat.

Bake uncovered at 350° for 1-1/4 to 1-1/2 hours, basting occasionally. Serves 8.

NOTE

Charleen's recipe was for two flank steaks. If I were you, I'd go ahead and make two, freezing one for a later date if that's more than your family can eat.

If you prefer, you can cut the recipe in half. I don't know if you can get all of the can of tamales in the middle of one flank steak or not, so you may have some tamales left over.

Serve this with spanish rice, pinto beans and hot tortillas. Excellent for entertaining. Can be made and refrigerated or cooked day before; reheats well.

NICE TO KNOW . . .

A tablespoon of oil or butter added to the water you cook noodles or pasta in will prevent most boilovers.

Mom's Lasagne

This lasagne is quicker than most to prepare. It may not be as traditional as some recipes, but I grew up with it. Every time I serve it, people rave.

1	box (8-oz.) lasagne noodles	2	cans (4-oz.) mushrooms (do not drain)
1-1/2	lbs. lean ground beef		
1/2	tsp. *each* oregano and sweet basil	1	can (14.5-oz.) tomato sauce
1	tsp. garlic powder	1	lb. Mozzarella cheese, grated (more to taste)
	Salt to taste		

Cook lasagne noodles according to directions on package, leaving them just a bit underdone. Drain, rinse and set aside.

Sauté ground beef until well done; drain thoroughly and season with oregano, sweet basil, garlic powder and salt. Add mushrooms, juice and all, then tomato sauce. You may add a little water if the sauce seems too thick.

Grease a shallow 9" x 13" baking dish. Spread several spoonfuls of sauce in dish. Layer noodles, sauce, then cheese; repeat layers. The more cheese in this dish, the better.

Bake uncovered at 350° for 30-35 minutes, until it is bubbly and browned on the top. Let rest for 10-15 minutes before cutting.

Serves 6-8.

My Favorite Pot Roast

I'm not going to presume to tell you how to make a pot roast if you've been following your mom's or grandmother's recipe for years. About the only thing you can do wrong with a pot roast is to cook it too fast, so that you toughen the meat.

I will, however, suggest that if you've never tried using diced vegetables — in French, *mirepoix* — as the base for cooking your roast, you will be pleased at the rich flavor they add. And you can use them to make an especially low-calorie gravy if you're counting calories.

ROAST

1	large carrot, diced	1	chuck roast, about
1	large celery rib, diced		1/2 lb. per
1/2	large onion, diced		serving
2	tbsp. oil (more or less		Salt to taste
	to coat pan)		

Put diced vegetables in large stew pan coated with oil. Stir until vegetables are coated with oil and place over medium heat. Stir until vegetables seem to sweat, about 2-3 minutes.

Add roast. Some people sear their meat first, browning all sides quickly over high heat. I don't, and my roasts are delicious, so I'm convinced it isn't necessary.

Cover with water and return to heat. Add salt to taste. Cover pot and bring to a boil over high heat. Reduce heat and simmer for 2-3 hours, or until meat is fork tender.

Remember, the secret of cooking less tender cuts of meat such as pot roasts is *long, slow*

cooking, whether you're simmering on top of the stove or baking in the oven.

VEGETABLES AND GRAVY
Carrots, Onions, Potatoes

During last 20-25 minutes of cooking, add scraped carrots, peeled onions, and potatoes. Add carrots first, then after they've cooked five minutes, add onions and potatoes.

When vegetables can be pierced by a fork, remove roast and vegetables to platter and cover with foil. Keep warm in oven.

GRAVY
Strain cooking liquid, reserving chopped vegetables. Return liquid to pot for gravy.

It isn't necessary, but I put the reserved diced vegetables into my blender along with a couple of cups of the cooking liquid and purée them to include in the gravy. If you are counting calories, you can skim off the fat and use these puréed vegetables to thicken the gravy without adding flour.

If you like, shake flour and water in a jar until well mixed and stir into cooking liquid. Heat until it boils, stirring frequently.

How much flour and water? Measure — or estimate — your liquid. Use one tablespoon flour for each cup liquid, adding more or less to preference.

Simmer thickened gravy for 3-4 minutes before serving to be sure flour is cooked. Add salt as needed.

Nano's Easy Dinner

Nano was my mom's mother, and this is one of her favorite casseroles. When I serve it, everyone wants the recipe.

1	lb. ground beef
1	medium onion, chopped
	Salt, freshly ground pepper, garlic salt to taste
1	cup uncooked rice
2-1/2	cups water (or as much water as your rice calls for)
1/2	tsp. salt
1	can (1-lb.) bean sprouts, drained
1/3	cup soy sauce
1	can cream of mushroom soup, undiluted

Brown meat and onion; season with salt, pepper and garlic salt and drain well.

Put uncooked rice in bottom of three-quart casserole and add as much water as the rice you use calls for; add salt. Spoon meat over rice and spread bean sprouts over meat. Sprinkle on soy sauce, and then spoon on the undiluted mushroom soup.

Cover and bake at 350° for 30 minutes to an hour. Vary time to suit rice. If you're unsure, taste to see if rice is done. The cooked casserole should be moist, but not juicy.

Serves 4-6.

Rouladen

I can't remember the first time I had this wonderful, inexpensive steak roll, but my mom has baked it for years. It's my Auntie Max's recipe, and she declares it's worth making just for the gravy. She may be right.

1	boneless round steak, 1/2" thick, trimmed of fat
	Salt and freshly ground pepper to taste
	Uncooked bacon strips, enough to cover steak
1	can (4-oz.) mushrooms, drained, chopped
1/3	cup chopped green onions
2	tbsp. bacon fat or oil

Trim steak and, if you like, tenderize with meat tenderizer and meat mallet.

Season one side of steak with salt and pepper, then cover with uncooked bacon slices, placed diagonally. Cover the steak entirely with bacon.

Combine mushrooms and green onions and pile them in a lengthwise row down the middle of the steak. Roll the steak like a long jelly roll with the mushrooms and onions in the center.

Tie the roll with string and brown it in the bacon fat. I like to use my electric skillet set on high for the browning. I bake it in the same skillet, covered, for three or four hours at 250°. You may bake it in your oven if you prefer. Be sure to cover it.

At serving time remove the steak roll to a platter to keep warm while you make the gravy.

You should have just over a cup of pan drippings. Shake four tablespoons flour in one cup water and stir into drippings. Simmer until thickened, about 3-4 minutes. Add more water as needed.

Serves 4.

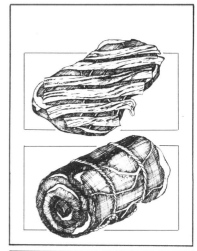

Spaghetti Casserole

Similar to lasagne and equally good. First time I served it my family made me promise to do it again soon. Thanks to Vi Moslein for sharing the recipe.

6	oz. spaghetti (use half the standard 12-oz. pkg.)
1	lb. ground beef, cooked and drained
1/2	cup chopped onion
	Garlic salt to taste
	Salt and freshly ground pepper to taste
1	small can (8-oz.) tomato sauce
1	lb. cottage cheese, drained
1	pkg. (10-oz.) frozen chopped spinach, thawed and drained
8	oz. Mozzarella cheese, sliced or grated
1/2	cup grated Parmesan cheese

Cook spaghetti in rapidly boiling salted water to the *al dente* stage (it should still have some texture).

While spaghetti cooks, brown beef and onion; drain. Add garlic salt, salt, pepper and tomato sauce to meat.

Oil an 8" x 12" casserole and layer half of spaghetti, meat sauce, cottage cheese, spinach and Mozzarella cheese. Repeat layers and top with Parmesan.

Bake uncovered at 350° for 30 minutes, until bubbling and lightly browned on top.

Serves 4-6.

NOTE

It won't hurt a thing to use more spaghetti if you want to stretch this dish a little further. Be sure to use a larger dish if you do, such as 9" x 13".

When you cook pasta for casserole-type dishes to be baked, rinse it in cool water and drain before combining with other ingredients.

Don't rinse pasta that is to be eaten immediately, as it will cool too quickly. Instead, briefly drain and toss immediately with melted butter, oil or sauce.

Summer Sausage

My mom came up with this recipe. If I hadn't known she'd made it herself, I would never have guessed.

4	lbs. regular ground beef (not premium or chuck)
2	tbsp. *curing* salt (available at large grocery stores or feed stores)
1	tsp. garlic salt
1	tsp. onion salt
1	tsp. favorite seasoning salt
2	tsp. freshly ground pepper
2	tbsp. Liquid Smoke
2	tbsp. mustard seed
1	cup water

Mix curing salt into meat, then add seasonings. Add water last. Form into four rolls and refrigerate for 24 hours before baking them.

Put sausage rolls on baking rack with pan underneath to catch drippings. Bake at 350° for an hour; turn sausage over and bake for another 30 minutes. Chill.

Each roll serves 4.

Tacos – Warren's Favorite

It's difficult to suggest a recipe for tacos, but at my son Warren's insistence, I'll do my best. He thinks they're wonderful.

1-1/2	lbs. ground beef, browned and well drained
1/2	tsp. *each* garlic powder, ground cumin, chili powder
	Pinch of oregano
1/3	cup taco sauce
12	6" taco shells, from the store or make your own
6-to-8	oz. Cheddar cheese, grated
	Chopped tomato, lettuce, jalapeño peppers
	Sliced avocado, optional

Combine ground beef and spices with taco sauce.

This recipe fills about 12 taco shells. Put a spoonful of meat mixture in each one and add some grated cheese. Twelve filled shells should fit into your 9" x 13" pan. Bake at 300° just long enough to melt cheese, about 5-7 minutes.

Serve them on plates with lettuce, tomato and peppers on the side. Slices of avocado are optional, but delicious.

Serves 4.

Taco Salad

The first time I had a taco salad was in the '60s when we were in a small college town. I was delighted to have found the dieter's answer to Mexican food — tacos without the shells! I loved it.

When I'm feeling very calorie conscious, here's how I make a taco salad at home. I broil ground beef patties and drain them thoroughly. Then I break them into pieces and add taco sauce and season well with garlic salt, ground cumin and chili powder.

For the salad, toss enough lettuce to fill a plate generously with just over a teaspoon of salad oil and a teaspoon of vinegar. Use the same seasonings as in the ground beef. Top the lettuce with the taco filling, sprinkle on some grated Cheddar cheese and some chopped green onion. It's a dieter's delight!

If you are not dieting, fix your taco meat like you always do, toss your lettuce with the oil and vinegar, and generously spoon on some chili con queso.

A bed of corn chips underneath all of this is wonderful, or top the whole plateful with crushed tostada chips.

I almost always serve myself a taco salad when I prepare tacos for the family. Same basic taste sensations, fewer calories. I don't leave the family out altogether, because it's one of their favorite meals, too. For the family, I include the optional ingredients. I'm the only calorie counter.

1	head iceberg lettuce, torn into bite-size pieces
1	lb. ground beef, browned, drained
1/2	cup taco sauce
1/4	cup oil
1/4	cup vinegar
	Salt and freshly ground pepper to taste
1/2	tsp. ground cumin or cilantro
2	medium green onions, chopped
2	cups queso (see Page 137), optional
1	cup crushed tostada chips, optional

Place iceberg lettuce in salad bowl. Brown and drain ground beef; stir in taco sauce.

Toss lettuce with oil until each piece glistens. Toss with vinegar, salt, pepper, ground cumin and chopped onions. Divide among four plates.

Top each plate with 1/4 meat mixture. Serve as is for dieters. For everyone else, pour 1/4 queso over meat and top with 1/4 of the tostada crumbs.

Serves 4.

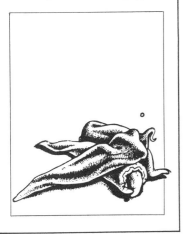

Tamale Pie

I was so thrilled when my friend Jean Jaggers shared this recipe. It's just like one I used to have years ago! Very plain, very simple, very filling, very *good!*

FILLING

1	lb. lean ground beef		1	tsp. salt
1/2	cup chopped onion		2	tbsp. chili powder
1	can (8-oz.) tomato sauce			(more if you like)
8	oz. water (use tomato sauce can to measure)			

TOPPING

1-1/2	cups water		1	tsp. salt
1	cup cornmeal			

Brown ground beef in a skillet with onion; drain. Add tomato sauce, water and seasonings. Put this mixture in a three-quart casserole.

Combine topping ingredients in a medium saucepan and cook, stirring, over low heat until very thick. Drop by spoonfuls onto the meat mixture. Do not stir; it should sit on top of the meat.

Bake at 400° for 45 minutes, until cornmeal topping is firm and filling is bubbling.

Serves 6.

Brandied Curry Chicken

This is a stunning dish. I serve it in an elegant casserole dish — a bed of rice, topped with chicken and the delicate sauce. Always impresses guests.

1/2	cup butter
3	large onions, sliced
8	chicken breast halves, skinned and boned
	Salt and freshly ground pepper to taste
2	tbsp. brandy
1	tsp. curry powder (or more to taste)
1-1/2	cups heavy cream
1	tbsp. cornstarch (optional)

Melt butter in electric skillet and add onion slices. Season chicken with salt and pepper and put on top of the onion. Simmer, covered, for about 20 minutes or until chicken is done (no pink). Add brandy, curry powder and cream; simmer ten more minutes.

Remove chicken to a warm platter. Reduce sauce until thickened, or add cornstarch if you like. (Mix cornstarch in 1/4 cup water before adding to prevent lumps.) Strain sauce, mashing onions to get all the juice out. Spoon sauce over chicken and serve with rice.

Serves 8.

Chicken with Almonds and Vegetables

This recipe is quick and easy. It stretches a little bit of chicken to easily feed four — deliciously!

MARINADE

1	tsp. soy sauce
1	tsp. cornstarch
2	tbsp. dry sherry
1	egg white
1/2	tsp. sugar
	Pinch of salt

CHICKEN

1-1/2	cups diced uncooked chicken
	Oil for stir-frying
1/2	cup sliced fresh mushrooms
2	cups chopped fresh broccoli
1	large onion, chopped
1/2	cup toasted slivered almonds

Mix ingredients for marinade. Marinate chicken while chopping vegetables.

In wok or heavy skillet, heat one tablespoon of oil and stir-fry each of the vegetables separately, adding another tablespoon of oil when needed. Be sure to allow oil to get very hot each time and to remove vegetables while they are still a little crispy. Put cooked vegetables in a large bowl.

When vegetables are ready, put chicken with marinade into wok and stir-fry until done. Add vegetables to chicken, stir for a minute to be sure vegetables are hot and serve immediately with rice. Sprinkle with almonds.

Serves 4.

I often buy packages of skinned, boneless chicken breasts. I dice and freeze them in plastic sandwich bags, measuring one to 1-1/2 cups each. Sure makes last minute meals a snap.

NICE TO KNOW . . .

The best way to store fresh mushrooms is to keep them in the carton they come in (or in a dish) and cover with a damp paper towel.

They keep for two or three days this way. Try to remember to dampen the paper towel whenever it dries out.

If you close the mushrooms in plastic bags, they get too damp.

Paprika and cayenne pepper are affected by heat and light. Store in the refrigerator and buy in small quantities.

When you are calorie conscious, you can make yourself a delicious fried chicken substitute by skinning chicken thighs and cooking them over medium heat in a non-stick skillet. I've found that cooking them uncovered makes them brown and crisp, and they are usually done in 10-15 minutes. Cut into the largest thigh near the bone to see if it's done; you don't want any pink meat.

You can use other pieces, but I've found that thighs are best. They are not only shaped for even cooking, but they are more moist than white meat. Also, thighs don't seem to get tough and dry the way breasts can when cooked this way.

Chicken Bits in Creamy Mustard Sauce

I do a lot of cooking with chicken, and I do a lot of cooking in a hurry, so I keep plastic bags of frozen bite-size boneless chicken breasts on hand.

I've discovered that a standard package of four to five boneless chicken breasts will usually equal about two cups of cubed chicken. If I make a casserole dish, one cup is really enough to serve the four of us. When you cut up one package, you might as well cut up two and freeze them for quick dinners later. Chicken tastes better if cooked fresh for each recipe.

The easiest thing to do with these bits of chicken is to quickly stir-fry them, either in a wok or a non-stick skillet. Combine with your favorite vegetables, all sliced into thin bite-size pieces, and mix into pasta or rice.

There are several sauces that work well with this combination.

MUSTARD SAUCE with SOUR CREAM

1	cup sour cream	1-to-3	tsp. Dijon mustard

Combine and add to the chicken mixture and heat through. Take care not to boil.

LOW-CAL SAUCE

1	cup chicken broth	1/2	cup plain yogurt
1	tbsp. cornstarch	1-to-3	tsp. Dijon mustard (optional)

Heat chicken broth and thicken with the cornstarch. Stir in the yogurt and mustard, if you like, and combine with the chicken and vegetables.

Chicken Enchiladas
(Calorie Conscious)

Almost everybody can benefit from trimming calories; and if you don't have to trim flavor too, why not?

FILLING

2	cans (6-oz.) chicken	1	rib celery, chopped
1/2	medium onion, chopped	1/4	cup chicken broth
1	small green pepper, chopped		

SAUCE

1	cup chicken broth		Garlic powder, chili powder
1	tbsp. cornstarch		and ground cumin to taste
1	cup plain yogurt	8	6" corn tortillas
4	oz. Monterey Jack cheese, grated	3	jalapeño peppers, sliced (optional)

Drain and chop chicken; place in mixing bowl. Simmer vegetables in 1/4 cup chicken broth until barely cooked, about ten minutes. Add to chicken.

For the sauce, thicken one cup broth with cornstarch over medium heat, stirring constantly until it bubbles. Let cool slightly and add yogurt, *half* the cheese and seasonings.

Mix 1/2 cup sauce into chicken mixture to bind it together. Distribute filling equally among tortillas. Roll and place seam side down in 8" x 12" dish.

Top with remaining sauce and cheese; sprinkle with sliced peppers.

Bake at 350° for 20-25 minutes, until cheese melts and it's bubbling around the edges.

Serves 4.

NOTE

When adding cornstarch to hot liquid, always dissolve in a little cool water first to prevent lumping.

NOTE

Briefly steam tortillas to make them pliable before filling and rolling.

Chicken Fricassee with Dumplings

The outstanding part of this dish is the sauce, so I'm going to present it in reverse order, sauce first for those of you who know how to make your own chicken and dumplings. Try this sauce instead of your usual gravy, and I think you'll love it.

FRICASSEE SAUCE

3	tbsp. butter	1	egg yolk
3	tbsp. flour	1	tsp. lemon juice
2	cups chicken broth		Salt to taste
1/2	cup heavy cream		

Melt butter and stir in flour; cook over medium heat for two minutes. Stir in broth; heat until bubbling. Combine cream and egg yolk. Stir slowly into hot broth, heat to simmering and add lemon juice. Taste and add salt if needed.

Ladle sauce over chicken and dumplings.

Serves 4.

CHICKEN

4	pieces of chicken breast (or other pieces)
4	large carrots, cut into 1-1/2" chunks
2	large ribs celery, cut into 1-1/2" chunks
1	large onion, cut into quarters
6-to-8	cups chicken broth
	Salt to taste

Simmer vegetables in broth for 15 minutes. Add chicken pieces and simmer five minutes more. Season and add dumplings.

DUMPLINGS

1	cup flour
2	tsp. baking powder
1/2	tsp. salt
1/2	cup milk
2	tbsp. oil

Combine dry ingredients, add milk and oil, stirring only to moisten.

Drop by tablespoonfuls into simmering broth. When broth returns to simmer, cover pot and simmer *without lifting lid* for 12-15 minutes (depending on size of dumplings).

SERVING

When you serve, simply lift the chicken, vegetables and dumplings onto deep plates or shallow soup bowls without the cooking broth. Ladle the fricassee sauce over chicken and dumplings. Complete your meal with a simple fruit salad.

Chicken Hash

This is an inexpensive, impressive dish. Call it "Turkey Hash" and it's a marvelous way to use up the leftover turkey.

1	3-lb. chicken, stewed and removed from bones
1	pkg. (10-oz.) frozen mixed vegetables
	Salt and freshly ground pepper to taste
2	cans cream of mushroom soup
1	soup can milk
1/2	cup butter
1	medium onion, chopped
2	ribs celery, chopped
1	pkg. (8-oz.) cornbread stuffing mix

Chop chicken into bite-size pieces; place in bottom of a three-quart casserole. Add salt and pepper to taste.

Cook vegetables according to package directions; drain and spoon over chicken. Combine soup and milk; pour over vegetables.

Melt butter in a skillet and sauté onion and celery until tender; add stuffing mix and toss until well mixed. Spoon over other ingredients in casserole.

Bake uncovered at 350° for 30 minutes, until browned on top, and bubbly around edge.

Serves 6-8. (Will serve more for a potluck buffet.)

Chicken Lasagne with Green Sauce

Serve this when you're in the mood to be creative — I promise your family will love it!

2-to-4	cups chopped chicken (about a 3-lb. fryer, stewed, or use canned)
8-to-16	oz. Mozzarella or Monterey Jack cheese, grated or thinly sliced
1	pkg. (8-oz.) lasagne noodles, cooked and drained
1	pkg. (10-oz.) frozen spinach, cooked and drained
1	can cream of mushroom soup, undiluted
1	cup sour cream
2	cans (4-oz.) green chilies, chopped (optional)
1/2	cup grated Parmesan cheese

Chop chicken and prepare cheese.

Cook lasagne noodles according to package directions, rinse and drain.

For sauce, cook and drain spinach, then purée in blender or food processor with soup, sour cream and chilies.

Assemble in 9" x 13" pan by alternating layers. Begin with a layer of sauce, then chicken, cheese and noodles. End with a thin layer of sauce and sprinkle with Parmesan cheese.

You may use a smaller pan if you like. The number of layers you have will depend on the amount of ingredients and size of pan. You should have at least two layers.

Bake uncovered at 350° for 30 minutes, until heated through and cheese has melted.

Serves 6-8.

Chicken Medallions Hollandaise

First time I tried this, I arrived at home at 6:00 p.m., started from scratch and had everything ready for guests who came at 7:00 p.m. It's so easy to prepare, I had time to trim artichokes, make a quick pâté and a splendid dessert.

4	chicken breast halves, skinned and boned
4	tbsp. flour
	Salt and freshly ground pepper to taste
4	tbsp. butter
1	envelope hollandaise sauce mix
1	pkg. frozen asparagus or spinach, cooked and drained
	Rice to serve four

Dust the chicken pieces in flour seasoned with salt and pepper. Sauté in melted butter over medium heat for about five minutes on each side — just long enough to lightly brown and cook through.

While chicken cooks, prepare hollandaise sauce according to package directions. Purée vegetables and combine with hollandaise.

Serve chicken breasts nestled into rice and glazed with sauce. It's a beautiful dish.

Serves 4.

Chicken with Peppers and Onions

NOTE

You may use any chicken pieces. Removing skin cuts calories.

VARIATION

Try adding some sliced carrots and celery to onion and peppers — use what you have on hand.

This is a great throw-together for a busy day. Vary to suit your family's tastes.

1	large onion, sliced
3	green peppers, sliced
1/4	cup butter
2	large potatoes
	Salt and freshly ground pepper to taste
4	chicken breast halves, skinned and boned
1/4	cup chicken broth
	Pinch of your favorite herb (sweet basil, parsley, cilantro, tarragon)

In large skillet sauté onion and green pepper in butter until tender, about 7-10 minutes. Peel potatoes and slice into thin circles and put slices on top of onion-pepper mixture. Salt and pepper generously.

Place chicken breasts on top of potatoes and pour broth over. Add more salt and pepper, along with pinch of herb. Cover and simmer until chicken is done — about 15-20 minutes.

Serves 4.

Chicken Tacos
(Calorie Conscious)

VARIATION

Bake the tortillas flat on a cookie sheet at 350° for 5-10 minutes, until crisp. (They will be tougher than fried tortillas, but for dieters, it's worth the saved calories.)

Substitute 1/2 cup cooked pinto beans for chicken. Mash beans and cook in non-stick skillet with onion, pepper, chilies and seasonings. Use two ounces grated Cheddar cheese in place of Jack cheese.

Spread bean mixture on toasted tortillas. Top with cheese and bake at 350° for 5-10 minutes, until cheese melts. Top with lettuce and tomatoes.

Dieting seems tougher when you have to give up Mexican food, so my theory is don't give it up. Measure carefully and cut unnecessary calories, and you can eat deliciously.

FOR EACH SERVING (Vary to meet diet requirements)

2	6" corn tortillas
3	oz. cooked chicken, chopped
1/4	medium onion, chopped
1/4	medium green pepper, chopped
1	can (2-oz.) green chilies, chopped
1	oz. Monterey Jack cheese, grated
	Salt, freshly ground pepper, garlic salt to taste
	Chili powder to taste
	Salsa

Steam tortillas briefly to soften. Chop chicken and set aside. Cook onion and pepper briefly in a little water or chicken broth. Combine chicken, onion, green pepper, chilies and cheese. Season to taste.

Divide filling between tortillas. Roll tortillas and place seam side down in baking dish, spoon on salsa to taste. Bake uncovered 20 minutes at 350°, long enough to heat through. Serve with tossed salad.

Chicken Tortilla Casserole

This is "from scratch" but worth the extra effort.

1	3-lb. fryer
1/2	cup chopped onion
2	tbsp. butter
1-1/2	tbsp. flour
1	cup milk
1/2	cup chicken broth
1	can (10-oz.) tomatoes and green chilies
12	6" corn tortillas
1/2	lb. Cheddar cheese, grated

Stew chicken; remove meat from bones and chop into bite-size pieces.

Sauté onion in butter over low heat until onion is transparent. Stir in flour and continue cooking for two to three minutes. Remove from heat and whisk in milk and broth. Return to heat and cook until it thickens, stirring with wire whisk to prevent lumps. Add can of tomatoes and chilies, breaking up tomatoes a bit, and mix thoroughly.

Tear tortillas into pieces.

Butter a three-quart baking dish and spread with a layer of chicken. Add a layer of tortilla pieces, a layer of sauce and a layer of grated cheese. Repeat layers ending with the cheese on top.

Bake uncovered at 350° for about 30 minutes, or until it bubbles around the edges and cheese has melted.

Serves 6.

VARIATION

I have been known to sauté 1/2 cup each of diced carrots and celery with the onion, or to add a box of mixed vegetables. I always chop vegetables into smaller pieces and the children never even notice them.

This goes together more easily than the list of ingredients indicates. Very good.

12	corn tortillas, or 1 pkg. tostada shells
3	cups chopped cooked chicken
	Garlic salt, ground cumin, salt and freshly ground pepper to taste
1	can (4-oz.) chopped green chilies
	Lettuce
	Chopped green onions
	Chopped tomato
	Oil and vinegar dressing
8	oz. Monterey Jack cheese, sliced
	Avocado slices
	Black olives

Bake tortillas on a cookie sheet, at 400° for about ten minutes, or heat the tostada shells according to package directions. While they are heating, season chicken with garlic salt, cumin, salt and pepper. Combine with green chilies.

Make a simple tossed salad with lettuce, green onions and tomatoes; dress with oil and vinegar. Season.

To assemble tostadas, divide chicken mixture among 12 tostadas; top with sliced cheese. Run these back in oven long enough for cheese to melt, about 5-7 minutes. Top with tossed salad. Garnish with avocado slices if you have some, or black olives, or both.

Makes 12.

Citrus Chicken

This recipe comes from Daniel MacEachron, and my family has found it to be outstanding. The rich sauce is a perfect blending of delicate flavors. Please don't be put off by the lengthy list of ingredients because it's not difficult at all.

8	chicken thighs, skinned (or other chicken pieces)
4	tsp. butter
	Salt to taste
1/3	cup orange juice (reserve half)
2	tbsp. lemon juice
1/2	tsp. grated orange rind

1/2   tsp. grated lemon rind
1/4   tsp. herb pepper (or tarragon or sweet basil)
1/2   cup heavy cream (or evaporated skim milk)
2   tbsp. white wine
2   tbsp. Madeira or port wine
1   tbsp. cornstarch
1/4   cup grated Parmesan cheese

Sauté chicken with butter in a non-stick skillet over medium heat until golden brown, about five minutes per side. Place in shallow 8" x 12" casserole and salt lightly.

Combine half the orange juice with lemon juice, orange rind, lemon rind and herbs. Pour into skillet. Stir to loosen browned bits and add cream (or milk) and wines. Simmer for two minutes.

Stir cornstarch into remaining orange juice and add to sauce. Cook until slightly thickened, about one minute. Taste, add salt if needed, and spoon over chicken. Sprinkle with Parmesan cheese.

Cover and bake at 325° for 30-40 minutes, until no pink remains in chicken. May be refrigerated overnight before baking; if so, increase baking time by 10-15 minutes. Ideal with rice or noodles.

Serves 4.

Curried Chicken Casserole

This is so good that even our "meat and potatoes" son ate it, bamboo shoots and all. My thanks to his great-aunt Libba Hanes.

    1   cup uncooked rice
    1   cup chopped celery
    1/2   cup chopped onion
    1   can (8-oz.) sliced water chestnuts, drain and reserve liquid
    1   can (8-oz.) bamboo shoots, drain and reserve liquid
    1   tsp. salt
    2   tbsp. curry powder
    1   can cream of chicken soup, undiluted
           Water, plus above reserved liquid, to equal 1-1/2 cups
    12   chicken thighs (or 6 breasts), skin removed

Butter a three-quart casserole. In the dish combine everything but the chicken; put the chicken on top.

Bake covered at 350° for one hour. Uncover and bake another ten minutes to brown chicken lightly. Rice should be tender and liquid absorbed.

Serves 6.

NOTE

Compare prices between chicken breasts and thighs. Thighs are more moist, easier to eat with knife and fork, and less expensive. I prefer thighs.

We don't use a lot of dressing with our salads. I drizzled enough over the lettuce to make pretty, set the remaining dressing on the table, and had enough left to put in the refrigerator for salads later in the week.

Edwardian Room Chicken Salad

This comes from the Plaza Hotel, New York City. My friend Margaret Sinclair used to live in New York, and she came up with the recipe. It's a lovely salad.

SALAD

2	cups chicken, bite-size pieces (about 4 medium pieces of chicken breast)
4	slices bacon, cooked and drained, 1" pieces
7	oz. romaine lettuce (about 1/2 a large head)
1	large avocado, diced
	Juice of one lemon
	Coarse salt and freshly ground pepper to taste

DRESSING

1/2	cup mayonnaise	3	tsp. crumbled blue cheese
1/4	cup sour cream		(add more or less to taste;
3	tbsp. chicken stock		original recipe called for 4 tsp.)
2	tsp. lemon juice		

Poach chicken breasts gently in barely simmering water; drain, cut into pieces and keep warm. Fry bacon; break into pieces. Wash and drain romaine; break into bite-size pieces.

For dressing, combine mayonnaise and sour cream with chicken stock and lemon juice. Whip with fork. Add blue cheese; taste.

Peel and cube ripe avocado. Toss with chicken and lemon juice. Place on bed of romaine, season with salt and pepper. Spoon on dressing, top with bacon.

Serves two as a one-dish entrée for a luncheon dish. You might serve four with smaller portions, adding a slice of melon, hot bread and perhaps a rice salad like the one on Page 64. The Puffed Cheese Ring on Page 38 is perfect with it.

Herbed Chicken Supremes

Perfect for a buffet dinner. Very easy to serve and manage on a plate that's balanced on your knees. It's also very good.

8	boneless chicken breast halves
	Salt, garlic salt, tarragon and pepper (or Spice Islands Herb Pepper) to taste

8 pats of butter
1 pint sour cream
1 cup salad croutons, crushed

Flatten each chicken breast slightly and sprinkle with seasonings. Place a pat of butter on each breast and roll chicken around it. Place in a buttered 8" x 12" casserole and spoon sour cream over them. Top with the crushed croutons.

Bake at 275° for two hours.

Serves 4-8.

Kevin's Sour Cream Chicken Enchiladas

My brother Kevin Patrick has been a professional chef, so his collection of recipes is outstanding. He finally shared this favorite with us, and it's wonderful.

1 chicken, poached and diced (I used a whole fryer; Kevin uses only chicken breasts)
2 tsp. ground cumin (1 tsp. plus 1 tsp.)
1 tsp. chili powder
1/2 cup butter
1/2 cup flour
1 cup chicken broth
1 cup half-and-half
1 tsp. salt
   Freshly ground pepper to taste
1 pint sour cream
1 pkg. (12) 6" corn tortillas
   Picante sauce
1 lb. Cheddar cheese, grated (I used 1/2 lb. and it was enough)

Poach your chicken, remove bones and chop. Season with one teaspoon ground cumin and chili powder.

Combine butter and flour in medium saucepan; cook over medium heat for two minutes. Remove from heat and stir in chicken broth, half-and-half, salt, remaining ground cumin and pepper. Return to heat and stir until thick and bubbling.

Remove from heat and stir in sour cream.

To assemble enchiladas, steam tortillas to soften, or heat briefly in 1/2" oil in skillet. Top with chicken and about one tablespoon picante sauce. Roll and place seam side down in large casserole. (They filled my 9" x 13" dish.) Top with sauce and sprinkle with grated cheese.

Bake uncovered at 350° for 30 minutes, until cheese has melted and it's bubbling around the edges.

Makes 12 large enchiladas.

Lemon Ricotta Chicken

This has a delightful citrus tang which sets off the flavor of the chicken beautifully.

1	lemon
2	tbsp. butter
1	carton (1-lb.) ricotta cheese
	Garlic salt to taste
6	chicken breast halves

Scrub lemon and slice into very thin slices. Chop slices into pieces and sauté in butter until lemon rind becomes translucent. Stir this lemon-butter into ricotta cheese along with the garlic salt.

To stuff the breasts, pull skin up from one side, leaving it securely hooked to the other side. Fill this pocket with as much of the lemon-cheese mixture as it will hold.

Place chicken breasts in a greased 8" x 12" shallow baking dish and bake at 300° for 40-45 minutes, depending on size of pieces. Run them under broiler for a minute if they need additional browning.

Serves 4-6.

Mandarin Chicken Salad

One of the most refreshing salads you can serve.

2-to-3	cups chopped cooked chicken
1	cup chopped celery
1	cup seedless grapes
1	can (11-oz.) mandarin orange slices, drained
1/3	cup mayonnaise
1	tbsp. lemon juice
2	tbsp. minced onion
1	tsp. salt
1/2	cup toasted almonds

Combine chicken, celery and grapes with orange slices. Dilute mayonnaise with lemon juice; stir in minced onion, salt and almonds. Combine with chicken mixture.

Refrigerate, covered, for several hours. Serve on pretty lettuce leaves or a bed of chopped lettuce.

Serves 4-6.

Onion-Crusted Chicken

So simple it's a joy. Ideal for guests.

4	large chicken breast halves, skinned and boned
	Salt and freshly ground pepper
1/2	cup butter, melted
1	tbsp. Worcestershire sauce
1	tsp. dry mustard
	Red pepper sauce (such as Tabasco), several drops to taste
2	cans (3-oz.) French-fried onion rings, crushed

Salt and pepper chicken; dip into mixture of melted butter, Worcestershire sauce, dry mustard and red pepper sauce. Roll in crushed onion rings.

Place pieces side by side in a 8" x 12" baking dish and spoon any remaining crumbs and butter sauce over the top.

Bake at 350° for 30 minutes (or less, if the chicken isn't very thick). Excellent with rice and a simple green vegetable.

Serves 4.

Orange Soy Chicken

Just a suggestion of curry is perfect for this quick chicken, but if your family doesn't like curry, use one-half teaspoon dry mustard in its place. Be flexible.

4	chicken breast halves (or 8 thighs)
	Salt and freshly ground pepper to taste
	Curry powder to taste
1/2	can (6-oz.) frozen orange juice concentrate, thawed
4	tbsp. soy sauce (or Worcestershire sauce)

Rinse and dry chicken. Place in a shallow pan and sprinkle with salt, pepper and curry powder. Spoon orange juice concentrate over chicken and shake about a tablespoon of soy sauce onto each piece.

Bake at 350° for 30 minutes, or until chicken is done.

Serves 4. Recipe doubles easily.

NOTE

Try this accompanied by the "Curry Stuffing" on pg. 98. It's unique and really makes the chicken special. If you'd rather make it easy on yourself, plain rice is good, too.

NICE TO KNOW . . .

The green leaves on the outside of lettuce contain more vitamins than the white ones, so don't throw away more than necessary.

Parmesan Chicken Medallions

This is an elegant specialty from my friend Rita Browning. Sometimes she serves the medallions topped with anchovy fillets rolled with capers.

8	boned, skinned chicken breasts
1/2	cup flour
1-1/2	cups fine toasted bread crumbs
1	cup grated Parmesan cheese
	Grated rind of 2 fresh lemons
1	tsp. salt
	Freshly ground pepper to taste
3	eggs, lightly beaten with 3 tbsp. water
1/2	cup butter
1/2	cup white wine

Flatten chicken breasts between sheets of waxed paper; use kitchen mallet or edge of saucer. Dredge in flour.

Combine bread crumbs, Parmesan cheese, lemon rind, salt and pepper. In separate bowl beat eggs with water. Dip chicken breasts in egg, and then in crumb mixture. Let rest ten minutes.

Sauté in butter in an electric skillet set at 350° until golden brown on both sides; remove to warm platter. Deglaze skillet with wine, adding extra butter to taste. Pour over chicken. Garnish with lemon wedges and parsley. Serves 4.

Quick Baked Chicken

This produces crunchy skin with tender meat — all with a minimum of effort and calories.

Chicken pieces your family will eat in one meal
Lemon or lime juice
Garlic salt
Seasoning salt or herb your family likes

Rinse and dry chicken pieces and place in a shallow pan. Sprinkle each piece with juice and then with the seasonings.

Bake uncovered at 350° for about 30-40 minutes or until all pieces are done (no pink left).

NOTE
I usually prepare breast or thigh pieces this way. An excellent seasoning is Herb Pepper, a blend of herbs which includes just a little tarragon.

Stuffed Chicken Breasts

These are really delicious. One of those entrées that impresses people because it's so rich — and it looks like it's a lot more complicated than it is.

4	chicken breast halves, skinned and boned
	Salt to taste
1/2	cup chopped onion
1/2	cup chopped mushrooms
1/2	cup chopped green peppers
6	tbsp. butter (2 tbsp. plus 4 tbsp.)
1	cup grated Swiss cheese
1/4	cup sherry
1/2	cup heavy cream (or canned skim milk)

Slice a horizontal pocket in each chicken breast; season with salt. Flatten the chicken breast pieces slightly with the edge of a saucer or the heel of your hand; it will make slicing them easier.

Sauté onion, mushrooms and pepper in two tablespoons butter until onion is translucent, about 5-7 minutes over medium heat. Set aside to cool.

Grate your cheese. When onion mixture has cooled enough to handle with your hands, add cheese and divide into four parts. Stuff each piece of chicken with this mixture.

You're going to sauté the chicken breasts and then bake them; but at this point, it looks like the stuffing will spill out for sure. What I do is put the chicken pieces on a cookie sheet and cover them with waxed paper and a weighted pan to press them flat. I set them in the refrigerator overnight before cooking. (You probably don't have to leave them that long, but it seems convenient to me to do it that way.)

When you're ready to cook the chicken, sauté in a skillet over medium-high heat in the remaining four tablespoons butter until they are browned on each side. Remove to a shallow casserole or pie dish.

Deglaze the skillet with the sherry, scraping up all the browned bits as it simmers for about one minute. Add cream or milk and simmer until it reduces to the consistency of a thin sauce. This should take 5-10 minutes; watch it carefully.

Pour sauce over chicken breasts and bake at 250° for about two hours. (You can bake them at a higher temperature for less time, of course, but they won't be as tender.)

Serves 4.

POACHING CHICKEN

Here are some general guidelines I'd like to share.

• One secret of flavorful chicken is to begin with one each medium size carrot, onion and celery rib, all coarsely chopped. Put them in the bottom of your largest stewing pot with one tablespoon oil, and stir to coat. Heat over medium heat until beads of moisture appear on the vegetables. Add chicken and water to cover. Bring to boiling and reduce heat to simmer.

• Always keep the water barely simmering. If you boil the chicken, it will be tough, dry and stringy.

• If you poach a whole chicken, it's easy to tell when it's done. The drumstick should be loose enough to wiggle when you pull it and, if you pierce it with a fork, the juice should run clear and not pink.

• One whole three-pound fryer will equal 3 cups chopped chicken. Compare that to canned chicken. One 6-oz. can chicken, drained, equals 1/2 cup.

• If you are removing skin and bones from poached chicken, you'll find it easier when the chicken is room temperature. If you can't get to it once it has cooled enough to handle, best put it in the refrigerator.

• I like to sort out my chicken pieces, using breasts or combinations of thighs and drumsticks in most recipes. I use the backs, necks, wings and giblets for chicken casseroles, salads and soups by poaching the pieces and picking the meat from the bones. There isn't as much meat on these pieces, but what there is, is especially good.

NICE TO KNOW . . .

Never add wine to a dish at the last minute. It needs to cook to evaporate the alcohol and leave the flavor.

Never use wine in cooking that is not of drinking quality. If the flavor isn't good enough for drinking, it will spoil your dish.

NOTES

_____
_____
_____
_____
_____
_____
_____
_____
_____
_____
_____
_____
_____
_____
_____

Sweet and Sour Chicken

The first time I served this very different — and very delicious — dish was to my father-in-law Alton Johns. I wanted something very special; and this chicken, with it's rich cheese filling and delicate sweet and sour sauce, was easy to make the night before and serve without effort. I recommend it for entertaining.

SAUCE

6	tbsp. sugar	1/2	cup white wine
1/4	cup butter	1	tbsp. Worcestershire sauce
2	cups white wine vinegar		Salt and freshly ground
1-1/2	cups finely chopped onion		pepper to taste

Place sugar in heavy-bottomed two-quart saucepan. Cook over low heat without stirring until sugar melts and caramelizes to a golden brown. Remove from heat; add butter and stir until melted.

Add vinegar to sugar and butter; mix well. Return to heat and bring to a boil, stirring constantly. Add onions and simmer until completely cooked, about 30 minutes, stirring occasionally.

Add wine, Worcestershire sauce, salt and pepper. Simmer three minutes; strain and cool. Discard onions.

CHICKEN

8	chicken breast halves, skinned and boned
1/2	cup flour
	Salt and freshly ground pepper to taste
1/4	cup butter
8	oz. Gruyère or other Swiss cheese, sliced
	Cooked rice to serve eight

Dredge chicken in flour seasoned with salt and pepper. Shake off excess and sauté in butter over medium-high heat until golden brown, about ten minutes per side, depending on thickness of chicken pieces. You want them cooked through, no pink left inside.

Cut horizontal pockets in chicken breasts and stuff with slices of cheese.

Put cooked rice in 9" x 13" or other appropriate casserole. Top with chicken pieces and cover with sauce. Bake at 250° until cheese melts, about seven minutes.

Serves 8.

Zesty Chicken Casserole

My mother-in-law Annie Johns is a terrific cook, and this recipe of hers is known around our house as "Grandmommy's Chicken". Need I say it's a favorite?

1 3 - 4 lb. chicken, stewed and removed from bones
1 large onion, chopped
1 jar (4-oz.) pimientos, chopped
1 can (4-oz.) green chilies, chopped
1 can cream of mushroom soup
1 can cream of chicken soup
1 lb. Old English cheese, cubed (don't substitute)
1 large pkg. (12-oz.) tortilla chips, crushed

Chop chicken into bite-size pieces. In a large saucepan combine onion, pimiento, green chilies, both soups and cubed cheese. Heat slowly, stirring occasionally, until cheese is melted.

Butter a shallow three-quart baking dish and layer chips, chicken and sauce, ending with sauce on top.

Bake uncovered at 350°, until bubbly around edges and heated through.

Serves 6-8.

Poached Eggs

1. You don't need a special egg-poaching pan. I use my regular saucepans with simmering water, varying the size pan for the number of eggs I want to poach at the same time.

2. You can poach several eggs at one time. In my medium saucepan I poach up to six eggs at a time. I've poached 12 in my large skillet.

3. The trick to poaching several eggs is to keep the water moving in a circle as you drop the eggs in one at a time. Keep it swirling with your spoon until they have set, and give the eggs a gentle nudge occasionally as they cook to prevent their sticking to the bottom of the pan.

4. If you want to poach eggs for a large group perhaps Eggs Benedict for brunch — you can fill your large mixing bowl with hot water and slip them into that bowl as you cook them. They will hold for half an hour or so and be hot enough to serve.

5. Eggs can be poached the day ahead of serving and stored in a bowl, completely covered with water. You slip them into simmering water for about one minute, just long enough to heat them before serving.

6. It's easy to tell if your eggs are cooked enough. My big fear for years was that I would have undercooked egg white, but it was a groundless fear. As the eggs cook, in *simmering* — not boiling — water, you can slip a slotted spoon under an egg, lift it out of the water and gently shake the spoon. When the white stops jiggling, it's cooked. After you've done a few, you can easily tell.

7. You can simmer your eggs in chicken broth or beef bouillon if you like, for added flavor. You can also add a little vinegar to the water to help them hold their shape, although I never bother.

8. It's best to lift the eggs from the water with a slotted spoon so the water drains away. I go one step further — I drain the eggs briefly on paper towels before putting them in the dishes. I hate watery eggs.

9. Serve your eggs with a pat of butter, salt and freshly ground pepper to taste, and a sprinkling of chives if you have them. Poached eggs are especially nice nested in corned beef hash, on a mound of grits, or in a dish of cooked rice. They take well to hollandaise sauce or a simple cheese sauce.

Basic Ricotta Fruit Sundaes
(Calorie Conscious)

NOTE

If you're using frozen fruit, be sure to buy the bags of whole fruit frozen without sugar — whole strawberries, blueberries, etc.

I serve the fruit frozen. By the time we begin eating, it is partially thawed, and is still cold enough to have ice crystals. Flavor and consistency seem better to me.

I don't peel peaches, even for cobbler. Saves time, adds roughage, and no one seems to care.

I frequently don't peel potatoes for casseroles or potato salads as others do, for the same reason.

Before you skip this, give it the benefit of the doubt.

My husband is one of those people who would, for the most part, rather do without a favorite fattening food than substitute something else that's low in calories. But I've won him over, at least partly, with various versions of this recipe.

I'm telling you, if he'll eat it and like it, you can trust his judgment. (I'll eat and like almost anything!)

1	cup (or 1 diet portion) of fruit (fresh, frozen or canned)
1/3	cup ricotta cheese (if using for breakfast; 2/3 cup if using for lunch or dinner entrée)
1/2	tsp. coconut, vanilla or almond extract
	Artificial sweetener to taste

I prefer artificial brown sugar substitute (Sugar Twin) to any other for dishes like this, and for my taste, I know that 1/2 teaspoon is perfect for each 1/3 cup ricotta cheese. I play it by ear where the fruit is concerned, adding sweetener only if the fruit is especially tart.

Whip the ricotta with the extract of your choice and sweetener to taste. Use a fork.

FRUIT SUGGESTIONS

My favorites include strawberries, blueberries, pineapple, bananas, plums, peaches, nectarines and apples. Use fresh or frozen without sugar.

Be sure to try different combinations with different extract flavorings in the ricotta cheese, and combine flavors. Banana especially works well with most other fruits.

SERVING

Depends on your mood. Sometimes I serve it with the cheese on the bottom, topped with the fruit. Sometimes I put the fruit on the bottom and use the ricotta like a whipped topping. Sometimes I layer it in a parfait glass.

Ricotta Breakfast Crunch
(Calorie Conscious)

I know it's a silly name, but I can't think of anything more appropriate. It's simply a variation of the Ricotta Fruit Sundae that is wonderful for breakfast or brunch.

HOT WITH GRAPE NUTS

If you add 3/4 oz. (between 1/4 and 1/3 cup) Grape Nuts cereal to the Ricotta Fruit Sundae, it adds both flavor and crunch. The crunch is important to me when I diet — I like to chew things.

Stir your fruit and sweetened ricotta together in a small baking dish and bake it for ten minutes at 350° or in the microwave oven on high for one minute. Top with Grape Nuts just before eating. If you stir the cereal in before you bake it, it won't be crisp.

Fruits which are especially good are peaches, nectarines, plums or apples.

COLD WITH GRAPE NUTS

Same idea, but use partially frozen fruit. Our favorite is frozen blueberries, but you may prefer strawberries or bananas. Yes, I freeze my bananas and use them partially thawed.

WHY RICOTTA CHEESE?

Okay, I admit it. Ricotta cheese, even sweetened and flavored, is not the same as whipped cream. Nothing is. But when you can't have whipped cream, it's a whole lot better than doing without. Try cultivating a taste for it, and it can be one of your best diet friends.

Most diets suggest 1/3 cup ricotta as a breakfast protein — that's roughly 100 calories, if you select part-skim milk ricotta. For

lunch or dinner you would use 2/3 cup, or just under 200 calories.

Frankly, the thing most people complain about with ricotta is the texture. I had a friend tell me once it felt "fuzzy on her tongue". Well, she's right. But with all the other pluses going for it, I think it makes sense to cultivate a taste for it. Start by using a little at a time with other foods to give it a more pleasing texture.

Ricotta Breakfast Danish
(Calorie Conscious)

You can't beat this for a quick, delightful breakfast, especially if you're counting calories. One-third cup part-skim ricotta cheese represents a breakfast protein in most diet exchange programs. I recommend experimenting with both the flavoring (vanilla, almond or coconut extracts) and the fruit topping — as well as the bread. Raisin toast is especially good!

1	slice bread	1/4	tsp. coconut extract, or
1/3	cup ricotta cheese		other favorite flavor
1/2	tsp. artificial brown sugar	1/2	cup frozen blueberries
	substitute (more or less		or other fruit
	to taste)		

Toast your bread. I prefer to toast mine on just one side, but that's up to you.

In a small bowl combine ricotta cheese, artificial sweetener and coconut extract. Spread evenly over toast and top with fruit.

If you have a toaster oven, heat the fruit-topped toast until the blueberries pop. Wonderful!

VARIATIONS

1. You may serve your ricotta Danish without fruit if you like.

2. Add a pinch of cinnamon or nutmeg or both to the ricotta mixture.

3. Fruit suggestions should follow personal taste preference and dietary guidelines, but my favorites include—
- 1/2 cup frozen blueberries
- 1/2 cup frozen strawberries
- 1/2 medium banana, diced
- 1/2 medium apple or peach, diced

4. The Danish doesn't have to be heated. Serve the cheese mixture cold on the toast and thaw the frozen fruit just enough so it's easy to eat.

Ricotta Breakfast Pancakes
(Calorie Conscious)

When you're dieting, you get very hungry for fattening favorites like pancakes. These make wonderful substitutes.

BATTER

1	slice bread	1/2	tsp. baking powder
1/4	cup skim milk	1/3	cup blueberries
1	tbsp. flour		

TOPPING

1/3	cup ricotta cheese
	Artificial sweetener to taste
1/2	tsp. vanilla extract

Combine bread, milk, flour and baking powder in blender; purée into smooth batter. Put blueberries into a small bowl and add batter, reserving a few berries for garnish.

Cook pancakes in a non-stick skillet.

People who frequently eat flaked cereal with milk for breakfast find it adds taste and variety to mix various types of cereal together. Experiment with your own combinations.

When children prefer sugared cereal, it's easier to get them to accept plain cereal if you mix the two together. Add just a little plain cereal at first and then gradually increase the percentage.

Works with adults, too.

Mix the topping ingredients and spread between the hot pancakes and on top, garnishing with the remaining blueberries.

Makes 4 four-inch pancakes.

Scrambled Eggs

Just a few basic rules make all the difference.

FOR EACH SERVING

2	eggs
1/2	egg shell of water
1	oz. easy-melting cheese (such as Velveeta)

The secret of scrambled eggs is to use the lowest possible heat and stir constantly.

Whip eggs with fork; add water and cheese. Lightly butter the pan and cook over *low heat, stirring constantly,* until fluffy. Serve immediately.

I usually use Velveeta because it melts so nicely; it's also salty enough that I don't add additional salt. Taste first, then season.

NOTE

If you use a non-stick skillet and you can afford just a few calories, scramble without butter and then top with a little butter when you serve them. This gives a lovely distinct flavor and doesn't take much butter to make a difference.

Steamed Eggs

If you prepare your eggs this way, they'll be sunny side up, with firm whites and liquid yolks. You don't have to flip them over, and you can cook them six to eight at a time if your skillet is large enough.

	Butter to coat bottom of skillet (about 1 tbsp.)
6	eggs
	Salt and freshly ground pepper to taste
1/4	cup water

Set your electric skillet on 325° and melt enough butter to coat the bottom of the pan. Break in the eggs, salt and pepper them, and pour water around edge of the eggs.

Cover and cook until eggs glaze over and whites are firm, about 3-5 minutes. It doesn't hurt to peek. Shake skillet if you aren't sure they are firm enough; whites should not jiggle. They cook quickly, so watch them closely.

Serves 3-6.

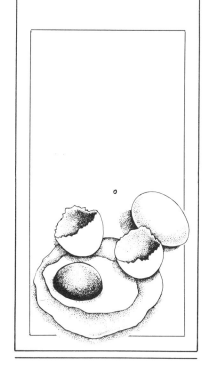

Baked Eggs

It's worth keeping cream on hand just for these eggs.

PER PERSON

1	tbsp. butter, melted		1	tbsp. heavy cream
2	eggs			Salt and pepper to taste

Put the melted butter in a large custard cup. Add eggs, cream, salt and pepper. Place on a cookie sheet in a 300° oven for about twenty minutes. Experiment with your oven and it won't take long to cook them just the way your family likes them.

NOTE

Grated cheese, bacon bits, chopped ham, chives or green onions can be added to the eggs.

Baked Potatoes & Poached Eggs

Don't you love potatoes and eggs together? And baked potatoes are so easy, especially when you're serving a crowd for brunch. These make a lovely buffet.

FOR EACH SERVING

1   medium-size baked potato (about 6-oz.)
1   egg, poached (or two soft-scrambled)
    Salt and freshly ground pepper
    Butter
    Chopped chives (or green onion tops)
    Crumbled fried bacon
    Grated Cheddar cheese

Poached eggs will hold well in a bowl of hot tap water; simply cook them and put them in the water. I hold mine that way for up to half an hour.

If you are serving a large group, you can usually poach 6-8 eggs at a time in a large skillet. Keep the water simmering and the eggs gently moving so they won't stick to the bottom.

If you are opting for scrambled eggs (really easier), leave them under-done — not runny, but soft.

SERVING

Open the potatoes and fluff them with a fork, adding salt, pepper and butter. Top with eggs and sprinkle on any of the extras you like — chives, bacon, cheese. If you are serving buffet-style, you may wish to have bowls of condiments so guests may serve themselves.

These will hold in a warm oven briefly after you've added the eggs, but don't leave them too long or the eggs will overcook.

NOTE

To estimate amount of condiments for large groups, figure for each serving: one tablespoon chopped chives, one slice of bacon to be crumbled, one ounce of cheese to be grated.

BACON FOR A CROWD

If you're cooking bacon for a large group, my first question is "Why?" If you're determined to proceed, then make it easy on yourself by using a roasting rack in the oven with a pan to catch the grease.

Cover the rack with pieces and bake at 400° for 15-20 minutes. Check periodically. Time will vary according to how you like your bacon.

Bruce's French Eggs

This rich egg dish, shared with me by my brother Bruce Patrick, may be the finest brunch dish I've ever tasted.

FOR EACH SERVING

1	tbsp. sour cream	2	eggs
1	oz. Swiss cheese, grated		Salt and pepper to taste
1	oz. ham, slivered (thin-sliced luncheon meat is fine)		

Pre-heat oven to 400° and put a water bath on the middle shelf — a cake pan 1/4 full of water.

Combine sour cream, Swiss cheese and ham; place in buttered large custard cups or individual soufflé dishes. Carefully break two eggs into each dish (it helps if you make an indention in the sour cream with the back of your spoon), and lightly salt and pepper the eggs.

Set dishes in the water bath and bake from 6-10 minutes.

The more dishes you have, the longer the baking time will be. Jiggle each dish to see if it's done; only the yolk and a little of the surrounding white should move. For firmer eggs, leave them until there is no jiggle at all. Some dishes in the same oven will cook faster than others, so check each one before serving.

Brunch Tacos

No, I'm not crazy! When you want an interesting — and delicious — brunch, why not?

7	eggs
2	thick slices easy-melting cheese (such as Velveeta)
1	can (4-oz.) chopped green chilies
1	recipe queso (see below)
6	flour tortillas (6"), steamed to soften

Scramble eggs with cheese until they are cooked but still very soft. Fold in the chilies. I don't add salt because cheese is salty. Taste to see what you think.

Steam tortillas, then roll each tortilla around a spoonful of eggs. Top with your favorite queso. Serves 3-6.

QUICK QUESO

1	can tomatoes and chilies	1	lb. easy-melting cheese

Melt together over a double boiler or in your microwave oven. You'll have some left over, which is good. Great dip.

NOTE

I always add an extra egg when I scramble them; two for each serving and one for the skillet. I'm sure I lose at least an egg in what sticks to the pan.

Jim's French Toast

This has long been my husband's specialty. We consider it a Saturday morning treat!

FOR EACH SERVING

2	slices rye, pumpernickel or sour dough bread	1-1/2	tsp. grated Parmesan cheese
1	large egg	4	drops red pepper sauce (such as Tabasco)
1	tbsp. Worcestershire sauce		Garlic salt to taste
1/4	cup milk		Bacon fat

Soak bread thoroughly in a well-blended mixture of other ingredients, then fry until brown on both sides in bacon fat. Keep slices warm in the oven until all are cooked.

Serve with butter, bacon and fried apples (see Page 92.) Wonderful!

JAM POCKETS

A French toast variation for anyone with a sweet tooth. Children love it.

FOR EACH SERVING

2	slices thick-sliced French or Italian bread	1/4	cup milk
1	egg	1-to-2	tbsp. favorite jam
			Butter

Slice lengthwise pockets in the bread and carefully spread jam in the pocket.

Dip bread in mixture of other ingredients, letting it thoroughly soak. Fry in butter until brown on both sides.

Serve with powdered sugar.

Kevin's Blintzes

Periodically my brother Kevin Patrick stops by Mom's and makes her a batch of his wonderful blintzes. She keeps them in the freezer and heats them in her microwave. Mom likes them for dessert, and we prefer them for brunch. Either way, they're wonderful.

1	cup grated Swiss cheese (4-oz.)
1	cup grated Cheddar cheese (4-oz.)
1	cup grated Muenster cheese (4-oz.)
1	cup drained cottage cheese
4	oz. cream cheese, softened
12	crêpes (see Page 29.)

Combine all the cheeses in a large mixing bowl. Use a heavy wooden spoon and prepare to work at it. If you have a food processor, you're home free. Use your chopping blade for the hard cheeses and blend in the cottage cheese and cream cheese.

This makes about three cups of filling. I use about 1/4 cup for each blintz. Place the filling in the center of your crêpe. Instead of rolling it like a tortilla, pull two sides of the crêpe over the ends of the filling, then lift a third side over the filling and roll it over the fourth side. You end up with a neat little package with no loose ends.

Bake the crêpes at 350° for about 15 minutes, just long enough to melt the cheese filling. Serve with dollops of sour cream and strawberry preserves.

Makes 10-12, depending on size of crêpes.

Omelettes

My dad taught me how to make omelettes his way, and I've never had a better one. I'll share a couple of favorite fillings.

BASIC OMELETTE TECHNIQUE   (for each omelette)
2   large eggs, whipped with fork
1/2   egg shell of water
    Salt and freshly ground pepper to taste
1   tbsp. butter, melted

Whip eggs with a fork, and add 1/2 egg shell of water (which makes them tender). Add salt and pepper.

Melt butter in omelette pan, and when it's foamy, pour in eggs. Cook over medium heat. Pull edges back as eggs begin to set, letting uncooked eggs in center pour out toward the edge of the pan. Be careful not to let the bottom of the omelette brown. Fill the omelette, give the cheese a moment to melt, and lift one side of omelette over filling. Roll onto plate and keep warm in the oven until all omelettes are ready to serve.

CHEDDAR CHEESE AND SOUR CREAM FILLING
1/4   cup grated Cheddar cheese
1/4   cup sour cream
1   tbsp. chopped chives or green onions

GRUYÈRE CHEESE AND TOASTED ALMOND FILLING
1   oz. grated Gruyère cheese
2   tbsp. toasted almond slivers
1   tbsp. chopped green onion

NUTRITION NOTE
I've only recently discovered that almost all of the protein in an egg is in the egg white, not the yolk. Did you know that?

What the yolk has is most of the calories and all of the cholesterol.

An average large egg has about 80 calories — 15 in the egg white, 65 in the yolk. For those who are either counting calories or watching cholesterol intake, it's obvious they're better off with egg whites.

You may substitute two egg whites for one whole egg in baked goods such as cookies, muffins, quick breads.

You can also experiment with herbs and various seasonings and come up with delicious scrambled egg whites, or omelettes made from egg whites.

If you try this, be sure to add a little yellow food coloring — I think it'll make you feel better about it.

If you really aren't sure how fresh eggs are, put them in water. Eggs with a tendency to float are well past their prime.

The fresher the egg, the better for frying, steaming or poaching. Not only for flavor, but the white of the egg is thicker and holds it shape better in fresh eggs.

EMBELLISHING EGGS

Maybe I should say a word about scrambled egg fillers.

I don't know what happens to scrambled eggs when you cook them, but is there anything more pitiful than one scrambled egg on a plate? Two aren't much better.

If you begin by heating a little leftover rice, spaghetti or noodles or some hash browns in a little butter before you add your eggs and cheese, the fillers stretch the eggs and add nice texture and flavor.

As a matter of fact, my favorite filler is leftover linguine tossed with sautéed fresh vegetables like mushrooms and asparagus.

The fillers you use, of course, must depend on the tastes of your family — but they are a nice, easy way to feed a crowd. If you have the time to turn them into this scrambled egg pie, fine. Otherwise, serve them as is.

I usually choose something like muffins or coffee cake to go with the scrambled eggs. Who wants to cook a couple of dozen pieces of toast?

And I don't serve bacon to a crowd either. Link sausages that can be tossed in a skillet and forgotten except for an occasional shake are much less hassle.

Scrambled Egg Pie

This is a nice change of pace from a quiche. It's a very different brunch dish that guarantees a crisp crust. The first time I prepared it, I used a dozen eggs, and they hardly filled the pie crust. I recommend fillers — they not only stretch the eggs, but add texture and flavor.

1	8" baked pastry pie crust
12	eggs
1	cup diced easy-melting cheese (such as Velveeta)
	Fillers, as suggested below

You may use a larger pie plate, and it's a good idea if you want to serve 6-8 people. If you do, add at least two cups filler.

Bake the pie crust and set it aside while you scramble your eggs with the cheese. Leave the eggs partly runny, fold in fillers, and spoon into pie crust.

Set in 350° oven for 7-10 minutes, until eggs have cooked firm enough to slice. Serve warm.

Serves 4-8, depending on size of slices and appetite of people served.

FILLERS
1. One cup cooked rice or leftover hash browns.
2. One cup cooked diced ham.
3. One cup cooked pasta

Cheddar Rice Patties

I like to keep cooked rice on hand in the refrigerator. Sure makes it easy to put together a quick dish like this favorite of ours.

2	cups fresh bread crumbs (reserve 1 cup)
2	cups cooked rice
1	cup grated Cheddar cheese
1/2	cup grated Parmesan cheese
1/4	cup finely chopped green onion tops
1/4	cup finely chopped green pepper
1/4	cup finely chopped celery
1/4	cup grated carrot
2	eggs
	Pinch of favorite herb (try sweet basil)
	Salt and freshly ground pepper to taste
4	tbsp. butter

Combine one cup bread crumbs with everything but butter. Form into patties, coating with reserved bread crumbs as you go. Mixture may be crumbly, but it will hold together when it cooks if you turn it carefully.

Sauté in butter until golden brown, about ten minutes per side over medium heat. Serve immediately.

Makes 8 patties; serves 4.

Cheese-Stuffed Pasta Shells

Pasta shells are as pretty to serve as they are delicious to eat. This recipe is easily made ahead. It smells divine as it bakes.

1	box (12-oz.) large pasta shells (about 36 shells)
1-1/2	lbs. ricotta cheese
1	cup grated Parmesan cheese (1/2 cup plus 1/2 cup)
1	tsp. salt
1	tsp. garlic powder
1/2	lb. Mozzarella cheese, diced
2	eggs, lightly beaten
1	pkg. frozen chopped spinach, cooked and drained
1	can (4-oz.) sliced mushrooms, drained (optional)
3	cups tomato sauce (1-1/2 cups plus 1-1/2 cups)

Cook pasta shells according to package directions to the *al dente* stage — still fairly chewy. Rinse, drain and put them on paper towels to dry.

Mix together remaining ingredients, except tomato sauce and half the Parmesan cheese. Stuff shells with this cheese mixture.

Cover bottom of a large shallow baking dish with half the tomato sauce, then set shells in it in a single layer. Spoon the rest of tomato sauce over top and bake covered at 350° for 30 minutes. Sprinkle with remaining Parmesan cheese and let dish sit for a few minutes until cheese melts.

Serves 6-8.

BACON IN THE MICROWAVE

If you're lucky enough to have a microwave, by all means experiment with the various microwave bacon pans available. They're sensational if you cook a lot of bacon — quick and foolproof.

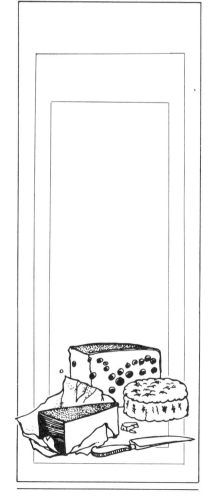

Fettuccine Alfredo

NOTE

You can buy wonderful fresh pasta noodles frozen in the grocery store. The ones I find are in 12-oz. packages.

If you wish to serve three or four people, use 12 ounces of noodles and this same sauce recipe; it'll work. If you serve four, consider it a side dish rather than an entrée.

This is so wonderful and rich, you won't believe how easy it is. Holds well in the oven.

    1   pkg. (8-oz.) egg noodles, cooked *al dente* and drained
    1/2 cup unsalted butter
    1/2 cup heavy cream
    1/2 cup Parmesan cheese, grated (6 tbsp. plus 2 tbsp.)

While the noodles are cooking, put butter and cream in a wide, shallow serving dish and warm in a 200° oven.

When butter has melted, stir in six tablespoons Parmesan cheese. Toss hot noodles in cream sauce and sprinkle with remaining Parmesan cheese.

Serves 2. Doubles or triples easily.

Gruyère Quiche with Crispy Crust

NOTE

Brushing unbaked pie crust with beaten egg and pre-baking it assures a crisp crust. Makes all the difference in the world, so take the extra minute to do it.

The crust stays crisp and the cheese oozes from the filling when you serve this outstanding quiche.

    1   10" pastry pie shell (see Page 192.)
    6   oz. Gruyère cheese, cubed
    3-to-4 green onions, chopped (green part only)
    1/2   cup chopped mushrooms
    6   eggs, lightly beaten
    1-1/2 cups half-and-half
           Salt to taste

Paint inside of pie shell liberally with beaten egg. Bake at 450° about 7-10 minutes, just until it is beginning to brown. Set aside to cool. It will remain crisp without getting soggy from the filling.

Place cubed cheese, green onions and mushrooms in bottom of pie shell. Beat eggs with the half-and-half and pour this carefully over cheese and vegetables. Salt to taste.

Bake at 375° for 30 minutes, or until filling no longer jiggles in the center.

Let rest ten minutes before cutting. Serve at room temperature.

Serves 6.

Italian Macaroni & Cheese

Without question, the best I've ever tasted!

1	lb. macaroni, parboiled, rinsed and drained
6	tbsp. butter (2 tbsp. plus 4 tbsp.)
2	tbsp. flour
2-1/2	cups milk
	Salt to taste
	Freshly grated nutmeg to taste
1/4	cup heavy cream, optional
1/2	cup grated Parmesan cheese
8	oz. whole-milk Mozzarella cheese, sliced into 1/2" thick slices (more or less)
1	cup fresh bread crumbs

Parboil macaroni, boiling it until you can bend it, but it's still too hard inside to eat. Rinse briefly in cold water; drain.

Make a thin sauce by melting two tablespoons butter and stirring in flour; cook two minutes and remove from heat. Whisk in milk; return to heat until it boils. Add salt, nutmeg and cream (if desired). I recommend adding the cream.

Put macaroni in a large mixing bowl. Sprinkle Parmesan over macaroni; add white sauce. Gently stir until well mixed.

Butter a large casserole (at least three-quart) and put half the macaroni mixture into dish. Cover macaroni with thick slices of Mozzarella cheese, then cover cheese with the rest of the macaroni.

Put enough day-old bread or dinner rolls (even hamburger buns will work) into your blender to make at least one cup of crumbs. Combine crumbs with four tablespoons melted butter and sauté until they begin to brown. Sprinkle over macaroni and cheese.

Bake at 350° for 40 minutes covered, then uncover and bake about ten minutes more — long enough to brown the bread crumbs.

This is very rich and very filling. I would serve it as an entrée with a steamed green vegetable and tossed salad.

Serves 6-8.

Whole-milk Mozzarella cheese is excellent in recipes which call for slices or cubes of cheese which melt during cooking. It has a higher fat content which means it melts better (not as stringy) — and which guarantees more calories per ounce. Believe me, if calories don't count, it's worth it.

If you have room in your freezer, it's a good idea to keep a bag of bread pieces there to accumulate the tag ends from loaves. The more different kinds of bread, buns and dinner rolls, the better. Thaw them and make bread crumbs.

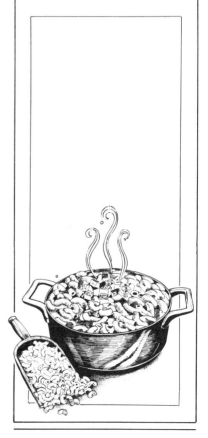

Kugel
(Calorie Conscious)

For those who count calories, it's easy to make this reduced calorie version of kugel. You may want to bake it in individual casserole dishes.

4	oz. noodles, cooked *al dente*, rinsed and drained
4	eggs, lightly beaten
2	cups skim milk
1	can (4-oz.) sliced mushrooms, drained
2	oz. Gruyère cheese, grated (or 4-oz. reduced calorie Gruyère cheese)
1	pkg. (10-oz.) frozen chopped spinach, cooked and drained
	Salt and freshly ground pepper to taste

Cook and drain noodles. Combine eggs, milk, mushrooms, cheese and spinach; season to taste with salt and pepper. Stir in noodles and pour into baking dish sprayed with low-calorie oil, such as Pam.

Use 10" pie plate, 8" x 12" baking dish, or four individual casseroles. Bake 30-40 minutes, covered, at 350°. Test for doneness by inserting knife in middle; blade should come out clean.

Serves 4.

Linguine with Bacon and Cheese

In our family we prefer our pasta without tomato sauce. This recipe is a good example of the variety of non-tomato things you can do with pasta. Try it, your family may enjoy it as much as mine does.

6-to-8	slices bacon
4	green onions (green portion only), chopped
1	pkg. (8-oz.) linguine
1	cup grated sharp Cheddar cheese
1/3	cup grated Parmesan cheese

Slice bacon into small pieces and fry. Drain and reserve fat. Chop onion tops and grate cheese.

Cook linguine to *al dente* stage — with some texture left. Dip out 1/2 cup cooking water and reserve. Drain linguine in colander and return it to cooking pot. Add about four tablespoons bacon fat and the 1/2 cup cooking water; toss thoroughly. (The water keeps the linguine a good consistency so that it neither sticks together nor is runny. Sounds strange, but try it.)

Add bacon and green onion, toss thoroughly and serve on warm plates. Sprinkle cheese on top.

Serves 4-6.

Mock Quiches
or Little Egg Pies

This recipe eliminates the pie crust calories and can be baked in a standard pie plate or individual custard cups.

1	cup grated Cheddar cheese
1	cup chopped meat or vegetables
4	eggs
1/2	cup milk
	Salt and freshly ground pepper to taste

Press the grated cheese into the bottom of buttered custard cups or pie plate. Put chopped meat or vegetable filling over cheese. Whip eggs, milk, salt and pepper together with a fork and pour over filling.

Bake at 350° until puffed and browned.

Serves 3-4 as entrée, 8 as appetizer or side dish.

Rich Creamed Eggs

Lovely luncheon or buffet dish; very delicate sauce. I still remember the first time I ate these, at a church dinner over 20 years ago. Father John Worrell made them, and he recently wrote me it's still a favorite dish.

6	eggs, hard-cooked and peeled
1	can cream of mushroom soup
1/3	cup mayonnaise
	Parsley, chopped

Hard cook the eggs and peel. While they are still hot, slice them in half lengthwise and place them in a pretty dish.

Mix soup and mayonnaise together and heat carefully; *do not boil.* Spoon sauce over eggs, sprinkle with parsley and serve.

Good over rice or on toast.

Serves 3 - 6.

Have you ever forgotten which eggs are hard-cooked? Simply spin one on the counter. If it's hard-cooked, it will spin evenly. If it's uncooked, it will wobble.

VARIATIONS

1. Cheddar cheese with canned chili peppers or crumbled bacon.

2. Swiss cheese with mushrooms or chopped ham.

3. Mozzarella cheese with sautéed onion and green pepper or olives.

Ricotta Spinach Bake _(Calorie Conscious)_

This is like a low-calorie lasagne — without noodles. It's very good, even without the noodles, and delicious for dieters.

2	pkgs. (10-oz.) frozen chopped spinach
	Garlic salt to taste
	Pinch of Italian herb blend
1	can (4-oz.) chopped mushrooms, drained
1	lb. ricotta cheese
4	oz. Mozzarella cheese, grated
1	can (8-oz.) tomato sauce with mushrooms

Cook spinach according to package directions; drain. Spread in the bottom of an 8" x 12" baking dish. Sprinkle liberally with garlic salt and the pinch of Italian herbs. Layer the mushrooms next.

Combine the ricotta and Mozzarella and spread it over the mushroom layer. Top with tomato sauce.

Bake at 350° for 30 minutes, or until it's heated through. Serves 4.

NOTE:

Sometimes I experiment with vegetables, using yellow crookneck squash or zucchini. You might also try Italian-cut green beans or chopped broccoli.

You may reduce the amount of ricotta or Mozzarella cheese to meet your diet requirements.

Roll-up Lasagne _(Calorie Conscious)_

This is one of the prettiest dishes you'll ever serve. Also one of the lowest in calories — without anyone noticing. Make it on a day when you'll enjoy working with your hands in the kitchen.

6	lasagne noodles, cooked _al dente_ and drained
1-1/3	cups ricotta cheese
1/2	cup grated Mozzarella cheese
1	cup grated Parmesan cheese (1/2 cup plus 1/2 cup)
1	pkg. (10-oz.) frozen chopped spinach, cooked and drained
	Garlic salt to taste
	Salt to taste
1	can (4-oz.) chopped mushrooms, drained
1	can (8-oz.) tomato sauce

Cut each lasagne noodle crosswise into two short pieces.

In a medium-size mixing bowl, combine ricotta, Mozzarella, and 1/2 cup Parmesan cheese. Drain the cooked spinach thoroughly in colander, pressing out the excess liquid with the back of your spoon.

Put the spinach in a small bowl and add garlic salt and salt to taste.

Assemble each piece of lasagne by putting half a noodle on flat surface. Press some of the ricotta cheese mixture over the noodle; the cheese will be about 1/4" thick. Top with some of the spinach and a few of the mushrooms. Frankly, I don't bother to measure the spinach or mushrooms other than estimating that 1/4 each covers three noodle pieces.

Roll each lasagne noodle jellyroll style. Pour half your can of tomato sauce in the bottom of an 8" x 12" casserole, and place the lasagne rolls in the dish with the noodle edge tucked under. Top with remaining tomato sauce and the rest of the Parmesan cheese.

Bake uncovered at 350° for 20-25 minutes, until cheese is beginning to brown and sauce is bubbling around the edge. This can be made ahead and stored overnight in the refrigerator. If so, increase baking time 10-15 minutes since ingredients will be chilled.

Serves 4.

Strata

Delicious, filling, and much easier than a quiche. Great for overnight guests and holiday brunches.

8	slices bread	1/2	tsp. dry mustard
4	slices American or Old English cheese		Dash of red pepper sauce (such as Tabasco)
4	eggs		Salt and pepper to taste
2	cups milk		

Make four sandwiches with the bread and cheese and fit into a shallow casserole. The size dish depends on size and shape of bread. I usually use an 8" x 12" dish.

Beat eggs with milk and seasonings; pour over sandwiches. Refrigerate overnight.

Bake at 325° for an hour or until nicely puffed and browned. Eggs should be set and cheese melted.

Serves 4.

VARIATION

1. Add thin slices of ham.
2. Use rye or pumpernickel bread with Swiss cheese.

Straw and Hay

This is a favorite with children as well as adults, perhaps because it is such a pretty dish. It's also very rich and full of flavor. A good company dish.

1	pkg. (8-oz.) thin white noodles
1	pkg. (8-oz.) thin green noodles
1/2	cup butter
1/4	lb. ham, cubed
1	pkg. (10-oz.) frozen peas, thawed
1	cup half-and-half
1	egg yolk, lightly beaten
1	cup grated Parmesan cheese (3/4 cup plus 1/4 cup)

Cook the noodles according to the package directions to the *al dente* stage — with some texture left. Drain and put in a well-buttered three-quart casserole.

Melt the butter in a skillet and sauté the ham. Stir in the peas. Whip egg yolk into half-and-half with fork. Reduce heat and stir in the half-and-half. Add 3/4 cup Parmesan cheese and blend well. Pour over noodles and sprinkle with remaining 1/4 cup Parmesan cheese. Bake at 400° for about 10 minutes, just until it's lightly browned and bubbly.

Serves 6-8.

Vegetable Pasta Pie

NOTE
1. Always use a strong-flavored cheese in casseroles or you'll lose the flavor, especially with a strong-flavored vegetable such as broccoli.

2. Vary vegetable if you like. Well-drained squash, mushrooms or asparagus would each be good.

3. Add crumbled bacon, chopped ham, tuna or chicken.

This recipe is a creative change from usual casseroles. Pretty to serve, keeps well. Very popular at our house.

3	cups cooked linguine (about 6-oz.)
1/2	cup chopped onion
2	ribs celery, chopped
1	pkg. (10-oz.) frozen chopped broccoli
2	eggs
1/2	cup milk
6	oz. cheese grated (Parmesan or sharp Cheddar)
	Salt and freshly ground pepper to taste
	Pinch of garlic salt

Cook linguine to *al dente* stage, and drain.

Add onion and celery to broccoli and cook according to package directions. Drain well.

Beat eggs with milk and cheese; season with salt, pepper and garlic salt. Combine with broccoli and linguine; pour all into a 9" or 10" buttered pie plate.

Bake uncovered at 375° for about 40 minutes, or until knife blade in center comes out clean. Let stand for about ten minutes and it will cut nicely.

Serves 4-6.

Nano's Liver

NOTE
Liver is best when served slightly pink in middle. Overcooking is what turns it into shoe leather.

This is my favorite liver recipe. I learned it by watching my grandmother, Maude Grandstaff, make it.

1	lb. sliced calf liver
2-to-3	eggs, lightly beaten
1	medium-large sack (12-oz.) of potato chips, crushed
	Bacon fat to cover skillet about 1/4" deep

Dip the pieces of liver into beaten eggs; roll in crushed potato chips.

Fry in bacon drippings, turning once, and being careful not to overcook. If you are using an electric skillet, set it at about 350°.

Serves 4.

Garden Spaghetti

We had driven in from out of town, tired and hungry. Thirty minutes later we sat down to eat this lovely, colorful dish — created, frankly, from leftover bits of this and that. It tasted planned!

1	pkg. (12-oz.) spinach spaghetti, cooked *al dente*	2	chopped small yellow squash
1	chopped medium onion	6	tbsp. butter (2 tbsp. plus 4 tbsp.)
2	chopped medium carrots	1/2	cup heavy cream
		1/2	cup grated Parmesan cheese

While spaghetti cooks, sauté onion, carrots and squash in two tablespoons butter. Like the spaghetti, they should be *al dente* — with texture.

Drain spaghetti and toss with four tablespoons butter; add cream and Parmesan cheese and continue tossing until cheese melts.

Put spaghetti on plates, then top with vegetables. The green spaghetti and the yellow and orange vegetables make a beautiful presentation. And delicious!

Serves 4.

NOTE

You'll want three to four cups chopped vegetables. Vary them as you like — zucchini, mushrooms, asparagus, cauliflower, green beans. Use what's on hand.

Mexican Bean Casserole

This is an unusual casserole with a Southwestern flair. Keeps and reheats well.

3	cans (15-oz.) kidney beans, drained and rinsed
1	cup chopped celery
1/2	cup chopped green pepper
1/2	cup chopped onion
1	cup chopped tomato (2 small)
1	can (4-oz.) green chilies, chopped (1/2 cup)
2	cups grated Cheddar cheese
2	tsp. chili powder
1	tsp. salt
1	cup mayonnaise
1	cup crushed tostada chips

Combine everything except crushed tostada chips; mix carefully, but thoroughly. Place in 8" x 12" baking dish and top with crushed tostadas.

Bake 40 minutes at 350°, uncovered. Allow additional baking time if you have held it overnight in the refrigerator before cooking.

Serves 6-8.

NOTE

Vegetables should be cooked, but with some texture. Use firm tomatoes; they really make the difference in this recipe.

Corned Beef Casserole

This is one of those dump-and-bake casseroles that are so good for quick family dinners.

1   can (12-oz.) corned beef
1/2 onion, finely chopped
1/2 green pepper, finely chopped
1   cup grated Cheddar cheese
1   can cream of mushroom soup
1   small can (5.33-oz.) evaporated milk
1   pkg. (8-oz.) noodles
1   cup crushed potato chips

Crumble corned beef into a three-quart casserole. Add the onion, green pepper, cheese, soup and milk. Stir together.

Cook noodles and drain. Add noodles to corned beef mixture; stir together and top with potato chips.

Bake at 350° about 20 minutes, or until it's bubbly around the edges.

Serves 4. Easily doubled or tripled.

VARIATION

1. Substitute two (6-oz.) cans chicken, turkey or tuna for corned beef. Drain well.

2. Use another creamed soup (celery, chicken, onion).

3. Stretch it by adding one (10-oz.) package frozen vegetables (chopped spinach, broccoli, mixed vegetables) cooked and well drained.

4. Use other crunchies on top, such as crushed salad croutons or a mixture of bread crumbs and grated Parmesan cheese (1/2 cup each).

Favorite Pot Pie

I love dishes I can serve a dozen times in different ways, using what I have on hand. This is one of the best.

2   cups chopped cooked chicken (ham, beef, lamb, fish)
2   medium potatoes, peeled and chopped
1   medium onion, chopped
1   pkg. (10-oz.) frozen vegetables (mixed vegetables, chopped broccoli, chopped spinach)
1   can cream of mushroom soup (cream of celery, chicken), undiluted
1   can (16-oz.) tomatoes, well drained and chopped (optional)
1   cup grated cheese (optional)
1   pie crust

Chop chicken. Put potatoes, onion and frozen vegetables in medium saucepan, add water to cover, and simmer until potatoes are barely done, about 7-10 minutes.

Drain vegetables and combine with chicken. Stir in can of soup (don't add extra milk), and put in bottom of a three-quart casserole dish. Cover with the chopped tomatoes, then grated cheese.

VARIATIONS

1. Use two well-drained cans of chicken, turkey or tuna.

2. Add 1/4 cup of any of the following: chopped green pepper, celery, chilies, olives, pimiento, toasted almond slivers.

Top with your favorite pie crust recipe, or use a frozen crust which you've re-rolled. You could also use crescent roll dough, canned biscuits, homemade biscuits, cornbread batter or puff pastry shells which you've re-rolled. Make it easy on yourself; they are all delicious.

Bake at 425° for 30 minutes, or until crust is golden, and it's bubbling around the edges.

Serves 4-6.

Fried Rice with Chicken

Fried rice is one of the quickest, easiest dishes to put together. Feel free to vary the ingredients according to your family's tastes and what's on hand. A delicious, one-dish meal in a snap.

2	tbsp. butter
2	tbsp. oil
1	rib celery, chopped
1/2	medium onion, chopped
1/2	medium green pepper, chopped
1	cup chopped chicken, cooked or uncooked (beef, pork, fish)
3-to-4	cups cooked rice
	Salt and freshly ground pepper to taste
	Assorted garnishes — see below

Heat butter and oil in large skillet and sauté vegetables over fairly high heat until onion begins to turn translucent. Add chicken and stir until cooked or completely warmed. Add rice and stir until mixture is very hot. Salt and pepper to taste.

Serve with toasted almond slivers, sliced avocado, grated cheese, alfalfa sprouts or anything else you feel that your family will enjoy.

Serves 4.

When you want to sauté something in butter over high heat, it's a good idea to use half oil. It keeps the butter from burning. Another way to prevent the butter from burning is to clarify it.

When you melt butter, it separates into a clear, yellow oil and milk solids. One reason for clarifying butter is that it won't burn as quickly if it doesn't have the milk solids in it.

The easiest way to clarify your butter is to melt it and set the liquid in the refrigerator long enough to solidify. You can simply lift off the clarified part and discard the rest.

Frozen Rice and Vegetable Casserole

NOTE

Keeping several packages of the frozen rice and vegetable combinations in the freezer and some cans of various meats in the pantry can lead to many combinations that are delicious. The extras, like chopped pimiento, sliced black olives and grated cheeses, greatly expand the possibilities and add a touch of class to a meal. The cheeses are available already grated in cans — Parmesan, Romano and American.

This is not a recipe so much as a guideline for quick meals you can almost throw together.

2 pkgs. frozen rice and vegetable combinations
 (French, Spanish, Oriental, etc.)
1 small can (5-6-oz.) ham, chicken or tuna
1 small can (4-oz.) sliced ripe olives
1 small jar (2-oz.) chopped pimiento
 Grated cheese (optional)
 Toasted slivered almonds (optional)

Cook two packages of rice and vegetables according to directions on package. Add meat, olives and pimiento, and heat through. Top individual servings with cheese and almonds . . . or not, if you don't have them. Either way is good.

Serves 4.

Ground Beef & Potato Bake

NOTE

Casseroles like this keep well in the refrigerator before and after baking. They always taste better the next day, after the flavors have had a chance to blend.

VARIATIONS

1. Add a package of cooked, drained frozen vegetables such as chopped broccoli, spinach, asparagus or mixed vegetables.

2. Substitute 2-to-3 cups of chicken, ham, roast beef, turkey or fish (cod, turbot) for the ground beef.

3. Instead of mushroom soup, try Cheddar cheese soup, cream of celery, cream of onion, or cream of chicken.

This one goes together quickly and smells wonderful while it's baking. My kids, who are not fond of casseroles, think it's great.

1 lb. ground beef, cooked and drained
1 medium onion, sliced
3 medium potatoes, scrubbed and sliced 1/2" thick
1 can cream of mushroom soup
1/2 soup can milk
 Salt and freshly ground pepper to taste

Spread ground beef over bottom of a three-quart casserole dish. Season with salt and pepper; cover with onion slices. Add a layer of potato slices; salt and pepper.

Combine soup and milk and pour over potatoes.

Bake uncovered at 350° for 50-60 minutes, until potatoes are tender.

Serves 4.

Hamburger Pie

Predictably, children love this hamburger pie. So do adults, with good reason. A delicious change from the usual casserole. Try both versions.

2	lbs. ground beef, cooked and drained
1/2	large onion, chopped
1/4	tsp. dill weed, plus a pinch for garnish
	Salt and freshly ground pepper
1	10" pastry pie crust, pre-baked (optional)
1	carton (1-lb.) creamed cottage cheese
3	eggs
	Sour cream for garnish
1	pkg. (10-oz.) frozen mixed vegetables, cooked and drained (optional)

FIRST VERSION — WITH PIE CRUST

Brown and drain meat and onion. Season with dill weed, salt and pepper to taste. Put meat in bottom of pre-baked pie shell. (Bake pie shell at 450° for 7-10 minutes — long enough to cook but not brown.)

Combine cottage cheese, eggs, pinch of dill; mix with blender or electric mixer until fluffy. Pour over meat mixture.

Bake uncovered at 375° for 30 minutes. Cheese topping should be puffed and golden brown, and firm to the touch. Serve with a dollop of sour cream and a dusting of dill.

Serves 6.

SECOND VERSION — WITHOUT PIE CRUST

Brown and drain meat and onion. Season with dill weed, salt and pepper. Put meat in bottom of 8" x 12" baking dish. Stir in mixed vegetables.

Combine cottage cheese, eggs and a pinch of dill. Mix in blender or electric mixer until light and fluffy; pour over meat.

Bake uncovered at 375° for 30 minutes. Cheese topping should be puffed and golden brown, and firm to the touch. Serve with dollop of sour cream and dusting of dill weed.

Serves 6.

NOTE

If you don't care for dill, use parsley or sweet basil.

If you use a lot of ground beef, you may find this will save you time. Brown the meat and drain it thoroughly — in the pan and on paper towels. Scatter the cooked ground beef loosely on a cookie sheet and freeze it. You can store the frozen pieces in a freezer container and spoon out as needed.

I frequently use a combination of chopped fresh onion, green pepper and celery in dishes. I've found it's a real time-saver to chop these in quantity and freeze small portions in plastic sandwich bags.

I don't have a magic remedy to keep you from crying while slicing onions but it will help if you hold the onion under cold running water while you cut and peel it, and if you will set it cut side down on your chopping block while you slice it.

Once sliced, keep onions covered with plastic wrap until you actually use them.

Tater Tot Casserole

VARIATIONS

1. Instead of ground beef, use one chicken, stewed and boned; or one pound frozen fish, barely cooked and flaked.

2. Instead of mushroom soup, use almost any creamed soup — cream of celery, onion, chicken, cheese. With fish use cream of shrimp.

3. Instead of onion, pepper and celery (or in addition to those vegetables) use mushrooms, chilies, or frozen vegetables such as mixed vegetables, chopped broccoli or spinach.

4. Instead of Cheddar cheese, use Swiss, Monterey Jack, Mozzarella or Parmesan — or a combination of what you have on hand.

Use this as a guideline — it's hard to go wrong. You are limited only by your imagination, and the ingredients on hand!

1	lb. ground beef
1/2	large onion, chopped
1	medium green pepper, chopped
1	large rib celery, chopped
1	can cream of mushroom soup
2	cups grated Cheddar cheese (about 8-oz.)
1	box (1-lb.) frozen potato nuggets (such as Tater Tots)

Brown the meat with onion, pepper and celery; drain. Stir in mushroom soup and pour into a three-quart casserole. Cover with grated cheese and top with potato nuggets.

Bake, uncovered, at 400° for 40 minutes.

Serves 4-6.

Anne's Pork Chops

One of my favorite recipes for years has been my sister-in-law Carol's broccoli. I've put it on the air, served it at home and taken it out, proudly telling everyone it was Carol's.

Last time my other sister-in-law Anne came to visit, she said it was her broccoli recipe — she'd given it to Carol years ago. So she gave me another good one, and this time I want to be sure Anne gets the credit she deserves. These pork chops are very, very good and twice that easy.

4	pork chops, about 1/2" thick
	Salt and freshly ground pepper to taste
1	medium onion, sliced
1	can cream of chicken soup
3	tbsp. catsup
3	tsp. Worcestershire sauce

Brown pork chops briefly on each side and season with salt and pepper. Place in 8" x 12" casserole dish, and top with onion slices.

Combine soup, catsup and Worcestershire sauce; pour over pork chops. Bake uncovered at 350° for 30 minutes, or until pork chops are done.

Serves 4, but easily doubled or tripled to feed a crowd. Wonderful with rice or noodles for the gravy.

Busy Day Casserole

Next time you're at the grocery store, check out the packages of boxed, dehydrated potatoes. Some are shredded and dried for hash browns, some sliced for scalloped potatoes. You can find them with assorted sauces, ranging from a Cheddar cheese sauce to sour cream with chives.

I recommend keeping them on the shelf at home because they make such easy last-minute casseroles.

Prepare each basic potato mix according to package directions, and then add any of the following combinations of ingredients.

1)
1 can (6-oz.) chicken, well drained
1/3 cup chopped green olives with pimientos (or ripe olives)

2)
1 cup chopped ham
1/3 cup chopped toasted almonds
1/2 cup cubed Swiss or Monterey Jack cheese (optional)

3)
1 pkg. (10-oz.) frozen mixed vegetables, cooked and drained

4)
2 eggs, hard-cooked and chopped
1/3 cup chopped dill pickles

Carlie's Spareribs

Years ago when I was in college, I had a friend who lived in her own apartment while I lived in a dorm. That meant she had her own kitchen, and I can still remember her serving her grandmother's spareribs with sauerkraut and apples. They were wonderful! I hadn't found a recipe for them until my friend Carlie Rodgers gave me this one. It's been in her family for years, and the ribs are as good as I remember my college friend's being those long years ago.

2-1/2 lbs. spareribs, cut into serving-size pieces
1/4 cup oil
1 quart sauerkraut (such as Vlasic)
3 medium red apples, cored but not peeled
3 tbsp. brown sugar, packed
1 tbsp. caraway seeds

In large, heavy skillet (or roasting pan) brown spareribs in oil over medium-high heat. Remove ribs from pan and turn down heat.

Add sauerkraut, apples cut into eighths, brown sugar and caraway seeds. Put ribs on top, cover, and let simmer on top of the stove for 45-60 minutes, until ribs are fork-tender and thoroughly cooked. If you prefer, bake covered in oven at 350° for 45-60 minutes.

Carlie recommends serving the ribs with mashed potatoes, but we love them just like they are.

Serves 4-6.

Cold Sausage Pie

If you will line your favorite casserole dish with heavy-duty aluminum foil before you fill it, you can easily freeze the contents and then lift them out. Fold the foil around them securely and label. Takes up less room in the freezer, and lets you use dish in the meantime.

Outstanding for picnics or weekend munching.

PASTRY

2	cups flour	4	tbsp. milk
1	tsp. seasoning salt	1	egg, lightly beaten
2/3	cup butter		

Cut butter into flour and seasoning salt, add milk and egg all at once, stir until dough forms. Roll for double crust pie.

FILLING

1	lb. hot pork sausage, browned and drained	1	medium green pepper, chopped
2	tbsp. sausage drippings	1	clove garlic, minced
1	large onion, chopped	1	large potato, scrubbed and grated

Brown and drain sausage leaving a little sausage fat in the skillet. Sauté onion, bell pepper, and minced clove of garlic in the sausage drippings.

Add grated potato to sausage and sautéed vegetables; pat into unbaked pie shell. Roll top crust and crimp into place. Cut steam vents in top.

Bake at 400° for about 30 minutes, until golden brown.

Chill several hours or overnight; serve cold or room temperature. Great for picnics.

Serves 6-8.

Ham Kugel

A kugel is a noodle custard. You combine eggs and milk with noodles — and go from there. It's a wonderful way to use up leftover vegetables or meats.

Kugels can be baked in traditional casseroles, round gelatin molds or pie plates. After baking, they are firm enough to hold their shape and slice.

1	pkg. (8-oz.) wide egg noodles, cooked *al dente*, rinsed and drained	1	can (4-oz.) sliced mushrooms, drained
		1	cup chopped ham
4	eggs	6-to-8	oz. cheese, grated
2	cups milk		Salt and freshly ground pepper to taste
1	tbsp. instant minced onion		

Cook and drain noodles. Combine eggs, milk and minced onion, add mushrooms, ham and cheese, stirring well. Add noodles, and mix thoroughly.

Pour into well-greased three-quart casserole or 8" x 12" pan. If you use a pie plate, be sure to use a large 10". If you use a gelatin mold, measure the capacity by pouring water in it first.

Bake at 300° for 30-40 minutes, covered. (If you leave it uncovered, some of the noodles get too dry.)

Test for doneness by inserting knife in center. The knife blade should come out clean. Baking time will vary depending on size and shape of dish.

Serves 4-6.

Ham Stroganoff

It's as good as you think it's going to be!

2	cups ham, diced	1	can cream of mushroom soup
1/2	cup onion, chopped	1	carton (8-oz.) sour cream
4	tbsp. butter (2 tbsp. plus 2 tbsp.)	1	pkg. (12-oz.) noodles, cooked *al dente* and drained
1	can (4-oz.) mushrooms, drained		Salt and pepper to taste
		2	tbsp. poppy seeds

Sauté the ham and onions in two tablespoons butter until onions are cooked. Add mushrooms and soup, stir until heated through. Add sour cream and heat thoroughly without letting it boil. (If it boils, it will separate.)

Cook and drain noodles. Toss immediately with remaining two tablespoons butter and poppy seeds. Serve ham over noodles.

Serves 4-6.

Oven-Barbecued Pork Chops

This is my friend Charlotte Wooldridge's favorite pork chop recipe.

PER PORTION

2	pork chops	1	tsp. brown sugar
	Salt and pepper to taste	2	thin slices lemon
2	tbsp. catsup		

Score pork chops and place on a baking sheet. Season and top each chop with the catsup, brown sugar and lemon slices, in that order.

Bake at 325° for 45-60 minutes, depending on how thick they are. There should be no pink left; check by cutting into thickest part of meat.

Party Ham Patties

All mothers have recipes they pull out when certain children come home for a visit, and you know those are the very best recipes in the world. This is my mom's recipe; for years and years she's made it especially for my brother Bruce. I love it for entertaining because it's different, can be made ahead, and is beautifully attractive on the table.

HAM PATTIES

1-1/2	lbs. ground ham	1	egg, slightly beaten
1	lb. ground fresh pork	8	slices canned pineapple
1/2	cup fresh bread crumbs	8	maraschino cherries (optional)
1/2	cup milk		

Combine first five ingredients and shape into eight patties about one inch thick. Top each patty with a pineapple ring and a cherry. Place on a rack in a roasting pan to allow the fat to drip away.

Bake at 350° for 45-50 minutes, basting occasionally with the sauce. Patties should be well browned and cooked in the middle.

SAUCE

1/2	cup brown sugar	1/4	cup vinegar
1/2	cup water		

Place in a small saucepan and boil for five minutes. Pour over patties before baking and occasionally as they bake.

Sausage Casserole

This is a wonderful brunch dish, especially for overnight guests. If you're serving children or those with tender palates, use mild sausage.

6	slices stale bread, cubed	1	cup grated sharp Cheddar cheese
1	lb. sausage, spicy hot	1	tbsp. dry mustard
1/2	medium onion, chopped	1	tsp. salt
8	eggs	1	can (4-oz.) chopped green chilies
2	cups milk		

Set bread out so it will be fairly dry and stale. Brown sausage with chopped onion; drain well.

Beat eggs with milk; stir in cheese. Add dry mustard, salt, bread. Stir in drained sausage and chilies. Pour into a well-buttered three-quart casserole or 8" x 12" baking dish. Refrigerate overnight, covered.

Bake uncovered at 350° for about one hour. It should puff and be lightly browned across the top, and firm when touched in the middle.

Serves 8-10.

Sausage Upside-Down Cornbread

1	lb. bulk sausage	1-1/2	cups grated Cheddar cheese
1	cup chopped onion	1	can (4-oz.) sliced ripe olives,
1/3	cup chopped green pepper		drained
2	tbsp. flour	2	pkgs. (8-1/2-oz.) cornbread
1	can (6-oz.) tomato paste		muffin mix, batter
1	can water (tomato paste can)		prepared according to
1	tsp. salt		package directions
1	tsp. chili powder		

Brown sausage, onion and pepper in skillet until sausage is well done. Drain as thoroughly as possible.

Stir in flour, tomato paste, water, salt and chili powder.

Pour into three-quart casserole and stir in Cheddar cheese and olives. Prepare cornbread batter and pour over sausage mixture.

Bake uncovered at 400° for 30-35 minutes, until cornbread topping is completely cooked and browned on top.

Let sit for five minutes before serving. If you have a platter large enough, invert and serve with sausage on top. It's pretty that way, but I usually just spoon it out of the dish.

Serves 6.

NOTE

The first time I made this unusual one-dish was for a family gathering of both adults and very young children. Age made no difference — there wasn't one bit left.

When recipes call for "stale" or "day-old" bread and all you have is fresh, leave several slices out to dry on a wire cake rack (so the air can circulate under them).

You might also set them on the rack in your oven for a few minutes. Turn the oven on and as soon as you feel any heat at all, turn it off. Leave the oven door shut.

The point of this is to get the moisture out of the bread.

Sautéed Ham and Zucchini

This is an easy, nutritious one-dish meal. Good for those evenings when you get home late and need to make a meal in a hurry.

1	cup chopped onion	2-to-3	cups cooked rice
1/4	cup butter	1/4	cup grated Parmesan cheese
2	cups chopped zucchini		
1	pkg. (8-oz.) boiled ham slices, chopped		
	Salt and freshly ground pepper to taste		

In large skillet over medium heat sauté onion in butter until translucent, about 5-7 minutes, stirring occasionally. Add zucchini and ham and continue cooking for another 3-5 minutes until zucchini is cooked and ham is hot. Season. Stir in rice and continue cooking until completely warmed through.

Serve hot sprinkled with Parmesan cheese. Cottage cheese and fruit salad complete the meal.

Serves 4.

NOTE

This recipe is easily adapted to calorie-conscious cooking. Cut butter back to four teaspoons; use two cups cooked rice.

Surprise Pie

This is a wonderful way to use up leftovers. Use it as a guide to your own variation.

CRUST

1	recipe pastry pie crust (see Page 192.)
3	tbsp. sesame seeds
1	tbsp. dry salad seasoning mix
2-to-3	tbsp. grated Parmesan cheese

Prepare pie dough according to recipe, adding sesame seeds, salad seasoning mix and Parmesan cheese to dry ingredients.

Roll out for double-crust pie.

FILLING

1-to-2	ribs celery, chopped		Mushrooms, sliced
1-to-2	carrots, chopped	1-to-2	cups leftover ham
1/2	medium onion, chopped		(chicken, roast beef,
1	medium potato, chopped		turkey)
1	medium squash (zucchini		Salt and pepper to taste
	or crookneck), sliced	1	recipe cheese sauce

Combine vegetables and meat with seasoning. Place in unbaked pie crust; top with remaining crust and flute edges. Be sure to cut steam vents in top crust.

Bake at 450° for ten minutes; reduce heat to 350° for 30 minutes. Cool five to ten minutes before slicing.

Serve slices with cheese sauce ladled over. (See Page 53.)

Serves 4-6.

Auntie Max's Fish

Auntie Max and Uncle Artie retired and live in the Ozarks beside a small lake. This is their favorite recipe for the crappie and bass Uncle Artie catches.

2	eggs, lightly beaten
4	tbsp. lime juice (or lemon juice)
1	lb. fish fillets
	Cracker crumbs
	Butter or oil

Combine eggs and lime juice. Dip the fillets in egg; roll in cracker crumbs. Fry in butter or oil. Serve with slices of lime.

Serves 4.

Baked Turbot Fillets

If you aren't familiar with turbot, do yourself a favor and get acquainted. It's a very mild and slightly buttery flavored fish that lends itself to a variety of recipes. This one is especially delicious.

    1   lb. (1" thick) turbot fillets, frozen
    1/2 cup orange juice
    1   pkg. dry ranch-style dressing mix
         Hickory Salt

Place frozen fish pieces in a shallow baking dish and spoon orange juice over them. It will freeze to the fillets. Sprinkle with dry ranch-style dressing and hickory salt to taste.

Bake uncovered at 450° for 20-25 minutes. Fish is done when it flakes with a fork (be careful not to overcook). This fish should be crisp on outside and moist inside.

Serves 3-4.

Great American Casserole

My son Warren named this casserole with what he thought was a clever name. For some reason it stuck — perhaps because so many people like it.

    1   large rib celery, diced
    4   medium carrots, diced
    1   large onion, diced
    2   large potatoes, scrubbed and diced (skins on)
    1-to-2 lbs. mild frozen fish fillets (turbot, cod)
    3   cups thick cheese sauce (or two cans Cheddar cheese soup
             thinned with a little milk)
    1   cup bread crumbs or crushed potato chips

Steam vegetables in a little water until barely done. Set aside.

Poach fish in about an inch of water until it just begins to flake. Drain on paper towels and cut into bite-size pieces.

See Page 53 for thick cheese sauce recipe, or use canned soup.

Combine vegetables, fish and sauce. Turn into a buttered casserole and top with bread crumbs or crushed potato chips. Bake at 350° for 30 minutes, or until it bubbles around the edges.

Serves 4-6.

COOKING WITH FISH

When I'm baking or poaching fish, whether it's fresh or frozen, I try to prepare more than we'll eat so that I can use it the second night in a casserole such as the one on this page.

Actually, you may substitute cooked, flaked fish with a very mild flavor (cod, turbot, snapper) in most casseroles calling for tuna or chicken. Leftover baked fish also makes delicious salad (patterned after tuna salad).

If you don't bake or poach fish often, it may be helpful to call a local fish market and talk to an expert about the different types of fish.

For instance, I recently learned that the thickness of the fish isn't the only criterion for how long you bake them — the texture of the fish has a lot to do with it.

To give you an example, these fish all bake at 350° —

Scrod	18-22 minutes
Snapper	12-15 minutes
Turbot	12-15 minutes
Sole, rolled	20-25 minutes

Note that you wouldn't bake sole without rolling it because the fillets are too thin; cooked flat, they're better broiled or sautéed.

Whether fresh or frozen and thawed, fish should never have an unpleasant aroma. If it does, pitch it out.

Frozen fish, when thawed, should not have evidence of freezer burn — dry, white spots. If it does, be sure to trim it off. I prefer to cook frozen fish while it is only partially thawed.

Fish is cooked when the flesh has turned a milky, opaque white. This is a better rule of thumb than checking to see if it flakes with a fork. Some fish is really overcooked by the time it flakes.

JFK Seafood Casserole

My friend Margaret Sinclair shared this elegant recipe with me. We can only presume it was, at one time, a JFK favorite.

1	lb. mixed crab meat and lobster, cooked
1	lb. shrimp, cooked
1/2	cup finely chopped green pepper
1/4	finely chopped onion
1-1/2	cups finely chopped celery
1	cup mayonnaise
	Pinch of salt
1	tbsp. Worcestershire sauce
2	cups crushed potato chips (about 3-oz.)

Pull crab and lobster into bite-sized pieces, put into large mixing bowl with shrimp.

Chop vegetables and add to seafood. Stir in mayonnaise, salt, Worcestershire sauce. Mix well, as though for salad.

Put into three-quart casserole and top with crushed potato chips. Bake at 400° for 20-25 minutes.

Serves 6-8.

NOTE

Vary the seafood according to taste and availability. You may use only crab and lobster, or perhaps all crab.

VARIATION

Refrigerate overnight and serve as a salad the next day. Omit potato chips.

Quick Baked Fish

A friend of mine got this recipe from a favorite restaurant. She's on a low-fat diet, so she uses low-calorie mayonnaise and says it is equally good.

1	lb. frozen fish fillets, thawed
3	tbsp. chopped fresh parsley
3	tbsp. mayonnaise, regular or diet

Rinse and dry fillets and place in shallow flat baking dish, approximately 8" x 12".

Mix parsley and mayonnaise and spread over fish.

Bake at 400° for about 20 minutes or until flakes easily with a fork.

Serves 3-4.

NOTE

If using dry parsley, mix 1-1/2 tablespoons together with mayonnaise and let stand for 5-10 minutes to soften.

NICE TO KNOW . . .

For a delicious sauce to serve with fish or beef, drain bottled horseradish and blend to taste into sour cream or whipped cream. For roast pork, blend into applesauce.

Salmon Mousse

Very light, perfect for luncheons. . . my mother-in-law Annie Johns' favorite.

1	large can (15-1/2 oz.) salmon
1	envelope (1 tbsp.) unflavored gelatin
1	cup sour cream with chives
1	cup mayonnaise
1	cup dill pickle relish
1/3	cup chopped onion
1/3	cup chopped celery
1	tbsp. Worcestershire sauce
	Salt and freshly ground pepper to taste

Drain salmon and pick out bones (unless you like them); reserve liquid in small saucepan. Sprinkle gelatin over liquid.

Combine all other ingredients, adding salt and freshly ground pepper to taste.

Heat salmon liquid with gelatin in small saucepan, stirring until gelatin completely dissolves. Add flaked salmon to gelatin mixture and stir to combine. Add to rest of ingredients.

Pour into well-oiled gelatin mold (use salad oil or mayonnaise) and chill several hours until set.

Unmold on lettuce leaves; garnish with parsley and fresh lemon slices.

Serves 6-8.

NOTE

If you're concerned about being able to unmold a dish like this, simply don't bother.

There's nothing wrong with letting it gel in an ordinary mixing bowl or cake pan. You can either cut it into squares or spoon it onto lettuce leaves.

If you want to dress it up, use a simple garnish — a sprig of fresh parsley, dollop of sour cream with an olive slice or sprinkling of green onion.

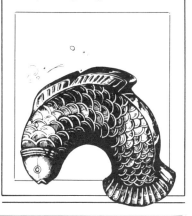

MENU BALANCING

It's important, when planning menus, to think in terms of the overall content and texture of each dish. The more variety, the more balance, the more appeal.

For instance, if I offer a casserole-type entrée with mixed ingredients (such as the seafood casserole or this mousse), I would likely want simple side dishes — sautéed cherry tomatoes or green beans. With the mousse, a simple asparagus salad might be good.

To complement a simple baked fish, I might serve an elaborate vegetable casserole such as my Squash or perhaps Stuffed Zucchini. (see Pages 87 and 88.)

With a soft-textured entrée like mousse, I'd want the contrast of crisp crackers or a chewy, full-bodied bread.

Plain entrées, such as the fish, may be followed by a rich dessert. When the entrée is smothered in rich sauce, I prefer fruit for dessert, perhaps with a thin slice of angel food cake.

Something cool as an entrée, such as the mousse, would be nice with a cup of hot soup. A hot entrée is presented well with a chilled soup, especially in warm weather.

Seafood Thermidor

NOTE
You may use 1/4 cup milk or half-and-half in place of wine.

This is an outstanding entrée. Certainly elaborate enough for guests and relatively inexpensive.

1	small onion, chopped	1/4	cup white wine
2-to-3	slices lemon	1/4	cup grated Mozzarella cheese
1	lb. frozen cod fillets, cubed (or any mild white fish)	1	tbsp. chopped parsley
		1	cup fresh bread crumbs
3	tbsp. flour	1/4	cup grated Parmesan cheese
1	can cream of shrimp soup	2	tbsp. butter, melted
1/4	cup milk		

Put chopped onion and lemon slices in a buttered skillet. Top with slightly thawed fillets cubed into 1/2″ pieces. Add just enough water to cover fish and simmer gently until it flakes easily — five minutes or so.

In medium saucepan blend flour into soup; add milk and wine. Heat until thick and bubbly, then stir in Mozzarella cheese and parsley. Carefully drain fish and fold it into this sauce.

Combine bread crumbs, Parmesan cheese and butter. Add half the crumbs to fish mixture and pour into a buttered two-quart casserole. Sprinkle with remaining crumbs.

Bake at 350° until it bubbles around the edges and is heated through, about 20-25 minutes. This can be made ahead and reheated just before serving, but increase heating time to 30-40 minutes.

Serves 4-6.

Sensational Shrimp Salad

NOTE
1. You may think this is not enough mayonnaise but it is.

2. Sammye's family prefers this salad topped with a little Catalina-style French salad dressing. I prefer it with lemon.

This is my friend Sammye Tucker's favorite salad. It's wonderful.

3	cups cooked rice, chilled or room temperature
1	cup cooked shrimp
1/4	cup *each:* chopped green pepper, celery, green onion, pimiento, and green or ripe olives
3	tbsp. mayonnaise
	Lemon slices
	Paprika
	Catalina-style French salad dressing (optional)

Mix rice, shrimp and chopped vegetables together with mayonnaise. Chill overnight to allow flavors to blend and serve on pretty lettuce leaves; garnish with lemon slices and paprika.

Serves 4-6.

Sherried Scallops & Sole

When you're in the mood to splurge, this recipe is ideal.

SEAFOOD

1-1/2 lbs. fresh scallops, uncooked
1-1/2 lbs. fresh sole, uncooked, bite-size pieces

SAUCE

1/2	cup butter	1/2	cup heavy cream
1/2	cup flour	1/2	cup dry sherry
1-1/2	tsp. chicken bouillon granules	2-to-3	cups crushed potato chips
3	cups milk		

In medium saucepan melt butter and stir in flour. Cook over medium heat for at least two minutes. Remove from heat and stir in chicken bouillon granules, milk, cream and sherry. Stir with a whisk to blend, and return to heat, stirring until bubbly and thick.

Place uncooked seafood in three-quart casserole. Pour sauce over seafood, mix carefully, and top with crushed potato chips.

Bake uncovered at 350° for 40 minutes and serve with rice.

Serves 10-12.

NOTE

My three-quart casserole is fairly shallow, and the sole and scallops were perfectly done. If your casserole is relatively deep, check middle of casserole to be sure seafood is done (does it flake easily with fork?) Don't add salt; the bouillon is salty enough.

Tuna Trash

When I created this casserole years ago, my family thought they were being funny when they named it. The name stuck, but I haven't minded because it's become such a family favorite.

4	medium potatoes, sliced
4	tbsp. butter
	Salt and freshly ground pepper to taste
2	medium onions, sliced
2	cans (7-oz.) tuna, drained (or chicken, turkey)
1	can cream of mushroom soup, undiluted
1/2	lb. easy-melting cheese (such as Velveeta)

Scrub and slice potatoes into pieces about 1/4" thick. You may peel the potatoes or not (sometimes I do and sometimes I don't).

Butter a three-quart casserole and divide all the ingredients in two. Make two layers in the following order — potatoes, dotted with butter and seasoned with salt and pepper; onions, tuna, mushroom soup and cheese. Finish with cheese on top.

Cover and bake at 350° for 40-45 minutes, or until potatoes are tender.

Serves 4-6.

COOKING FOR COLOR

When you serve entrées like either of the ones on this page, be sure that you plan colorful vegetables — bright tomatoes, carrots or beets and something green.

The reason is that most casserole-type dishes are pretty bland in color. If you put them on a plate with corn, baked onions, or yellow squash, everything would look drab and unappetizing.

Bright colors with casseroles add visual appeal which translates to appetite.

A scallop isn't always seafood.

Small pieces of other types of meat, trimmed of all fat and gristle and flattened with the heel of your hand, the edge of a plate, or a meat mallet are also called scallops. They are usually no more than 1/4" thick.

You'll frequently find recipes calling for chicken, turkey or veal scallops.

Whole Meal Salad

It's a whole meal in itself. That's how they named this salad entrée that dates back to my husband's youth in East Texas.

1	pkg. (12-oz.) large shell macaroni cooked *al dente* and drained
2	cups chopped cooked shrimp
1/2	cup chopped green onion tops
1/2	cup chopped celery
1/2	cup chopped pimiento-stuffed green olives
1/2	cup chopped dill pickle
1	cup mayonnaise
1/4	cup dill pickle juice
1/4	cup olive juice
	Dash of garlic salt
	Salt and freshly ground pepper to taste

Combine and cover; chill overnight. It's very important to give it several hours for the flavors to blend. Stir before serving, adding more mayonnaise if needed. Taste and correct seasonings. *Serves 6-8.*

Veal Scallops with Bourbon Sauce

This is an incredibly easy, but very impressive, recipe. Don't worry if you don't like bourbon. The sauce has a wonderful flavor but it really doesn't taste like bourbon.

8	veal scallops
	Salt and freshly ground pepper
1/2	cup flour (approximate)
1/4	cup butter
2	tbsp. bourbon whiskey (or Scotch or brandy), warmed
3/4	cup heavy cream

Season scallops lightly with salt and pepper; dust with flour. Be sure to shake off excess flour. In a large skillet melt butter and sauté scallops for two minutes on each side. They should be golden brown.

Remove scallops to warm platter and add warmed whiskey to skillet. Ignite it and shake the pan gently until flames go out. Stir in cream, scraping the pan, and heat until it thickens a bit. Serve as a sauce over the scallops.

Serve with rice so you don't lose any sauce; it's too good! Serves 4.

Desserts

Chocolate Mayonnaise Cake

One way to save yourself money, time and effort is to plan your holiday parties, dinners, or open houses back to back on consecutive days.

Now, I know when you first think about it, it sounds awful — you don't have time to recover!

But look at it this way. You only have to clean the house and polish the silver once. The decorations are in place, the candles are out and the centerpiece is on the table.

You can even let your menu do double service. It's usually easier, and sometimes cheaper,

to double recipes and serve them twice. Who's to know? Or to care?

Some dishes can be recycled, like this delicious pound cake. Present it whole and lovely the first evening. Slice it and serve with fudge sauce or crumbled with layers of rich pudding in pretty parfait glasses the next meal.

The really critical thing about food is to know what space will be required in your refrigerator and oven. After planning the menus, physically put the dishes where they will be stored to be sure that everything fits.

Please don't let the mayonnaise alarm you. This is my favorite chocolate cake. It's not only ridiculously easy; it is light, moist, and rich in flavor.

2	cups flour	1/2	tsp. salt
2	tsp. baking soda	1	cup mayonnaise
1/2	cup cocoa	1	cup strong coffee
1	cup sugar	1	tsp. vanilla extract

Combine dry ingredients in large mixing bowl, tossing lightly with a spoon to mix. Combine mayonnaise, coffee and vanilla in smaller bowl, then add to dry ingredients and beat on medium speed with electric mixer for three minutes.

I've baked this cake as a layer cake, sheet cake and Bundt cake — you can, too. Grease your cake pan or pans generously, dust with cocoa (instead of flour) and bake at 350°. Time will vary according to pan, so test carefully for doneness.

Layer cake, check after 20 minutes; sheet cake, check after 25 minutes; Bundt cake, check after 45 minutes.

Chocolate Pound Cake

My friend Helen Titus has a stack of recipes like mine. It took her ages to find her favorite recipe, and I'm grateful she kept looking. It's a wonderful cake.

3	cups flour	1	cup vegetable oil
3	cups sugar	1/2	cup butter, softened
1/2	cup cocoa	5	eggs
1/2	tsp. baking powder	1-1/4	cups milk
1/4	tsp. salt	1	tsp. vanilla extract

Sift flour, sugar, cocoa, baking powder and salt together. Set aside.
Combine oil and butter; add eggs, one at a time, beating constantly. Gradually add milk and vanilla.

Slowly mix dry ingredients into egg mixture. Pour batter into a well-greased Bundt or tube pan, and bake at 325° for one hour and 15 minutes or until cake tests barely done. Cool in pan for ten minutes and invert onto cake rack until cool.

Coconut Cream Cake

This cake is a cool, moist treat with an extra coconut taste. It's simple to prepare and oh, so good!

1	pkg. white cake mix		1	can (16-oz. or 8-1/2-oz.) cream of coconut
3	egg whites		1	carton (8-oz. or 12-oz.) whipped topping, thawed
2	tbsp. oil			
1-1/3	cups milk			
2	cans (3-1/2-oz.) coconut			

Combine cake mix, egg whites, oil, milk, and one can coconut. Bake in greased 9" x 13" pan (one layer) at 350° for 20-25 minutes, until center springs back when touched.

Make holes in warm cake with fork; pour cream of coconut over the cake. When cool, combine second can of coconut with whipped topping and frost cake, still in pan.

Chill several hours or overnight. Keeps well in the refrigerator.

NOTE

You don't have to be precise with this recipe, I've learned from experience.

1. Use either size can of Cream of Coconut; with the larger can cake will be more moist. Look for the cans next to tonic water and other drink mixes in grocery stores.

2. Use either size carton whipped topping. One gives more icing, but either is plenty.

3. One time I even forgot to put the can of coconut in the cake batter — and everyone still raved about how good it was!

Coconut Pecan Bundt Cake

I've made this for years for my coconut-loving family. It doesn't need icing.

1	box yellow cake mix
1	box instant vanilla pudding (four-serving size)
1/2	cup oil
4	eggs
1	cup milk
1	can (3-1/2-oz.) shredded coconut
1/2	cup chopped pecans

Combine cake and pudding mixes. Add oil, eggs and milk and beat at medium speed 2-3 minutes. Add coconut and pecans; beat until blended and pour batter into a well-greased Bundt pan.

Bake at 350° for 40-45 minutes. Do not overbake. Great with vanilla ice cream.

Cream Cheese Pound Cake

This is a vanilla-rich, flavorful pound cake that goes well with ice cream, fresh or frozen fruit, custard sauce — or nothing!

2	cups butter, softened	3	cups cake flour (or regular flour)
1	pkg. (8-oz.) cream cheese, softened	2	tbsp. vanilla extract (*tbsp.* is correct)
3	cups sugar		
6	eggs		

Whip butter and cream cheese together in large mixing bowl. Gradually add sugar and beat until thoroughly dissolved.

Add in eggs one at a time until well mixed. Blend in flour gradually, then vanilla.

Batter will be light in texture, but too thick to pour into pan. Grease and flour a Bundt pan, spoon in batter and bake at 325° for one hour, to one hour and 15 minutes. Check cake after an hour and remove when it is slightly underdone, as it continues cooking for a few minutes after being removed from oven.

Let cool in pan for ten minutes; invert over plate. Serve warm or cool.

Dark Chocolate Pecan Bundt Cake

So simple, but so good. Doesn't need icing.

1	box devil's food cake mix
1	box instant chocolate pudding (four-serving size)
1/2	cup oil
4	eggs
1	cup double-strength coffee
1/2	cup chopped pecans, toasted

Combine cake and pudding mixes. Add oil, eggs and coffee; beat at medium speed until thoroughly mixed. Add pecans and beat until well-blended.

Pour into a well-greased Bundt pan and bake at 350° for 40-45 minutes. Do not overbake.

Fresh Apple Cake

I first had this cake when a friend brought it to the office — about 20 years ago. It didn't last long then, and we still eat every crumb.

    2   cups brown sugar, packed (1-lb. box)
    1-1/4   cups oil
    2   eggs
    3   cups flour
    1-1/2   tsp. baking soda
            Pinch of salt
    1/2   tsp. *each* cinnamon and freshly grated nutmeg
    4   Winesap apples, peeled, cored and sliced
    1   cup chopped pecans
    1   tsp. vanilla extract

Blend sugar and oil until completely moistened; add eggs, one at a time. Whip with electric mixer until it's fairly light and fluffy. Gradually add flour as you beat, then add baking soda and spices. Use wooden spoon when batter becomes too stiff for mixer.

Stir apples, pecans and vanilla into the batter. Pour into a well-greased and floured Bundt pan. This is a heavy, moist cake, and requires long baking time. Bake at 300° for one hour and 15-20 minutes, or until firm when touched in center. Don't overbake.

Pecans and other nuts keep best in the refrigerator or freezer. Once opened, packages of nuts can get rancid if stored at room temperature, especially if kept in a cabinet that stays very warm.

Pecans are an ingredient that often can be adjusted to suit your own taste — and budget. One-half cup is ample for most dishes, and you can usually cut that back to 1/4 or 1/3 cup.

Grasshopper Cake

This is delicious, easy and so pretty to serve. You can also use another liqueur if you like — how about Amaretto or crème de cacao?

    1   box white cake mix
    6   tbsp. crème de menthe liqueur (4 tbsp. plus 2 tbsp.)
    1   jar (11-oz.) hot fudge sauce (the kind for ice cream
            sundaes)
    1   carton (8-oz.) frozen whipped topping, thawed

Prepare cake mix according to directions, adding four tablespoons crème de menthe. This adds a light mint flavor and a lovely color. Bake the cake in a 9" x 13" sheet cake pan as directed on the box and cool.

When cake is cool, spread top with fudge sauce (don't heat it). Fold remaining two tablespoons of the liqueur into whipped topping and frost over fudge sauce.

Refrigerate until ready to serve.

NOTE
If you prefer, use eight ounces heavy cream whipped with two tablespoons liqueur instead of whipped topping. It won't keep as long, but I prefer it.

Hawaiian Cake

My friend Vi Moslein left this recipe on my desk with a short note — "So good — so quick — and so moist!" She's so right!

1   pkg. yellow cake mix
3   eggs
1/3   cup oil
1   cup sour cream
1   can (8-oz.) crushed pineapple with juice (measures 1 cup)
3/4   cup coconut
3/4   cup brown sugar, packed

Combine cake mix with eggs, oil, sour cream and crushed pineapple. Be sure to use juice. Beat with electric mixer for a full three minutes.

Pour batter into well-greased 9" x 13" pan. Combine coconut with brown sugar and spread over unbaked batter.

Bake at 350° for 35 minutes, or until cake is firm in center.

Serves 8-12.

Pumpkin Cake

Ideal for holidays, but good year round. So easy!

3   cups sugar
1   cup shortening
3   eggs
1   can (1-lb.) pumpkin
3   cups flour
1   tsp. *each:* salt, baking soda, vanilla extract, cinnamon, nutmeg, and pumpkin pie spice

Cream sugar and shortening until light and fluffy. Add eggs one at a time, then the pumpkin. When this is well blended, add flour gradually, mixing well. Finally, add seasoning and spices.

Pour batter into a well-greased and floured tube pan or Bundt pan. Bake at 350° for about one hour, until firm in center.

NOTE

This is a rich, moist cake that we prefer without frosting. If you want to frost yours, try the cream cheese frosting on pg. 175 used with the Tomato Soup Cake.

Quick Macaroon Cake

Delightful chewy coconut topping. Keeps beautifully.

1-1/2	cups biscuit mix	1/2	cup milk
1/2	cup brown sugar, packed	1	tsp. vanilla extract
1	egg, lightly beaten	2/3	cup coconut
2	tbsp. oil	1/3	cup brown sugar, packed

Combine biscuit mix and first 1/2 cup brown sugar. In smaller bowl mix egg, oil, milk and vanilla. Stir into biscuit mix and pour into greased 8" x 8" baking pan.

Combine coconut and remaining 1/3 cup brown sugar; sprinkle over cake batter.

Bake at 350° for about 35 minutes, until cake bounces back when touched in the center.

Serves 6-8.

NOTE

Served warm, the topping has the delightful, chewy texture of macaroons. Covered, the cake keeps well, but the topping absorbs moisture and loses its chewiness. Good both ways.

Red Velvet Cake

What a beautiful cake — it's deep red with a white frosting that's different and not too sweet. It is delicious, and keeps well in the refrigerator.

CAKE

1/2	cup shortening	2	tsp. cocoa
1-1/2	cups sugar	2-1/4	cups flour
2	eggs, lightly beaten	1	cup buttermilk
1	oz. red food coloring	1	tsp. baking soda
1	tsp. vanilla extract	1	tbsp. vinegar

With your electric mixer, cream shortening and sugar until light and fluffy. Beat in eggs one at a time.

In a small bowl make a paste of red food coloring, vanilla and cocoa. Blend this paste into shortening mixture. Gradually mix in flour and buttermilk, alternating each. When flour is completely mixed in, combine baking soda and vinegar; add to batter.

Grease and flour two 9" cake pans. Fill 2/3 full and bake at 350° for 25-30 minutes, until center springs back.

FROSTING

1	cup milk	1	cup sugar
3	tbsp. flour	1	tsp. vanilla extract
1	cup butter, softened		

Stir milk and flour together over low heat until fairly thick. Cool *completely*. Cream butter with sugar until it is fluffy and sugar is completely dissolved; add flour mixture and stir in vanilla.

NOTE

I keep this cake in the refrigerator. Frosting seems better chilled.

Simple Sponge Cake

A simple, easy cake that is ideal with fruit or ice cream. Also wonderful with butter, hot out of the oven!

3	eggs	1	cup milk
2	cups sugar	1/4	cup butter
2	cups flour	1	tsp. vanilla extract
1	heaping tsp. baking powder		

Beat eggs with sugar until light and fluffy, add in flour and baking powder beating until well blended.

Warm milk with butter until butter melts, but don't let it boil.

Gradually beat milk and butter into batter; stir in vanilla extract. Pour into well-greased and floured tube or Bundt pan; bake at 325° for about 40 minutes. Watch carefully to avoid overbaking. Remove from oven when firm to the touch in the center.

Sour Cream Poppy Seed Cake

One of the most delicious cakes I've ever tasted. I shared this recipe with my friend Diana Craft and every time her family gathers for a special-occasion dinner, someone asks her to bring it. Her two-year-old son Roger has been known to bring her a cake mix, saying, "I like cake." It's his favorite, too.

1	box yellow cake mix
1	small box instant vanilla pudding mix (four-serving size)
4	eggs
1/2	cup oil
1	cup sour cream
1	tsp. vanilla extract
1/4	cup poppy seeds

Combine dry cake mix and dry pudding mix in large bowl. Add eggs, oil and sour cream; beat at medium speed several minutes until batter seems very light and fluffy. Add vanilla and poppy seeds and beat until well blended.

Pour batter into a well-greased Bundt pan. Bake at 350° for 35-45 minutes. Remove from oven about five minutes before you think it's done, as it will continue to cook in the pan. It should be marvelously moist.

Tomato Soup Spice Cake

It doesn't taste like tomato soup. It's a delightful spice cake — moist, not too sweet. Thanks to my friend Sue Dill for sharing it.

CAKE

3/4	cup butter	2-1/2	cups flour
2	cups sugar	1	tsp. allspice
3	eggs	1	tsp. cinnamon
2	tsp. baking powder	1	cup pecans, chopped
1	tsp. baking soda		(optional)
1	can tomato soup		

Cream butter and sugar. Add eggs, one at a time, mixing well. Add baking powder, baking soda and tomato soup (undiluted).

In another bowl combine flour with allspice and cinnamon. Gradually add to creamed ingredients, beating constantly. Add pecans, if you like. (I like!)

Pour batter into a greased and floured Bundt pan and bake at 350° for about an hour. Remember to take it out of the oven about five minutes before you think it's done — heat from Bundt pan will continue to bake it, and this helps ensure a moist cake.

FROSTING

1	pkg. (8-oz.) cream cheese, softened	1	tsp. vanilla extract
1/2	cup butter, softened	1/2	tsp. *each* brandy and rum flavoring
1	box (1-lb.) powdered sugar	1/2	tsp. almond extract

For frosting, cream the cheese and butter with powdered sugar. Add flavorings. Frost cake when it's cool.

Note the illustration. When I frost cakes, I frequently take this easy way out. Don't you think it looks elegant?

What do you do with a cake that's been baked too long and is dry? Or perhaps it's simply several days old and has dried out?

• Serve it with ice cream — that's easiest.

• Slice it and put it in the bottom of a casserole dish and top with pudding. (If it's an iced cake, scrape off the icing and trim it first.)

• Slice and sprinkle with a little sherry or liqueur. Smother with whipped cream.

• Crumble and alternate with layers of pudding or softened ice cream in pretty parfait dishes.

• If it's a pound cake, toast it with a little butter, or slice and serve with a juicy fruit.

Caramel Nut Brownies

This recipe is from my friend Barb Reschley. When she gave it to me, she wrote across the top of it, "Fabulous!" She's right. They're so rich, they're almost like candy — brownies with a slightly chewy caramel center.

50	caramels (14-oz. pkg.), unwrapped	1	German chocolate cake mix
2/3	cup evaporated milk (1/3 cup plus 1/3 cup)	3/4	cup butter, melted
		1	cup chocolate chips
		1	cup chopped pecans

Melt caramels with 1/3 cup milk in top of double boiler over barely simmering water. Stir frequently.

While slowly melting caramels, combine cake mix with melted butter and remaining 1/3 cup milk, stirring to blend well. Spread half this mixture into thin layer in greased 9" x 13" baking dish. It will be a fairly stiff batter, so pat it out with your hand or the back of a spoon.

Bake 6-8 minutes at 350°, until it is barely firm to the touch but not done.

Remove from oven and sprinkle with chocolate chips and pecans. Drizzle melted caramels over chips and nuts, then cover with remaining cake batter. The batter will be very stiff, so drop it like drop cookie batter and smooth it lightly with the back of your spoon. It may not cover the caramel sauce completely, but that's okay.

Continue baking at 350° for 15 minutes, until brownies are firm to the touch and pulling away from sides of the pan.

Cool in the pan. If they are too warm when you slice them, they fall apart. They are so rich that very small pieces are fine.

Makes 3-4 dozen.

Eggs separate best when cold. The warmer they are, the runnier the whites are.

Chocolate Meringue Cookies

Light and crisp on the outside, moist and chewy in the center. No one guesses your "secret" ingredient!

1	pkg. (6-oz.) semisweet chocolate chips	1/2	tsp. vanilla extract
3	egg whites, room temperature	1	cup sugar
1/4	tsp. cream of tartar	1	cup saltine cracker crumbs (about 25 crackers)

Melt chocolate chips in microwave or double boiler. Cool to lukewarm, stirring occasionally.

Whip egg whites with cream of tartar and vanilla to stiff peaks. Gradually beat in sugar until you have very stiff, glossy peaks.

Fold in chocolate until well blended. Fold in cracker crumbs until thoroughly mixed.

Drop by rounded teaspoonfuls onto oiled cookie sheet. Bake at 350° for 10-12 minutes. Baked for ten minutes, cookies will be chewy; twelve minutes, crisp.

Remove cookies to cool on wire rack.

Makes about three dozen two-inch cookies.

Chocolate Oatmeal Cookies

These have a very rich chocolate flavor and are not too sweet. This is a fairly small recipe, so you may want to double it — they don't last long.

1/2	cup butter, softened	1	tsp. baking soda
1	cup brown sugar, packed	1/4	cup cocoa
1	egg, lightly beaten	1-1/2	cups rolled oats
1	tsp. vanilla extract	1/2	cup toasted almond slivers
3/4	cup flour		

Cream butter and brown sugar; add egg and vanilla, then stir in flour. Once flour is well blended, add the baking soda, cocoa and rolled oats. At this point the batter will be very stiff. Add almonds and drop by teaspoon onto an ungreased cookie sheet.

Bake at 350° for 8-10 minutes for soft cookies or 12-15 minutes for crisp cookies.

Makes about 2 dozen.

Coconut Shortbread Cookies

These delicious cookies melt in your mouth, as shortbread should. They have the added bonus of texture from the coconut.

1	cup butter, softened		Pinch of salt
6	tbsp. sugar	2	cups flour
1	tsp. vanilla extract	1	cup flaked coconut

Cream butter and sugar with a pastry blender. Add vanilla and salt; gradually work in the flour. This makes a stiff dough, so use your hands if you like. When flour is well blended, mix in coconut.

Divide dough into thirds. Roll each piece into a log, cover with plastic wrap and chill until firm enough to slice. May be frozen.

Slice cookies about 1/4" thick and bake at 350° for about ten minutes. Watch them carefully because they are best when they are just beginning to brown around the edges.

Makes 3-4 dozen.

NOTE
Be sure to toast almond slivers first. Makes a great difference in flavor. You could substitute toasted pecans.

When baking cookies, use a sheet of aluminium foil cut to fit the cookie sheet. This not only makes clean up easier, but if you have only one cookie sheet, you can be dropping dough on foil while first batch bakes. Simply slide foil with baked cookies off the cookie sheet and slide the foil with the unbaked ones onto it.

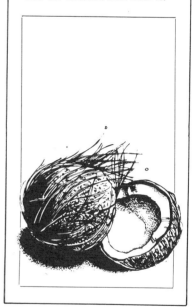

Flaky Oat Cookies

NOTE

This dough is delicate like pie crust, so be gentle with it and handle it as little as possible. I prefer to cut mine into squares rather than reroll it. You can slice diamonds instead of squares.

The pastry-like texture of the cookie contrasts with the chewy texture of the rolled oats. Delicious without being too sweet.

3	cups rolled oats	1/2	tsp. baking soda
1-1/2	cups flour	1	cup shortening
1/2	cup sugar	2-to-3	tbsp. cold water
1/2	tsp. salt		

Combine dry ingredients; then cut in shortening as you would for pie crust until the pieces are smaller than English peas. Add cold water a little at a time, stirring, until dough sticks together; add more if necessary.

Roll out dough between pieces of plastic wrap to about 1/4" thick. Slice into squares or use a cookie cutter. Bake on an ungreased cookie sheet at 375° for 15-20 minutes, or until lightly browned on top.

Makes about five dozen.

Jelly Turnover Cookies

NOTE

I always prefer to use a jelly that is not very sweet for these cookies, something like red currant jelly or apricot preserves. Actually, any favorite would do.

I could eat my weight in these delicate cookies. They take a little time to make, but they're worth it.

1	cup butter, softened
2	small pkgs. (3-oz.) cream cheese, softened
2	cups flour
	Jelly or preserves
	Powdered sugar

Whip butter and cream cheese together; gradually stir in flour until you have a smooth dough.

Chill dough until it rolls easily. Roll about 1/3 of it at a time between pieces of plastic wrap. Cut out circles of dough with your cookie cutter and put a small spoonful of the jelly or preserves in the middle. Fold over and crimp the edges with a fork, or fold two sides up over middle and pinch together.

Bake on an ungreased cookie sheet at 350° for 10-15 minutes, until they are a light golden brown and the jelly is beginning to ooze out temptingly around the edges.

Dust with powdered sugar.

Makes 40 two-inch circles.

Kiss Cookies

If you have a sweet tooth, don't even think about baking these — they're too irresistible!

1	cup butter, softened	1	cup chopped pecans
1/2	cup sugar	1	pkg. (9-oz.) chocolate
1	tsp. vanilla extract		candy kisses
1-3/4	cups flour		Powdered sugar

Cream butter and sugar together with vanilla. Add flour gradually until well blended; stir in pecans. Chill the dough.

Unwrap the chocolate kisses and mold about one tablespoon of cookie dough around each chocolate kiss, covering candy completely. Bake on cookie sheet at 375° until they just turn golden around the edges, about ten minutes. Let cool slightly before removing from cookie sheet.

When completely cool, dust with powdered sugar. Store in air-tight container.

Makes about 3 dozen.

Madeleines

These cookies are really lovely little French sponge cakes. Gourmet shops carry special madeleine tins which are traditional. You can use muffin tins, but they aren't as much fun.

1	cup sugar
3	small eggs
1	cup flour
1/2	tsp. baking powder
	Pinch of salt
1/2	cup butter, melted
1	tsp. *either* vanilla extract or grated lemon peel

Beat sugar and eggs until light and lemon-colored. Stir in flour, baking powder and salt. Add melted butter and vanilla extract or lemon peel.

Fill buttered madeleine tins and bake at 325° about 20 minutes until lightly brown around the edges. If you're using regular muffin tins, fill only about 1/4 full.

Makes 24.

NOTE
These are relatively low calorie cookies, about 77 calories each.

When soft cookies dry out, you might try putting them in an airtight container with a piece of fresh bread. Check them periodically because sometimes the bread releases so much moisture they crumble.

Praline Cookies

These may be the most unusual cookies you've ever tasted. The simple graham cracker base is the perfect balance for the rich praline topping.

48	graham crackers (break 24 doubles in two)
1	cup finely chopped pecans
1/2	cup butter
1/2	cup margarine
1/2	cup sugar
1	tsp. vanilla extract

This recipe is basically very simple, but I've made it three times, and I've learned some important lessons.

First, let me caution you that once you make your praline sauce, it doesn't hold very well for a second batch of cookies. This means you should have your 48 crackers already in pans. The ideal pan is a large jellyroll cake pan with a 1/2" side; it takes two of them. You can use other pans. If you can't fit in 48 crackers, don't worry about it. You'll simply have some praline sauce left over.

Second, it is important that you time the sauce exactly.

Third, don't crowd your oven when you bake the cookies. It's better to bake them in batches.

Now for the recipe. Place your crackers in the pans. Chop the pecans. Melt butter, margarine, sugar and vanilla together in a small saucepan. When mixture comes to a rolling boil you can't stir down, time it for *exactly three minutes* and remove from heat. Stir it constantly during the three minutes.

Stir in the pecans and spoon sauce over graham crackers. I put one heaping teaspoonful of sauce in the middle of each cracker. As it bakes, it spreads out to coat the crackers evenly.

Bake at 325° for 8-12 minutes. Remove from oven as soon as they begin to brown around the edges. Cool cookies on waxed paper.

Makes 36-48 cookies.

Shortbread Cookies

These crisp, delicate cookies melt in your mouth. The recipe is so simple that it is ideal for children — they love to help pat out the dough.

1-1/2	cups sugar
5	cups flour
2	cups butter, softened

Butter Cookies

Cookie baking directions almost always say something like "about 10 minutes" or "10-12 minutes." This is because baking time varies according to the size of the cookies; you may drop more from your spoon than I do.

Experiment with your own timing. In general, cookies baked the minimum amount of time will be more moist. Another minute or two and they're crisp. Vary each recipe to suit your family tastes.

Mix sugar and flour and add butter, mixing with hands or spoon until all the flour and sugar mixture is absorbed.

Press dough into a 9" x 13" pan or a 10" x 15" cookie sheet to a thickness of about 1/3". Sprinkle with sugar. Chill, cut into squares and bake at 325° for 18 - 20 minutes.

Or, if you prefer, simply pat the dough into two circles on a cookie sheet. Bake as above. Remove from oven and cut into pie-shaped wedges while still hot.

Makes approximately 2 dozen.

Simple Butter Cookies

Our family loves this rich, buttery cookie. It's one of my favorites because it's so simple.

1	cup unsalted butter, softened
1/2	cup sugar
2	egg yolks
2	cups flour
	Low calorie apricot preserves (optional)

Cream butter and sugar, add egg yolks and blend. Gradually stir in flour — and that's it!

Chill dough until it's easy to handle and roll into marble-sized balls. Put them on cookie sheets and flatten with bottom of a glass you've dipped in sugar. Dampen the glass with a little water to get sugar to cling.

These cookies are good plain, but even better if you make an indentation with the back of a spoon and fill it with preserves. I used low-calorie apricot preserves because they aren't too sweet, and they were perfect.

Bake cookies on ungreased cookie sheet at 325° for 10-12 minutes, until they begin to brown around the edges. They're delicious!

Makes 3-1/2 dozen two-inch cookies.

This Shortbread Cookie recipe is a good example of the importance of making sure you understand recipe directions. Years ago a friend shared it with me, telling me to "combine" the sugar, flour and butter.

When I got home I realized I didn't know whether to melt the butter, soften it, or cut it into the flour and sugar as though for biscuits or pie crust.

I opted to melt it, and the cookies were as hard as brickbats! And, if I had cut the butter in with a pastry cutter, they would have flaked and crumbled like pastry instead of melting in your mouth as they should. So there were three options, but only the correct one worked.

Technique is critical.

NOTE
    For quick chilling of cookie dough, press it around the inside of a glass mixing bowl to a thickness of about one inch. Set bowl in the freezer for 10-15 minutes.

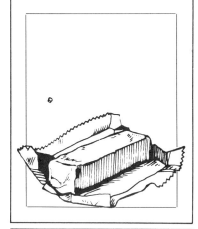

Square Peanut Butter Cups

I baked these to send to my daughter Shannon's class. They were a tremendous hit!

16   double squares of graham crackers, crushed
1   cup butter, softened
1   cup peanut butter
1/2   lb. powdered sugar
1   pkg. (12-oz.) chocolate chips

Put crushed graham crackers into a bowl and, with your hands, mix in butter, peanut butter, and powdered sugar. When thoroughly mixed, press into an 8" x 8" pan and bake uncovered at 350° for 15 minutes, until lightly browned. Remove from oven and spread chocolate chips over top. Return to oven just long enough to melt chips so they spread like frosting.

Cool to room temperature and cut into small squares.

Makes 16-25, depending on how you cut squares.

The next time your inexperienced child wants to cook something, offer one of these two recipes.

I don't know why so many recipes geared for children are for ridiculous and basically unappetizing things like clown salads.

It makes more sense to me to encourage beginners with adult recipes that are sure to be truly enjoyed by almost everyone who eats them.

Set your children up for compliments and praise — and they'll want to learn to cook.

They're no different than we are.

Susan's Coconut Brownies

My first taste came from the plate of goodies sitting next to the office coffee pot, and I couldn't resist. My only consolation was that they were so rich a very *small* piece was enough. Thanks to Susan Yoes for her recipe.

1/2   cup butter, melted
1   cup graham cracker crumbs
1   pkg. (6-oz.) chocolate chips
1   cup coconut
1   cup chopped pecans
1   can (14-oz.) sweetened condensed milk
      (such as Eagle Brand)

Pour melted butter into 9" x 13" glass baking dish. Add graham cracker crumbs; mix with fork and pat them down. Sprinkle chocolate chips, then coconut, and then pecans over crumbs. Do *not* stir. Drizzle sweetened condensed milk over the whole thing and bake uncovered at 375° for 25-30 minutes, until lightly browned on top.

Makes 2-3 dozen.

Baked Fruit with Brandy

A simple, lovely dessert. Very unusual.

1   can (16-oz.) Freestone peaches, drained
2   medium bananas, fairly green, sliced
2-to-4 tbsp. brandy
    Cinnamon to taste
    Freshly grated nutmeg to taste
2   tbsp. brown sugar, packed
1   tbsp. butter

Combine peaches and bananas in a baking dish. Stir in brandy, cinnamon and nutmeg.

Sprinkle with sugar, dot with butter. Bake at 350° for 15 minutes; serve warm.

If you like, you may top with a dollop of sour cream lightly sweetened with brown sugar or with ice cream.

Serves 4.

Brian's Peaches

This is a remarkably simple dessert my brother, Brian Patrick, created.

4   fresh peaches, peeled and sliced
4   tbsp. Kirsch or Triple Sec (more to taste)
8   oz. heavy cream, whipped

Place peach slices in large wine goblets or parfait glasses. Sprinkle with liqueur. Top with whipped cream.

Serves 4.

Cornbread Pudding

It may sound strange, but it sure is good. It's not only an excellent way to use up leftover cornbread or muffins, but it has more texture than most bread puddings.

2	cups milk
1	cup brown sugar, packed
4	cups cornbread or other muffin crumbs
	(one muffin = 1/2 cup crumbs)
1/2	cup butter, melted
4	eggs, lightly beaten
1/2	tsp. cinnamon
	Freshly grated nutmeg to taste

Combine milk and brown sugar; stir to dissolve sugar. Put crumbs in another bowl and drizzle with butter; toss lightly. Combine crumbs with milk mixture and let it sit a few minutes until crumbs absorb milk. Stir in eggs, cinnamon and nutmeg.

Pour mixture into a well-buttered casserole or cake pan. Bake uncovered at 350° for 45-60 minutes. Baking time depends on size and shape of pan. I used an 8" x 8" cake pan and baked it for about 55 minutes. Test for doneness by inserting knife in center; when blade comes out clean, it's done.

Serve this pudding warm or room temperature for best flavor, but don't leave it out of the refrigerator for longer than an hour; puddings spoil quickly.

Serves 8.

VARIATION

Use any muffins you have left over. If you have only four muffins, then halve other ingredients and use a smaller pan, like a loaf pan.

You can also use leftover unfrosted cake crumbs. If you do, reduce sugar to 2/3 cup since cake crumbs are already sweet.

Gingerbread

Gingerbread is something I don't bake too often, but when I do, this recipe yields an extremely delicate gingerbread.

1-1/2	cups flour		1/2	cup sugar
	Pinch of salt		1/2	cup hot water
1	tsp. *each* baking soda,		1/2	cup molasses
	ground ginger, cinnamon		1/2	cup mayonnaise

Combine dry ingredients and mix well. Mix hot water and molasses and add to flour mixture along with mayonnaise.

Pour batter into a greased 8" x 8" pan. Bake at 325°for 25 - 30 minutes, until center springs back.

Serve with butter, hot from the oven.

Layered Pudding Dessert

This is a large dessert which keeps well for several days. It's so rich you'll prefer small pieces. It makes an elegant presentation.

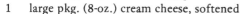

- 1/2 cup butter, melted
- 1 cup flour
- 1 cup chopped pecans
- 1 large pkg. (8-oz.) cream cheese, softened
- 1 carton (8 or 9-oz.) frozen whipped topping, thawed (set aside one cup)
- 1 cup powdered sugar
- 1 pkg. instant vanilla pudding (4-serving size)
- 1 pkg. instant chocolate pudding (4-serving size)
- 3 cups milk (1-1/2 cups plus 1-1/2 cups)

CRUST

Pour melted butter in bottom of 9" x 13" baking dish; stir in flour and pecans. Carefully press this cookie-like dough over bottom of dish. It will be very thin, but it will be enough.

Bake at 350° for 15-20 minutes (until lightly browned). Cool before filling.

FIRST LAYER

Mix cream cheese, one cup of the whipped topping and powdered sugar together until light and fluffy, about two minutes. Spread over cooled cookie crust.

SECOND LAYER

Mix instant vanilla pudding with 1-1/2 cups milk for about two minutes, until it begins to thicken. Spread over cream cheese layer.

THIRD LAYER

Mix instant chocolate pudding with 1-1/2 cups milk for about two minutes. Vanilla layer should be set by the time you spread chocolate layer over it.

Top with remaining whipped topping. Garnish with grated chocolate or more chopped pecans if you like. Slice and serve in squares.

Serves 12-15.

I picked up this wonderful dessert recipe from another mother at the Girl Scout garage sale. It's an annual affair, in the scout leader's home.

And what a gem she is to take on these girls, year after year. They're the most active troop in our area.

What a sensitive soul she is, this Scout leader Laura MacIlvaine, who called to say, "We're going to make sure our girl makes First Class (that's like an Eagle Scout), even if she can't do everything the others do. So long as she does her best and works hard at her level, I'll see that she makes it." And she did.

Laura gives so much more than time to her troop. She gives her heart, her mother's understanding. "Thank you" is precious little to say.

And while I'm at it, what about our soccer coach? Our son has grown up with him.

Warren has learned that soccer's just a game, and that life is for leaders and for working to be a part of the team.

Thanks to Bob Henninger and his wife, Vivian, who mothers those boys like her own.

And thanks to the rest of you, out there, who give so much of yourselves to thousands of children, coast to coast.

We're grateful.

Ma Neal's Fruit Cobbler

Harriet Douglas sent me this recipe which she says dates back 145 years. Recipes which survive that many years must be good — and this one is!

1/2	cup butter	3	tsp. baking powder
1-1/2	cups flour	1	can (1-lb.) fruit (crushed
1-1/2	cups sugar		pineapple, peaches,
1-1/2	cups milk		apricots, etc.), partly drained

Melt the butter in the bottom of cast iron pan or 9" x 13" baking dish.

Combine flour, sugar, milk, and baking powder into batter, and pour over melted butter. Add one can of fruit. Stir to mix.

Bake at 350° for 30-40 minutes if using glass dish. Bake at 400° for 30 minutes if using cast iron. Cobbler should be browned on top and firm in center. Serve warm or room temperature with ice cream or unwhipped heavy cream.

Serves 6-8.

These two recipes represent the thing I love most about my radio program — people love to share with me as much as I enjoy sharing with them.

I've never met Harriet Douglas, but she's listened to my program for a long time, and she's quick to send me interesting recipes.

Marie Legault is the mother of a close friend, and like so many others, she scouts good recipes for me.

Hardly a day goes by that someone doesn't send a recipe, and I love it.

Thank you, all of you.

Marie's Cream Cheese Cake

My friend's mom Marie Legault is famous for this cake. One bite and you'll know why.

CRUST

1	pkg. yellow cake mix	1/2	cup butter, melted
1	egg, lightly beaten		

Combine cake mix with egg and butter; press into bottom of a 9" x 13" cake pan.

FILLING

1	pkg. (8-oz.) cream cheese, softened	1	cup powdered sugar
		2	eggs
1	cup brown sugar, packed	1	tsp. vanilla extract

Beat cream cheese with two sugars, eggs and vanilla. Pour filling over the crust and bake uncovered at 325° for about 45 minutes, until filling poofs up and is browned a bit on top. It should be firm enough not to jiggle when you shake the pan. The filling settles as it cools.

Very rich, so cut the pieces small.

Nano's Date Rolls

This is a rich confection literally out of my childhood. Nano always made it at Christmas. I found my recipe recently in my 14 year-old scrawl. Do you suppose my grandchildren will remember it as well?

1	box (1-lb.) graham crackers, crushed	1-1/2	lbs. English walnuts, ground
3	lbs. dates, ground	1/2	cup butter, melted
		1/2	pint heavy cream

Crush graham crackers and grind dates and walnuts; food processor or an old-fashioned meat grinder do very well. Combine graham cracker crumbs, dates and nuts with melted butter.

Add cream a little at a time until crumbs are completely moist and dough is of consistency to mold with your hands. Divide dough into pieces and form into logs. Wrap logs in plastic wrap and keep them in refrigerator; slice as needed.

Makes 6-8 logs, 1-1/2" in diameter, 12" long. Keeps well in the freezer.

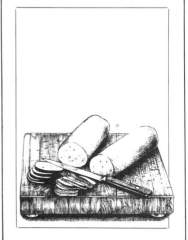

Peach Cheesecake
(Calorie Conscious)

Unlike most low-calorie desserts, this one has a rich, satisfying texture and flavor.

2	large pkgs. (8-oz.) Neufchâtel cheese, softened
3	small (8-oz.) cans water-packed peach slices, drained
1/4	cup sugar
1	tsp. vanilla extract
3	eggs
1	pkg. (11 double crackers) graham crackers, crushed
1/4	cup butter, melted

If you have a food processor, whirl cheese, peaches, sugar, vanilla and eggs all at once until well blended.

If you don't, purée peaches in blender or push through sieve. Combine with other ingredients and beat with electric mixer until light and fluffy.

Combine graham cracker crumbs with butter; press into 10" pie pan. Don't bake. Add filling, pouring it over the back of a spoon so that it won't disturb the crumb crust.

Bake uncovered at 300° until set in center and browned around the edges, about one hour. Cool and serve.

Yields 16 diet portions of approximately 166 calories each.

NOTE

Neufchâtel cheese has 80 calories per ounce, compared to 100 per ounce for cream cheese. It makes an ideal substitute.

Rich Banana Pudding

I had no idea this pudding would be as extraordinary as it is. Neither whipped topping nor instant pudding are favorites of mine, but in this recipe they are wonderful. My family raved about it, and visiting sisters-in-law all wanted the recipe.

Vanilla wafers (most of a 12-oz. box)
4-to-5 medium bananas, peeled and sliced
2 small pkgs. vanilla instant pudding (four-serving size)
3 cups milk
1 can (14-oz.) sweetened condensed milk (such as Eagle Brand)
1 large carton (12-oz.) frozen whipped topping, thawed

Line bottom and sides of 9" x 13" dish with vanilla wafers. Cover wafers completely with sliced bananas, the more the better. Overlap them a bit.

Prepare pudding according to package directions, using three cups milk. Add sweetened condensed milk and fold in whipped topping. Pour over bananas; chill and serve.

Serves 12-15, possibly more because it is very rich. Keeps well overnight.

NOTE

1. The day I made this, my 9" x 13" dish was very full, perhaps because I was so generous with the bananas. I had enough pudding left to make another small 4" x 8" dish for our daughter to take home.

2. As with other recipes calling for frozen whipped topping, you can use 8-oz. heavy cream, whipped, instead.

Strawberry Fondue

What a lovely, casual way to end a meal with friends.

1 quart fresh strawberries, washed but with stems left on
1/2 cup sour cream
1/2 cup sugar (granulated, powdered or brown)
Ice

Clean the strawberries and pat dry. Put the sour cream and sugar into pretty little dishes (custard dishes will do).

Center the dishes on a platter or tray, and surround them with ice. Scatter the berries over the ice.

Serve on a small table so that everyone can comfortably reach everything. The idea is to hold the strawberry by its stem and dip it first into the sour cream, then into the sugar.

Serves 4, easily doubled or tripled.

When you wash fresh straw-berries, leave the stems on. If you remove them first, your berries may become a bit waterlogged.

If you can't use fresh berries immediately, you can store them in a shallow bowl in the refrigerator.

Cover the bowl with a damp paper towel.

If a few are still a little green, set those on the window sill to ripen.

Strawberry Angel Cake

This is a difficult dessert to describe. When my friend Billie Whidden served it, I knew I had to have the recipe. It's a frozen dessert — light, rich, and simply delicious.

    2   full-sized angel food cakes
            (already baked, from the store)
    1   large box strawberry gelatin
    2   pkgs. (10-oz.) frozen strawberries

FROSTING
    1   pint heavy cream, whipped
    1   tbsp. sugar
    1   tsp. vanilla extract

There is no need to make the angel food cakes from scratch. The first thing you do is tear them both into bite-size pieces and put them in a very large mixing bowl.

Make strawberry gelatin according to package directions and set it in refrigerator until it's partially set (the consistency of uncooked egg whites).

Thaw strawberries until they are juicy enough to stir; add them to chilled gelatin. Combine gelatin mixture with angel food cake pieces and toss lightly until they are completely mixed.

Pour this mixture into a one-piece tube pan and freeze it overnight.

Thaw cake on kitchen counter until loose enough in pan to unmold, about one hour. Whip cream with sugar and vanilla and frost cake. Leave out until easy to slice, a total of one to 1-1/2 hours.

Cake slices are dark red, like strawberries, with fluffs of white cake showing here and there. It's just beautiful. Leftovers can be frozen for a day or two, but it's best the first time around.

Sour Cream Peach Cobbler

I'd never tried peach cobbler with sour cream, but when my friend Lisa Hanes brought me her favorite recipe, I knew at a glance it would be wonderful. I was right. The filling has an almost caramel taste; absolutely delicious.

    3   cups sliced fresh peaches
    1-to-2 cups sugar (depending on how sweet
                peaches are)
    6   tbsp. flour
    2   cups sour cream
    6   egg yolks, lightly beaten
    1   unbaked pastry pie crust
                for double crust pie

Combine sliced peaches and sugar; let stand 30 minutes.

In medium saucepan combine flour, sour cream and egg yolks. Cook over low heat until very thick, stirring occasionally and watching carefully to be sure it doesn't burn. Should take 7-10 minutes.

Combine with peaches in an 8" x 12" baking dish, stirring until peaches are well coated.

Top with unbaked pastry pie crust; flute and cut steam vents. Sprinkle with a little sugar if you like.

Bake at 350° for 45 minutes, until crust is golden brown and filling is beginning to ooze temptingly.

Best served warm. Serves 8-10.

NOTE

1. You may like to dust them with powdered sugar or drizzle them with a little orange marmalade that you have heated with some butter.

2. The number of crêpes this will fill depends on the size of the crêpes— I usually do six-inch ones. Two make a nice size serving.

Vi's Custard Crêpes

My friend Vi has shared her favorite crêpe recipe which has a filling I really love. It is light, fluffy, rich, and slightly sweet, appropriate for lunch, brunch or a light dessert.

FILLING

1/4	cup butter, softened	3	egg whites, beaten to hold stiff peaks
1/4	cup sugar		
3	egg yolks		Chopped nuts, raisins, or chopped dates
1-1/4	cups dry cottage cheese		
6	tbsp. sour cream	12	crêpes (see Page 29.)

SAUCE

1   egg, beaten
1/2   cup milk

Stir together the butter, sugar and egg yolks. When they are well blended, add the cottage cheese and sour cream. Gently fold in the stiffly beaten egg whites and the nuts, raisins or dates.

Put about one-fourth cup of the filling on each crêpe, then roll it and place it seam side down in a shallow 9" x 13" baking dish.

Beat the milk and egg for the sauce together and pour over crêpes.

Bake, uncovered, at 300° for 30-45 minutes, until they are heated through and the custard is set.

Walnut Fudge Pudding

Back in the days before you could buy a packaged mix for almost everything, my mom had a special dessert that I just loved. You can buy mixes for similar puddings now, but they don't come close to being as good as hers.

BATTER

1	cup flour		Pinch of salt
3/4	cup sugar (or brown sugar, packed)	1/2	cup milk
		2	tbsp. oil
2	tbsp. cocoa	1/2	cup chopped English walnuts
2	tbsp. baking powder		

Combine dry ingredients; add milk and oil. Stir in walnuts and pour into an ungreased 9" square pan.

PUDDING SAUCE

- 1 cup sugar (or brown sugar, packed)
- 1-3/4 cups hot water (or coffee)
- 1/4 cup cocoa

Combine pudding sauce ingredients, mixing well. Pour over cake batter. <u>DO NOT STIR.</u> As the cake bakes, the batter rises to the top to form a brownie-like cake and the pudding makes a thick, rich fudge sauce under the cake.

Bake at 350° until edges of cake topping are pulling away from sides of the pan, about 20 minutes. Center may not be quite firm, but that's okay. Serve warm or cold, with fudge pudding sauce spooned over the cake. If you're tempted, add whipped cream.

Serves 6-9.

For a lovely seasonal touch in the autumn, set out bowls of your favorite nuts.

Everyone will appreciate it if you include an extra nutcracker or two.

Wynn River Cheesecake

I treasure this recipe which was given to me by Margaret Ackerman. She got it from the chef at the Wynn River Ranch in Colorado, and I agree with Margaret — it's the best cheesecake in the world!

CRUST
16	graham crackers, crushed	1-1/2	tsp. cinnamon
2	tbsp. sugar	1/2	cup butter, melted

FILLING
3	pkg. (8-oz.) cream cheese, softened	3	eggs
1	cup sugar	1/2	tsp. vanilla extract
		1/2	tsp. almond extract

TOPPING
- 1 pint sour cream
- 3 tbsp. sugar
- 1/2 tsp. vanilla extract

Combine graham cracker crumbs, sugar, cinnamon and butter. Press into 10" pie plate or springform pan.

Cream the cheese and sugar until light and fluffy. Add eggs one at a time, then vanilla and almond extracts. Pour into crust and bake at 350° for 20 minutes.

Combine sour cream, sugar and vanilla. When cheesecake has baked 20 minutes, take it out of the oven and turn oven up to 500° while you spoon on topping. Return to oven for five minutes. Let cool to room temperature and chill. Also freezes well.

Serves 12 (small, very rich pieces).

NOTE

If you use a pie plate, you may not have room for all the topping. You can easily cut topping recipe in half. It will still be outstanding!

Basic Pastry Pie Crust

I never make pastry for a single crust. If I'm baking a single pie shell, I make the double-crust recipe and freeze half to use later. It freezes beautifully before or after rolling. I don't roll it before freezing because I don't have that much room in my freezer.

Incidentally, there are usually a few leftover pie crust scraps. It takes just a minute to roll and cut them into decorative shapes for the top of your pie — such a nice finishing touch.

The final bits and pieces of dough can be rolled and dotted with butter. Sprinkle with cinnamon sugar and bake until golden brown.

So light and flaky it will float off your plate.

2	cups flour	3/4	cup shortening
1	tsp. salt	5-to-6	tbsp. ice water

Combine flour and salt in medium mixing bowl. Cut shortening in with pastry cutter until mixture resembles cornmeal.

Very important that you add ice water, not tap water — you want the pieces of shortening to stay solid. Add water one tablespoon at a time, stirring each tablespoon into one small part of the flour mixture. Stir only until moistened enough to cling together in a ball.

Chill dough before rolling. This is enough pastry for one large double-crust pie or two small ones. For unfilled pie shells prick before baking at 450° for 10-12 minutes, until golden brown. Cool before filling.

Quiche Pie Crust
(Vinegar)

This is a light, flaky crust that doesn't need delicate handling. It can be rolled and rerolled successfully. I don't even chill it before rolling it out.

3	cups flour	1	egg, lightly beaten
	Pinch of salt	4	tbsp. cold water
1	tbsp. sugar	1	tbsp. vinegar
1-1/2	cups shortening		

Measure flour into a mixing bowl; add salt and sugar. Cut in shortening with a pastry blender (or two knives) until size of cornmeal. Combine egg, water and vinegar and add all at once to flour mixture. Stir until dough clings together; roll out between sheets of plastic wrap.

This may be used as an unbaked shell. To partially bake crust as suggested in most quiche recipes, bake at 450° for 7-10 minutes until cooked but not brown. If your recipe calls for a baked shell, put into a 450° oven for 10-12 minutes, or until golden brown.

Makes two 8" or 9" pie shells, or one double-crust pie.

Cookie Crust

This is wonderful as the basis for any ice cream pie.

1/3	cup butter	1	egg yolk
2-1/2	tbsp. sugar	1	cup flour
	Pinch of salt	1/3	cup chopped nuts, any kind

Cream butter with sugar and salt. Add egg yolk and beat until smooth. Stir in the flour and nuts.

Press into a 10" pie pan and bake at 325° for ten minutes, until lightly browned.

Cool and fill with favorite ice cream, sundae topping, whipped cream and a cherry.

VARIATION
Add the following to crust ingredients:
1. 2 tbsp. cocoa, added to flour
2. 1/2 cup coconut, added to flour
3. 1/2 cup chocolate chips, chopped

Crumb Crust

A basic cookie crumb crust is quick and easy to do, and it can be used with any ice cream, pudding or meringue pie.

1-1/4	cups graham cracker crumbs (or crushed vanilla wafers or zweiback)
1/4	cup sugar
1/4	cup butter, softened

Mix ingredients together thoroughly and pour into a 9" pie plate. Shape with the back of a spoon into a crust. Bake at 375° for eight minutes. Cool before filling.

NOTE
There's nothing simpler when company comes than an ice cream pie — or more impressive. Use two or three flavors in different colors, add a favorite sundae topping and freeze. Garnish with chopped nuts and whipped cream when you serve.

Crunchy Pecan Pie Crust

Ridiculously rich! Thanks to my friend Libby Maus.

1	cup butter, melted	1/2	cup finely chopped pecans
2	cups whole-wheat flour		

Melt butter and stir in the flour and pecans.

This is not a rolled pie crust. Simply mix in 10" pie plate and press it over bottom and up the sides with the back of a spoon.

Bake it at 350° for about 20 minutes, until lightly browned. Cool completely before filling. This goes well with almost any pudding or ice cream filling.

Makes one large crust.

NOTE
Normally, I don't use straight instant pudding as a dessert by itself or as a cream pie filling. But the friend who gave the recipe to me swore that the crust was so rich, you couldn't tell if you used instant or cooked pudding. Sounded reasonable, so I tried it and, truthfully, I loved it.

Best Chocolate Pie

NOTE

1. Egg whites freeze nicely. Save them for a later day. (See Pecan Meringue Pie recipe, pg. 199.)

2. Be sure pie dish measures 10" as this is a lot of filling. That also means you can slice pieces smaller.

NICE TO KNOW . . .

A couple of chocolate chips dropped into your after dinner coffee cup will give a good mocha taste.

For years I have made pies as holiday desserts. I always have a fancy one for the adults and this chocolate one for the children. Or so I thought. What really happens is everyone has a piece of each because they can't resist this one!

1-1/2	cups brown sugar, packed
2/3	cup cocoa
6	tbsp. cornstarch
	Pinch of salt
4	cups milk
6	egg yolks, lightly beaten
4	tbsp. butter, softened
2	tsp. vanilla extract
1	10" pie shell, baked and cooled
1	cup heavy cream, whipped

Combine brown sugar, cocoa, cornstarch and salt in a large saucepan. Stir in milk. Cook over medium heat, stirring constantly, until it comes to a boil. Boil for two minutes and remove from heat.

Stir a spoonful of hot pudding into egg yolks, then gradually add yolks to hot pudding. Return to heat and boil for one more minute. Remove from heat and stir in butter and vanilla. Cool pudding slightly before pouring into cooled pie crust and chill completely before serving.

Serve with mounds of whipped cream and shaved chocolate.

Serves 8-10.

Chocolate Peanut Butter Pie

As easy as it is rich and delicious!

1	pkg. chocolate fudge pudding, not instant (*six-serving* size)
1	pkg. vanilla pudding, not instant (*four-serving* size)
2-1/2	cups milk
1-1/2	cups milk
1/2	cup chunky peanut butter
1	10" pie crust, baked and cooled
8	oz. heavy cream, whipped without sugar
	Chopped dry roasted peanuts and/or shaved chocolate for garnish

You'll need two saucepans. Combine fudge pudding with 2 1/2 cups milk in one, and the vanilla pudding with 1-1/2 cups milk in the other. Cook until they boil and thicken over medium heat.

Stir peanut butter into vanilla pudding.

Drop warm pudding into crust, alternating spoonfuls of chocolate and peanut butter vanilla. Swirl flavors together.

Chill. Just before serving, top with unsweetened whipped cream. Garnish, if you like, with chopped peanuts or shaved chocolate — or both!

NOTE

This is a lot of filling, so be sure to use a 10" pie plate. If you use a smaller one, put leftover filling into pudding dishes or layer into parfait glasses.

Creamsicle Pie

This ice cream and sherbet pie is wonderfully refreshing in warm weather. It goes together in about ten minutes, and it's absolutely beautiful when you slice and serve it.

CRUST

1   box flat chocolate wafers, crushed (such as Famous Chocolate
          Wafers) — reserve 1/2 cup crumbs for top of pie
1/2 cup butter, melted

Combine crumbs and melted butter in large ten-inch pie plate. Press into bottom and up sides of dish; do not bake.

FILLING

1   quart vanilla ice cream, softened slightly
1   quart orange sherbet, softened slightly
1   jar (11-oz.) fudge sauce, optional

Layer half the vanilla ice cream in the pie shell, add orange sherbet, and remaining vanilla. Sprinkle reserved cookie crumbs over top and freeze several hours.

If you wish to use the fudge sauce, drizzle about 1/3 of it over the crumbs in the bottom of the dish, then drizzle the remaining sauce between ice cream and sherbet layers.

Let the pie sit at room temperature for about ten minutes before slicing.

NOTE

The soft ice cream melts into the crumbs so they adhere nicely when you slice and serve pie. Makes it convenient to skip baking the crust.

VARIATION

There is no reason why you can't layer any two or three flavors of ice cream or sherbet. Just remember to select flavors for color as much as for taste.

With ice cream pies it's not always necessary to soften the ice cream first. If it's frozen very hard, spoon out small portions and chop with a spoon or whisk. I prefer this because sometimes the ice cream gets too soft before the recipe is completed.

Frosty Pumpkin Pie

NOTE
    You may substitute eight ounces of whipped heavy cream for whipped topping. I really prefer it.

The flavor of this frozen pie is so delicate that your family may not readily identify the pumpkin. It has a light texture and a rich flavor, and it's certainly easy.

    1   can (1-lb.) pumpkin
    1   pkg. vanilla pudding (six-serving size)
    1   cup milk
    1/2 tsp. *each* ground ginger, cinnamon and freshly grated nutmeg
    1   cup frozen whipped topping, thawed
    1   graham cracker pie crust, baked and cooled (see Page 193.)

Whip pumpkin, pudding mix, milk and spices together and fold in whipped topping. Pour into cooled, baked pie shell and freeze until serving time.

Fruit Tart

NOTE
    I've found a small paint brush is softer than a regular pastry brush and is easier to use.

This makes a lovely presentation at the table.

             Pastry for two-crust pie
    4-to-6   fresh apples or pears
    1   jar (10-oz.) red currant jelly, melted
             Sugar to taste

    Fit pie dough into a metal tart pan (bottom lifts up and away from sides). You will use all of the dough — there's no top crust. Prick with fork so it won't puff up, and bake at 450° for 7-10 minutes or until just beginning to brown. Cool crust.

    While crust cools, peel apples or pears and slice them as uniformly as possible.

    Paint the inside of tart shell with approximately half the melted currant jelly. Arrange sliced fruit in circles, turning slices one direction for one row and the other direction for next row. Sprinkle fruit with a light dusting of sugar; bake at 375° for 30 minutes, or until fruit is tender.

    After it has cooled slightly, paint the fruit with remaining melted jelly.

    Serve as is, or topped with whipped cream. I prefer it at room temperature.

    Serves 8-10.

Jim's Coconut Cream Pie

This has been my husband's favorite dessert for many years. It's not overly sweet.

FILLING

1/4	cup sugar
1/4	cup brown sugar, packed
4	tbsp. cornstarch
	Pinch of salt
2	cups milk
3	egg yolks, lightly beaten
2	tbsp. butter
1	tsp. vanilla extract
1	can (8-oz.) coconut (reserve 1/3 cup)
1	baked pie crust, cooled

Combine sugar, brown sugar, cornstarch, salt and milk in medium saucepan. Heat over medium heat, stirring gently but constantly. Bring to a rolling boil and boil for one minute, no longer. (If you boil it too long, the sauce may be thin.)

Remove from heat. Stir a spoonful of the hot mixture into egg yolks. Gradually add yolks to hot mixture, stirring constantly. When well blended, add in butter, vanilla, and all but 1/3 cup coconut. Cool filling slightly.

Pour cooled filling into baked and cooled pie shell. We prefer a pastry pie crust, but you may use graham cracker crust if you like.

MERINGUE

3	egg whites, room temperature
1/2	tsp. cream of tartar
1/2	tsp. vanilla extract
9	tbsp. sugar

Beat eggs with cream of tartar and vanilla extract until stiff peaks form. Gradually add sugar, beating after each addition until sugar has dissolved. Whip meringue until you have stiff, glossy peaks which still lean a little.

Spoon meringue over filling and sprinkle with remaining 1/3 cup coconut. Bake at 350° for 10-15 minutes, depending on thickness of meringue. It should be golden brown. You may use pie plates ranging from 8" - 10"; the smaller the dish, the higher the pie.

NOTE

Be sure meringue touches crust all the way around; it should keep it from shrinking as it bakes. Notice that I said "should". Frankly, I've made a lot of pies, and I have never found one of the traditional rules of thumb for meringue that worked all the time. Just don't worry about it — the pies are still delicious!

It's important to stir a little of the hot pudding mixture into uncooked egg yolks before adding the yolks to the pudding. If you don't they may cook into little bits of scrambled egg when they hit the hot pudding. Gradually warming them keeps this from happening.

For years I added more cornstarch to recipes than called for when I made cream pies from scratch. I couldn't seem to get the pies to stay firm enough to slice.

One day I read that cornstarch mixtures get thin if overcooked. Apparently, I'd been a little careless in timing my hot pudding. A more careful eye on the clock took care of it.

Lemon Ice Cream Pie

My friend Diana Craft created this luscious dessert — literally — from scraps in the kitchen. It was so good, she wrote it down and I'm glad to pass it along.

CRUST

2   cups crushed vanilla wafers
1/4   cup chopped pecans
1   tsp. apple pie spice
    Freshly ground nutmeg to taste
1/4   cup butter, melted

Combine crumbs, pecans and spices in ten-inch pie plate. Add butter, stirring until it's completely absorbed. Press into pie plate with your hands.

Bake at 350° for 7-10 minutes, until lightly browned. Cool completely before filling.

FILLING

3   lemons, juice only
1   can (14-oz.) sweetened condensed milk (such as Eagle Brand)
2   cups vanilla ice cream

Combine lemon juice and sweetened condensed milk. Stir until thick and well blended. Add ice cream and beat with whisk or electric mixer until thoroughly blended. Pour into cooled pie shell and freeze several hours, until firm. Serve frozen.

It takes about three heaping cups of vanilla wafer cookies to yield two cups of cookie crumbs. I counted, and I used 45 cookies.

When making pies with crumb crusts, it's a good idea to reserve 1/4 cup crumb mixture to sprinkle over top of pie for garnish. I usually forget, but it's nice if you can remember.

Mock Pecan Pie

This is a rich pie, very similar to pecan pie, but much less expensive.

3/4   cup sugar
3/4   cup dark corn syrup
3/4   cup rolled oats
1/2   cup canned coconut, shredded or flaked
1/2   cup butter, melted
2   eggs, lightly beaten
1   8" or 9" unbaked pie shell, your own or a frozen one

Combine filling ingredients and pour into shell. Bake at 350° for 45-50 minutes, or until set in center.

NOTE
    The rolled oats used in this recipe should be quick-cooking, but not instant.

Pecan-Glazed Cheesecake Pie

One of the most outstanding desserts I've ever served. Looks more complicated than it is.

CRUST

Make single pastry crust on Page 192, adding 1/3 cup minced pecans to ingredients.

Place in ten-inch pie plate; bake at 450° for 7-10 minutes, until baked but not brown.

FILLING

2	pkgs. (8-oz.) cream cheese, softened	1	egg, lightly beaten
		2	tsp. vanilla extract
1/3	cup sugar	1	cup chopped toasted pecans

Whip cream cheese with sugar. Blend in egg and vanilla. Pour into slightly cooled pie shells and top with toasted pecans.

GLAZE

3	eggs	2	tsp. sugar
2/3	cup light corn syrup	1	tsp. vanilla extract

In separate bowl whip together eggs, corn syrup, sugar and vanilla extract and pour glaze over pecans. Pour glaze over back of spoon, and it won't rearrange pecans.

Bake at 375° for about 40 minutes. Serve chilled . . . in very small slivers.

Toasting pecans and almonds in an oven at 300-350° for 5-10 minutes greatly intensifies their flavor. Watch them carefully, and stir occasionally as they bake. They are usually done when you can smell them baking.

Pecan Meringue Pie

This is not a meringue pie in the sense of meringue cream pie, but rather a light, airy meringue that is crisp all the way through.

3	egg whites, room temperature	1	tsp. baking powder
1	cup sugar	1	cup chopped pecans
1	cup saltine cracker crumbs	1	pint heavy cream, whipped

Whip egg whites until frothy. Gradually beat in sugar to make a stiff meringue. When sugar is completely dissolved and stiff peaks hold their shape, fold in cracker crumbs and baking powder, then pecans. Mixture will be pretty stiff.

Spread it in a well-buttered ten-inch pie plate. Use the back of your spoon to shape it and bake at 350° for 30 minutes, until firm and crisp and barely browned. Let it cool completely, then fill with the whipped cream and refrigerate for at least one hour before serving.

Serves 6-8.

VARIATION

Instead of saltine cracker crumbs, you might substitute one cup crushed chocolate wafer cookie crumbs.

For a mocha filling, you may add one tablespoon honey and one tablespoon instant coffee (or less) to whipping cream.

You can freeze egg whites and egg yolks as long as you separate the two.

Pineapple Meringue Pie

This is a recipe I developed some years ago for a friend. He'd had a similar pie in a long-lost truck stop restaurant, and couldn't ever find it again. He told me this comes pretty close.

3	eggs separated
1/2	cup brown sugar, packed
4	tbsp. cornstarch
	Pinch of salt
2	cups milk
2	tbsp. butter
1	tsp. vanilla extract
1	flat can (8-oz.) crushed pineapple, drained
1/4	tsp. cream of tartar
6	tbsp. sugar
1	baked 9" pastry pie shell

Separate eggs and set aside.

Into saucepan put brown sugar, cornstarch and salt. Add milk and stir over medium heat until it boils for two minutes — no longer. Remove from heat and add a little of the hot mixture to egg yolks; then add yolks to hot pudding and cook for two more minutes over low heat, stirring all the time.

Add in butter, vanilla and pineapple. Cool filling slightly and pour into baked pie shell.

Whip egg whites slightly, then add cream of tartar. Gradually adding in sugar, beat until meringue holds stiff peaks. Spread over pie and bake at 350° until golden brown, about 15 minutes.

Raspberry Cloud Pie

This frozen pie is light, rich, refreshing and almost too pretty to cut. It's an outstanding finale!

CRUST

1/3	cup butter, softened
2-1/2	tbsp. sugar
	Pinch of salt
1	egg yolk (reserve egg white)
1	cup flour
1/3	cup minced almonds

Combine crust ingredients and press into 8" or 9" pie plate. Mixture will be crumbly before you press it. Bake at 325° for about 10 minutes, until lightly browned. Cool completely.

FILLING

1	pkg. (10-oz.) frozen raspberries, partially thawed and drained
2	egg whites
1/2	cup sugar
1	tsp. vanilla extract
1	cup heavy cream, whipped

Put raspberries, egg whites, sugar and vanilla in large mixing bowl or food processor. Whip until mixture thickens and expands.

Fold in whipped cream and spoon into cooled crust. Freeze several hours or overnight.

NOTE

1. You may use 8", 9" or 10" pie plate. The smaller the dish, the higher the filling, and the more spectacular the dessert.

2. Be sure you don't over-thaw the raspberries. They should still have ice crystals in them. Completely thawed, they don't whip into as fluffy a meringue.

3. This is an outstanding crust, but you may use a graham cracker or vanilla wafer crust if you like.

Sour Cream Date Pie

What can you say about a pie with sour cream, pecans and dates — except that it's delicious?

CRUST

1	9" pie crust made with the addition of
1	tbsp. sesame seeds

Brush the crust with a little of the beaten eggs from the filling. Bake at 450° for 7-10 minutes. It should be cooked, but not brown. If you have not pricked it with a fork, it may buckle a bit, but the filling will push it down.

FILLING

1/2	cup butter, softened
1/2	cup brown sugar, packed
4	eggs
1	cup sour cream
1	tsp. vanilla extract
1	cup chopped pecans
2/3	cup chopped dates

Cream butter and brown sugar until light and fluffy. Beat in eggs, one at a time. Blend in sour cream and vanilla; add pecans and dates.

Pour into pre-baked crust and bake at 350° for 30 minutes. Let pie cool to room temperature before serving. Leftovers, if any, go in the refrigerator.

NOTE

One word of caution. This pie looks very much like a quiche when it's baked. Be sure everyone in the family knows what it is, or they may be surprised, as our son Warren was — he warmed up a piece for breakfast one morning. He doesn't even care for sweets.

Sweet Potato Pie

My husband grew up with his mom's sweet potato pie — it's the highlight of every holiday meal. This is her recipe. You'll find it similar to pumpkin pie, but lighter in flavor.

1-1/2	cups mashed sweet potatoes (canned or fresh)	1/2	tsp. salt
2	tbsp. butter, melted	2	eggs, lightly beaten
1	cup brown sugar, packed	1-3/4	cups milk
1	tsp. cinnamon	1	9" unbaked pastry
1	tsp. ground ginger		pie shell

When Jim's mom first gave me this recipe, I'd never made a sweet potato pie. I peeled, chopped and boiled the potatoes as I would white potatoes, and mashed them.

Later she told me she uses canned sweet potatoes. Certainly, that's easier. You do as you like.

Combine sweet potatoes with butter, brown sugar, cinnamon, ginger and salt. Beat in eggs and milk. Pour into unbaked pie shell and bake at 450° for ten minutes, then reduce the heat to 350° and bake about 45 minutes longer. When a knife blade inserted in the center of the filling comes out clean, it's done. Top with whipped cream.

NOTE

Please don't leave this pie sitting out for long, as it can spoil fairly quickly. Much better to keep it in refrigerator.

Spices such as cinnamon and ginger don't retain their freshness from one Thanksgiving to the next, so please buy small containers and replace them every three months or so. It may seem wasteful, but the difference in flavor is remarkable.

Toasted Almond Pie

The toasted almonds give this pie a wonderful flavor. Rich enough that small pieces are enough.

1	cup slivered almonds, toasted
1/2	cup semisweet chocolate chips, chilled
2-1/2	cups ricotta cheese
3/4	cup sugar
3/4	cup heavy cream, whipped
1	tsp. vanilla extract
1	9" graham cracker pie crust, baked and cooled

Grind toasted almonds in blender or food processor until they are a little coarser than cornmeal. Chop chilled chocolate chips the same way.

Next, whip ricotta cheese with sugar in a large mixing bowl. Stir in ground almonds and chocolate chips. Whip cream with vanilla and fold into ricotta mixture.

Spoon filling into cooled pie shell and refrigerate overnight. You may garnish with shaved chocolate or almond halves.

NOTE

Chocolate chips have to be *completely* chilled or the heat of the blades makes them melt. You might even freeze them.

The simplest way to crush corn flakes, crackers or cookies for crumbs is to put a few in a plastic sandwich bag and press with rolling pin. I like Glad bags because they have a top flap that tucks in quickly and contents don't spill out.

ORIGINAL KAYE JOHNS RADIO SCRIPTS

INDEX

APPETIZERS

BEVERAGES

BREADS

SOUPS, SAUCES & SANDWICHES

SALADS

VEGETABLES & SIDE DISHES

ENTRÉES

EGGS & CHEESE

BREAKFAST

BRUNCH

DINNER

LIVER

MEATLESS